KU-525-943

Fans, Feminisms and 'Quality' Media

Fans, Feminisms and 'Quality' Media considers how long-running and popular radio and TV programmes such as *Inspector Morse* and *The Archers* participate in contemporary debates about gender and feminisms, national identity and ethnicity, and tradition and modernity. Examining the connections between these programmes and heritage film, Lyn Thomas reveals how both programmes, in different ways, reflect tensions in postcolonial British culture and contribute to definitions of 'quality' in the media. Through in-depth research and interviews with listeners and viewers, she investigates the social construction of identities (particularly feminist identities) in talk about media texts, showing how popular radio and TV series become part of their audience's own personal narratives.

Lyn Thomas is Principal Lecturer in French and Research Director in the Faculty of Humanities and Education at the University of North London. She researches French and British media texts and audiences and their relationship with feminisms. She is the author of *Annie Ernaux: An Introduction to the Writer and her Audience* (Berg, 1999).

LIVERPOOL JOHN MOORES UNIVERSITY
Aldham Roberts L.R.C.
TEL. 0151 231 3701/3634

LIVERPOOL JMU LIBRARY

3 1111 01203 5059

Media, Education and Culture

Series editors:
David Buckingham, Institute of Education, University of London, UK and Julian Sefton-Green, Weekend Arts College, UK.

Cultural Studies has developed rigorous and exciting approaches to pedagogy. The **Media, Education and Culture** series extends the research and debate that is developing in this interface between cultural studies and education.

Digital Diversions: Youth Culture in the Age of Multi-Media
Edited by Julian Sefton-Green

Teaching Popular Culture: Beyond Radical Pedagogy
Edited by David Buckingham

Wired Up: Young People and the Electronic Media
Edited by Sue Howard

Teen Spirits: Music and Identity in Media Education
Chris Richards

The Making of Citizens: Young People, News and Politics
David Buckingham

Fans, Feminisms and 'Quality' Media
Lyn Thomas

Forthcoming

Researching Children's Popular Culture: Mapping the Cultural Spaces of Childhood
Claudia Mitchell and Jacqueline Reid-Walsh

Fans, Feminisms and 'Quality' Media

Lyn Thomas

London and New York

First published 2002
by Routledge
11 New Fetter Lane, London EC4P 4EE

Simultaneously published in the USA and Canada
by Routledge
29 West 35th Street, New York, NY 10001

Routledge is an imprint of the Taylor & Francis Group

© 2002 Lyn Thomas

Typeset in Baskerville by Taylor & Francis Books
Printed and bound in Great Britain by Biddles Ltd, Guildford and King's Lynn

All rights reserved. No part of this book may be reprinted or
reproduced or utilised in any form or by any electronic,
mechanical, or other means, now known or hereafter
invented, including photocopying and recording, or in any
information storage or retrieval system, without permission in
writing from the publishers.

British Library Cataloguing in Publication Data
A catalogue record for this book is available from the British Library

Library of Congress Cataloging in Publication Data
Thomas Lyn, 1953–
Fans, feminisms and 'quality' media/ Lyn Thomas.
    p. cm. – (Media studies)
Includes bibliographical references and index.
1. Inspector Morse (Television program) 2. Archers (Radio program) 3. Television and
women–Great Britain. 4. Radio and women–Great Britain. I. Title. II. Series.

PN1992.77.I56 T46 2002
791.45'72–dc21   2002024897

ISBN 0–415–26181–3 (hbk)
ISBN 0–415–26182–1 (pbk)

For Duncan Fraser

Contents

Acknowledgements

I would like to thank all the people who filled in questionnaires and/or took part in focus groups or telephone interviews for their interest in the study and willingness to participate. My research was entirely dependent on this goodwill, and I am very grateful. I would also like to thank my transcribers – Jackie Harnett, Betty Mitchell and Terry Doonan. I am particularly grateful to Terry, who, with the help of his late wife Betty Doonan, transcribed the earliest tapes, and took a great deal of interest in my work (and the latest narrative developments in *The Archers*). Their daughter, my friend Shelagh Doonan, helped distribute fliers in May 1997 and was enthusiastic and supportive, especially in the early stages of the research. Thanks are also due to Hedli Niklaus and the staff at Wood Norton Hall for their co-operation in the organisation of focus groups at an *Archers* fan club weekend, and to the National Film Theatre and 'a theatre in the south of England' for allowing me to distribute questionnaires.

The Humanities Faculty Research Committee at the University of North London awarded a sabbatical for the completion of this research in 1999. I am grateful for this crucial support. I would like to thank my colleague Karen Seago for her interest in the research and role as observer of *Morse* focus group 2. I would also like to thank another UNL colleague, Eileen Cottis, for her warm support and encouragement, for conversations about *The Archers* over many years, *Archers* books and press cuttings. My parents have also collected cuttings and kept an eye on *The Radio Times* and local (Midlands) press. The Director of the Irish Studies Centre at UNL, Mary Hickman, has heightened my awareness of questions of Irish identity, and has been a supportive and perceptive advisor throughout. I would also like to thank Sarah Morgan of the Irish Studies Centre for fascinating discussions of 'race' and ethnicity in *The Archers*. My PhD supervisor, David Buckingham, deserves a very heartfelt thank-you – for constructive criticism and consistent encouragement. Charlotte Brunsdon has been an enthusiastic and critical reader over several years, and I would like to express my appreciation of all the help she has given me. I would also like to to thank the anonymous readers who commented on the manuscript for their very helpful comments. In 1995 the then *Feminist Review* Collective published my article on *Morse*: I am grateful to them for their support of an unknown writer, and to the present Collective for intellectual stimulation and good company. Finally, I am deeply grateful to Duncan Fraser for his patience in reading and commenting on the manuscript, and for his companionship and support.

Transcription Conventions

...	text omitted
(.)	pause
]	overlap between utterances
= =	absence of discernible gap between speakers

Underlining for words which are spoken with added emphasis
Clarificatory material is placed in square brackets, e.g. [*Female laughter*]
Numbers in brackets after quotations denote transcript line numbers

Introduction

Why *Morse*? Why *The Archers*? Why Me?

> This book, then is about interpretations, about the places where we
> rework what has already happened to give current events meaning.
> It is about the stories we make for ourselves, and the social specificity
> of our understanding of those stories.
>
> (Steedman, 1986: 5)

Carolyn Steedman's description of her aims in *Landscape for a Good Woman* contains many elements which are essential to this study. The most significant of these is perhaps the idea that within the social and material constraints of our lives, we are constantly telling and retelling stories, giving meaning to the past and present. These stories, like the research which focuses on them, do not represent an authentic or final truth, but the study of their ebbs and flows can give some sense of a cultural and historical moment. The autobiographical dimension of this project is much less developed than Steedman's *Landscape*, but the 'I' of the academic researcher which is the dominant voice here does need some fleshing out, since like much academic work, this book has grown out of my own life-history: the links and cross-overs between the two narratives deserve some elucidation.

'The stories we make for ourselves' are constituted from the cultural and discursive resources available to us. In this sense individuals draw on what Graham Dawson has described as 'the narrative resource of a culture – its repertoire of shared and recognized forms – [which] therefore functions as a currency of recognizable social identities' (1994: 23).[1] It is surely uncontroversial to suggest that in the late twentieth and early twenty-first century media texts are an important part of this narrative resource. If new technologies permit new forms of communication, the content of communications can be just as significantly imbued with the public stories made available to us by those now old-fashioned media – television and radio. The main aim of this research is to explore *how* we use and appropriate these narratives in social interactions, the kind of social and psychic purposes which media texts and the stories we weave around them allow us to fulfil. The starting point for this analysis has to be the relationship between my narratives of my own life and the two media texts I have chosen to study. This interrelationship alone can explain fully the development of the project; it is also inevitably the case that the psychic level is more available to me in my own story than through the analysis of the accounts provided by others in social talk. Finally, this albeit brief narration is the first stage of my attempt to disrupt the notion of the objective researcher: following a well-established tradition of feminist research, I will throughout attempt to highlight my own stake in the research and the social specificity of the apparently neutral 'I'.

My own relation to both of these texts – *Inspector Morse* and *The Archers* – is a mixture of critical distance and emotional involvement. It can serve both to illustrate and to nuance the theory of the relationship between taste and social class developed by the French sociologist Pierre Bourdieu, which is discussed more fully in Chapter 1 (Bourdieu, [1979] 1984). I was brought up in a working-class family in Wolverhampton, and at 18 went from my comprehensive school to Oxford to study Modern Languages. My parents had both left school at 14, and I was the first person in my family to go to University. I effectively moved into middle-class culture, but at the same time retained a sense of not quite belonging, of being an outsider. It is perhaps not surprising, given this history, that my reaction to the beautiful images of Oxford in *Inspector Morse*, which I discovered in the early 1990s, twenty years after my time at Oxford, was ambivalent. On one level I found the images of middle-class life – tea on the lawn, sherry parties, Morse's own taste for classical music and good country pubs – reassuring. In the same way, the leisurely tea at 5 and supper at 7 which I consumed in my Oxford college seemed a more adequate protection from the collapse of civilised life than the hastily put together bacon and egg 'teas' – an amalgamation of both meals – that we had at home. These images, and the class trajectory of Morse himself, mirroring my own, made me feel that what sometimes seemed like a fragile veneer of middle-classness was not just a figment of my own imagination, but an external reality.

The representations of a cosy and aesthetically pleasing middle-class lifestyle which I found in *Morse* and *The Archers* were deeply, and strangely, reassuring, even though generic conventions required their constant disruption (albeit in different ways and to differing degrees). The programmes seemed to contain my anxieties about changing class, or about being rejected by my new class. My early interest in them cannot, however, be subsumed into the aspiration to middle-classness which Bourdieu's theory might suggest as a dominant motive; I was less concerned with the impact that such tastes might have on others' readings of me, than with my own search for a cultural home. If the Oxford location of *Morse* was significant for me, the rural Midlands context of *The Archers* was also a link with the past. The fictional county of 'Borsetshire' seemed very familiar, and a further link was provided by the small but significant number of exiles from Birmingham and Wolverhampton in the village of Ambridge.[2] The *Archers* 'Omnibus' on Sunday mornings provided an oasis of familiar Midlands voices in my southern 'exile'. Similarly, while the representations of middle-class life were a reassuring reminder of the solidity of the traditions I now aspired to, the popular genres – crime fiction and soap opera – which the programmes belong to, provided a connection with popular culture more broadly, and hence with my background.

At home during my childhood we watched *Crossroads* (my grandmother never missed an episode) and *Coronation Street* (which my mother still watches). After leaving home at 18 I never watched another episode of either until recently, when I have occasionally watched *Coronation Street* with my mother. Later, the theme tune alone of *EastEnders* would induce a kind of sinking feeling, and, on the few occasions when I have watched, depression, rather than distraction, was the result. If the East End of London seemed like dangerous territory, working- and lower middle-class Liverpool offered no greater attraction: I only watched *Brookside* during the winter of 1988–9 when I was staying in a friend's home, and could watch with the protection of her cultivated conversation and company. All these TV soaps were too close to the mark: both their representations of predominantly working-class communities and the act of watching TV soap reminded me too much of the culture of origin I had spent my life escaping from (and more recently 'reclaiming').[3]

We never listened to *The Archers* at home, so the radio soap, and the genteel voices of Radio 4 generally, for me carry mainly the ethos of my acquired culture. I began to listen in the late 1970s as a young married woman; I was introduced to the programme by the middle-class husband I had met at Oxford, and I listened while preparing meals in the kitchen of a Victorian house we were renovating. The end of the marriage, and of this period of my life, was accompanied by a rejection of *The Archers* which was as pronounced as my later reaction to *EastEnders* and *Brookside*, though of a different nature. The cosy tones of *The Archers* at this time of real insecurity failed to reassure, and could only irritate. My 'return to Ambridge' is associated with buying my own house and becoming involved in feminist groups in the 1980s; the reasons for this are not entirely clear to me, but being part of a feminist culture where listening to and making subversive readings of *The Archers* was a shared pleasure was doubtless significant.

Already in my teens I had found a form of soap opera, or romance, which was not accompanied by a depressing sense of claustrophobia and of the inescapability of the downward spirals I observed in my own extended family. The classic serial on television came to my rescue, providing all the pleasures of soap opera and romantic fiction in combination, but with the past and the literary to protect me from all too familiar realities. The televised version of Galsworthy's *The Forsyte Saga* (BBC, 1967) was the highlight of my week, and I read Jane Austen and the Brontës, rather than Mills and Boon or *Jackie*. My interest and pleasure in *Inspector Morse* can be seen as a continuation of this taste for gentrified romance and 'aesthetically superior' soap. In some ways the middle position of *Morse* and *The Archers* as popular culture with aspirations to 'quality' reflected my own 'inbetween' class position. However, this Bourdieuian reading is incomplete. The search for narratives of the personal described above indicates the gender-specific dimension of my cultural choice. The 'femininity' of the texts places them lower on the Bourdieuian hierarchy of taste than the high cultural forms which my Oxford education had introduced me to. In this sense *Inspector Morse* and *The Archers* are more a personally satisfying compromise than an expression of social aspiration.

An exception to this may be found in that dimension of my interest in these texts which results from my involvement in academic feminism. If ambivalence in relation to popular culture (and particularly 'women's genres') is the mark of the contemporary 'feminist intellectual' whose recent history has been charted by Charlotte Brunsdon, then I was no exception (Brunsdon, 2000). While watching *Morse* I became aware that I was simultaneously drawn both to the traditional side and to what I perceived as more subversive elements. As a single woman I was intrigued by the programmes' apparently obsessive concern with the social divisions operating between single people and couples; *Morse* seemed to be reversing the 'family values' of the 1980s by representing single people (particularly, of course, Morse himself) positively, while the married or attached people around them seemed to flounder in confusion, vice and immorality (see Chapter 2). On the one hand, I was reassured and entertained by the visual spectacle of heritage Britain, and on the other, delighted by subversive elements which seemed to form a critique of contemporary British society and reaffirm my own identity as an 'outsider'. Similarly, my 'solitary vice' of listening to *The Archers*, and being involved enough to cry with Shula when Mark died, was accompanied by social critique. With my feminist friends I would laugh at the characters whose company I craved enough to race across London to be home in time to listen on weekday evenings. We would speculate about the possibility of lesbian romance in Ambridge or of Pat ditching the awful Tony. These rather 'middle-brow' cultural tastes, in Bourdieu's terms, could be redeemed by an intellectual feminist deconstruction.

These complexities were surely not unique. I became interested, not only in the social identities constructed in talk about media texts, but also in the emotional investments revealed in such talk, particularly from 'outsider' positions of various kinds. This interest was one of the starting points of this project. Another was the pleasure I obtained from the texts themselves and my desire to write about them. In the rest of this chapter I will develop the academic history of the project and the particular combination of textual analysis and audience study which resulted from my initial interests.

The Texts: *Inspector Morse* and *The Archers* as 'Quality' Media

On the face of it, *Inspector Morse* (Zenith, 1987–2000) and *The Archers* (BBC Radio, 1951–) are separated by many differences – of medium, genre and audience (national in the case of *The Archers*, and international in the case of *Morse*). Despite these differences, these texts have in common the combination of a popular genre with an aspiration to 'quality'.[4] *Morse* is renowned for its high production values and standards of acting, its references to the literary canon and classical music. *The Archers* is broadcast on Radio 4, arguably the purveyor of middle-class talk to the nation, and was originally designed to educate farmers in post-war Britain; the contemporary programme may be less overtly didactic, but its remit nonetheless encompasses the exploration of social issues, particularly those affecting rural communities.

Even the national/international distinction is becoming increasingly blurred in the globalised context of the twenty-first century. Although *The Archers* is clearly playing to a home audience, the format of the programme has been adopted elsewhere, notably in Afghanistan, where the BBC's World Service has created a new soap – *New Home, New Life* – based on *The Archers*. The huge audience of circa 35 million people tuning in to this programme in Afghanistan and Pakistan would surely be the envy of British radio broadcasters at home (Brockes, 2001).

Questions of 'quality' are highly contentious in the contemporary British context, particularly in relation to broadcasting, which since the 1920s has been primarily defined as a public service with an educational and cultural mission (Scannell and Cardiff, 1991). The use of the term 'quality' media seems to be an instance of the hierarchy of cultural taste analysed by Bourdieu, and the contentiousness of the term is perhaps the result of efforts to resist or redefine the hierarchy it encapsulates. Geoff Mulgan has commented on recent manifestations of the 'quality' discourse:

> In Britain, perhaps more than anywhere else, a rhetoric of quality in broadcasting, the ritual equation of quality with *Brideshead Revisited* and *The Jewel in the Crown* (rather than with *Boys from the Blackstuff* or *The Singing Detective* or for that matter *Brookside* and *The Tube*), has consistently been used to legitimise, and disguise, the narrow tastes and prejudices of a small, metropolitan, cultural elite.
>
> (Mulgan, 1990: 5)

My question is how *Inspector Morse* has perpetuated and developed the discourse of 'quality' media: what exactly are the signifiers of 'quality' present in *Morse*? How are these signifiers articulated within the conventions of the crime genre? In relation to *The Archers*, the question poses itself slightly differently. Through the low status genre which it belongs to, the programme could be associated with the television soaps, acquiring their 'popular culture' connotations, but *The Archers* arguably has a rather different image. Hendy comments that 'public-service radio funded by licence fees has always had to perform a difficult balancing act of populism and elitism' (2000: 18). Radio 4's soap opera seems to play a crucial part in this – required both to attract a (for the medium) large audience and to maintain high standards of dramatic production. In Chapter 2 I explore how this delicate balancing of high and low cultural status is constituted, and how it is maintained, both in the texts and in the secondary literature. Mulgan's (and others') critique of 'quality' and Bourdieu's cultural hierarchy will be interrogated in this process.

Like many media texts which aspire to the 'quality' label, *Morse* and *The Archers* can also be linked to the heritage style of representation which since the 1980s has been identified as a significant feature of popular culture in Britain and elsewhere (Corner and Harvey, 1991a). There is now a substantial literature concerned with the analysis of heritage culture as it manifests itself in museums, country houses, cinema and television. The media texts which have been studied so far in this context are adaptations of classic literary works, whether for cinema or television. Like Mulgan, Charlotte Brunsdon has noted how two television series – *Brideshead Revisited* (Granada, 1981) and *The Jewel in the Crown* (Granada, 1984) – became flagships for 'quality' in the 1980s, contributing both to a certain ideology of national identity and to its economic dimension, through what she describes as the 'heritage export value' of the texts (Brunsdon, 1990). Higson (1993) has provided a detailed account of heritage films such as the Merchant–Ivory adaptations of Forster. All these discussions link the economic success of the genre to a nostalgic representation of Englishness: the last days of Empire, cricket on village greens, country lanes and Oxbridge colleges. In almost every case nostalgia is associated with a flight from the political realities of the present, and is seen as a reflection of post-colonial anxieties in relation to national identity.

My purpose is to develop these arguments by asking how texts which belong to genres not immediately associated with heritage – a TV crime series in one case, and a radio soap opera in the other – may nonetheless participate in the nostalgic mode of representation and attendant anxieties around Englishness. Chapter 2 will therefore extend the discussion of heritage text and culture by applying the concept to a new genre in the case of *Morse* and a new genre and medium in the case of *The Archers*. How are the textual features of 'heritage' inflected in these new and different contexts? How does the difference of medium and genre affect these representations? (The question of medium is particularly significant in relation to *The Archers*, since existing analyses all focus on visual culture.) How do these texts contribute to the ideological climate of contemporary Britain and to constructions of national identity and Englishness?

A related strand of enquiry is the place of such representations of a traditional 'heritage' culture in texts which, unlike most of the literary adaptations discussed by other analysts, are in fact set in the contemporary world. The argument of many of the discussions of heritage texts cited above is that although apparently focused on the past, in reality they are deeply concerned with the present. Thus, Cairns Craig (1991) reads Merchant–Ivory films as a reflection of the materialist and individualistic values of Thatcherism in the 1980s. In most cases this viewing of the present through the prism of the past is regarded as politically regressive and conservative. How are the traditional and modern elements in *Morse* and *The Archers* combined and balanced? What constitutes the 'modernity' side of the equation? In response to this question, my main focus will be the field of gender representation: can this be regarded as one of the significant areas in which the programmes' modernity is expressed? Can the programmes' combination of tradition and modernity be seen as participation in a deeply rooted ideological conflict in modern British society, rather than as a reinforcement of the latter's most conservative elements? In this sense, it could be argued that in the analysis of heritage culture the Academy has pursued its tendency to condemn popular culture as politically incorrect (Samuel, 1994). Are *Morse* and *The Archers* symptomatic of a more complex relation to contemporary British politics and society than many of the analysts of 'quality' popular culture have allowed for?

The question of gender representation in the two texts is a significant aspect of my research in its own right, as well as constituting an important element of the discussion of modernity. There is now a large and growing corpus of feminist analysis of popular culture: feminist researchers have tended to focus on Hollywood film, television soap opera and aspects of youth culture, such as female singers or groups. Frequently this analysis has paid particular attention to the perceived subversiveness of women's genres, such as the melodrama and the soap (Van Zoonen, 1994). In relation to the detective genre on television, most feminist work has concentrated on programmes with female leads, such as *Cagney and Lacey* (Mace Neufeld Productions, 1981; D'Acci, 1987, 1994; Gamman, 1988) or *Widows* (Euston Films, 1983; Brunsdon, 1987; Skirrow, 1987). The two detective heroes of *Morse* are men, the original books on which the series was based were written by a male writer, and the crime genre generally is often regarded as a 'man's genre' (Brunsdon, 1987: 185). In this sense *Morse* is not an obvious choice for feminist study. The representations of traditional Englishness which dominate the visual landscape of the programmes, and the associations with 'quality' discussed above, also make *Morse* an unlikely candidate for the exploration of subversiveness. Yet, it is this apparent inappropriateness which makes *Morse* the ideal choice for the analysis of the influence of feminisms on popular culture in a broad sense: to what extent can the influence of feminisms be identified in a programme as mainstream as *Morse*? If such influences are found, what form do they take – how are feminisms, and gender generally, represented in this context? Do these representations permit us to argue that in contemporary Britain feminisms in some form have infiltrated the most apparently 'establishment' areas of popular culture? Can it be argued that changing representations of gender in response to feminisms are in fact a significant aspect of the conventions of 'quality' programmes? The originality of my project thus lies in part in its search for feminism where one would not necessarily expect to find it, in programmes which are seen as part of a particularly static and even old-fashioned tributary of the mainstream.[5]

Similar questions pose themselves for *The Archers*, though the differences of genre and medium change their inflection. *The Archers* is a soap opera, the 'women's genre' *par excellence*, and in this respect it is not surprising to find that since 1991 it has had a woman producer and, many critics would argue, a feminist agenda (Pearson, 1994). Yet, *The Archers* is also associated with deeply conservative (and Conservative) elements of British society – the 'country way of life' of hunting, shooting and fishing for those who own the land, and toil for a pittance for those who do not. How do feminisms find a voice in this context? How do changing representations of gender contribute to the modernisation of a series which has been running since 1951? If almost all the analysis of negative or objectifying representations of women since the 1970s has focused on film and television, how relevant are these discussions to the analysis of changing representations of gender in radio?

The Audiences

In attempting to discuss the questions outlined above, I am very aware of the limitations of textual analysis. If *Morse* and *The Archers* are in some sense to become test cases for a discussion of the discourses of tradition and modernity, and of feminism, in contemporary British culture, it seems important to look beyond the programmes themselves. A highly popular media text can doubtless provide some indication of the ideological preoccupations and concerns of a culture, but it remains a professionally produced artefact, characterised by the gulf which exists between the worlds of its producers and those of its consumers. The academic reading of the text introduces another, equally separate, dimension; just as there is no guarantee that the text will be read according to the producers' intentions, the academic reading carries no automatic wider validity. Although textual analysis clearly has its place in contemporary cultural and media studies, here some of my major questions relate to the audiences of these programmes. I am not attempting a large-scale survey generating statistical information which would then be generalisable to the audience as a whole. It is not my aim to establish the class, ethnicity or gender profile of the 15 million or more people who are claimed to constitute the British *Morse* audience or the 4.5 million *Archers* listeners. Here I have taken small samples, recruited on the basis of their enthusiasm for the programmes, in order to look in detail at readings other than my own.

Although I have chosen a radio and a television text, comparison of audience practices in relation to the two media is not the main focus of this study. Insights in this area may emerge, and differences between the media must be taken into account in the analysis, but the identification of differences between radio and TV consumption, which would have required a much larger, context-based study, was not my main aim.[6] My questions originate either in the texts or in the audience–text dynamic. Doubtless, one of the questions underlying the research was whether the discourses I had identified in the programmes – the conflict between tradition and modernity, or the influence of feminisms – had some wider currency. However, as I have already indicated, I am also concerned with a still more fundamental question – the construction of social identities through and in talk about media texts.

My research is based on the notion that in interaction with others, individuals are perpetually constructing narratives which combine to form a particular social identity. Identity is not fixed, but may change, subtly or even dramatically, in the course of even one interaction.[7] It is inextricably linked both to the dynamics of the interaction, and to factors such as gender, 'race', ethnicity, class and sexuality which will always have a defining, if not immutable, impact on the interaction itself and on the identities which individuals construct or perform within it. In 'normal' social life (i.e. social interactions which take place outside a research context) media texts clearly play a role in the claiming and performance of identities, providing a shared culture and a focus for the crucial expression of likes and dislikes, allegiances and rejections. The aim of this research is to simulate this process in the context of talk about the two texts chosen for study. Clearly, the simulation can never be equivalent to spontaneous social interactions – the presence of a researcher and a tape-recorder must always play a determining role – but it will allow more insight into the nature of audience–text relations than text-based speculation. What kind of social identities do the particular textual characteristics of *Morse* and *The Archers* allow members of their audiences to claim in talk about the programmes? In the analysis of talk about these texts my focus will inevitably be on the social process, since this is more available for analysis than the inner worlds of the participants. The latter are, however, not systematically excluded from the discussion, and some insights may emerge.

Subsidiary, but in the end crucial, questions emerged from the first part of the research on the *Morse* audience. As I will argue in Chapter 4, the nature of the two focus groups suggested the characterisation of some readings as 'mainstream' (or, to use Stuart Hall's term, 'preferred'), and of others as 'oppositional' (Hall, [1973] 1996). This provided me with an initial model for the ensuing research on *The Archers*, but at the same time generated further questions – about the terms themselves, their usefulness and validity, and their exact meaning in this context. The encoding/decoding model was originally formulated by Stuart Hall. In his influential paper, Hall developed the notion of three codes of reading: dominant, negotiated and oppositional. A dominant or preferred reading 'decodes the message in terms of the reference code in which it has been encoded', producing an almost perfect correspondence between the meanings encoded in the text and the reading (ibid.: 47). The match is less perfect in a negotiated reading, where there is a mixture of acceptance of and resistance to the dominant meanings in the text. An oppositional reading completely replaces the dominant code with its own oppositional code, and therefore produces a reading which questions or contradicts the meanings encoded in the text. This model, translated by David Morley into empirical study, has been widely critiqued, most significantly by Morley himself. Morley has made a number of detailed criticisms of his earlier work, of which the most relevant here relates to the emphasis on acceptance or rejection of the ideological message of a text which the terms 'decoding', 'preferred' and 'oppositional' reading imply (Morley, 1980 and 1992: 119–30). He comments that the model 'assumes that one is dealing with a broadly political form of communication' (Morley, 1992: 126). This makes it difficult to apply it to entertainment genres such as soap opera, and may also lead to an excessive emphasis on the content of audience talk, with a consequent lack of attention paid to its form and context. These criticisms are developed by Barker and Brooks, who express the rather extreme view that the encoding/decoding model is 'a blight on contemporary audience research' (1998: 92).

My own use of some of Morley's terminology does not imply an acceptance of the model as a conceptual block. In Chapter 4 I have replaced 'preferred reading' with the perhaps equally problematic 'mainstream', though I have retained one of the original adjectives – 'oppositional'. The *Morse* research identified a reading of the programmes which was highly critical of them, and which deconstructed as well as admired their 'quality' connotations. 'Oppositional' was a convenient term to characterise this, while 'mainstream' was a useful (if crude) way of describing a more enthusiastic, or 'impressed by quality' mode. As this indicates, one of the defining points of my own appropriation of these terms is a difference in relation to the 'quality' discourse and the hierarchy of taste which it embodies. I am interested to explore whether these groups, as Bourdieu's work would suggest, attempt to enhance their own social status through the appropriation of 'quality' media texts. How might 'oppositional' and 'mainstream' reading strategies differ in this respect? What other characteristics of a mainstream reading of *Morse* and *The Archers* might be identified? How is it differentiated from the oppositional readings which in the first case I stumbled upon, and in the second set out to explore? These questions lead to a methodological development in the research. If 'mainstream' and 'oppositional' were found to be useful terms for the broad categorisation of the readings of *Morse* which I analysed, would my research on *The Archers* confirm or deconstruct this scheme? Would the study of aspects of a more institutionalised fan culture inevitably question the viability of this contrast, and particularly of the term 'mainstream'?

The particular kind of oppositional reading which I am concerned with here (and the second defining point of my use of the term) was in part determined by its emergence in *Morse* focus group 2, where feminist critique of the representation of women became a dominant discourse. This group's ironic jokes about *The Archers* played a role in the decision to research feminist and other fan cultures concerning the radio soap.[8] However, my interest in feminist readings also stems from my own analysis of the two texts, and the nature of my interest in them. If my textual analysis is at least in part motivated by the desire to explore the presence of feminist influences in mainstream, 'quality' popular media texts, my audience studies are based on the notion that textual analysis alone cannot provide a full picture of the place of feminisms in a culture. I am interested not merely in changing representations, but also in readings of these changes. How have feminisms influenced, not only the programmes themselves, but also talk about them? The broader corollary to this is the whole question of feminisms as a component of social and cultural identity, as well as a political position. Arguably, cultural identities informed by feminisms are well established in contemporary British social life, particularly in middle-class milieus: what might such identities consist of, both (and differently) for women and men, in the context of talk about media texts? My choice of texts allows me to refine this to a still narrower focus: how is enthusiasm for mainstream 'quality' media texts combined with an alternative, feminist reading? How are such alternative readings expressed and inflected? In this aspect of the study I am not suggesting that a fixed 'feminist identity' is assumed by individuals, but rather that feminisms may intersect with other factors in the adoption of subject positions in specific social contexts.

Thornton's term 'subcultural capital', which is based on Pierre Bourdieu's notion of cultural capital, is also relevant here (Bourdieu, 1984; Thornton, 1997: 200–12). The term is useful in the discussion of fan cultures generally, since it implies an assertion of difference and status which would not be recognised by the wider society, given the generally low cultural prestige of fan cultures (Jenkins, 1992: 208). For example, it will be relevant in the discussion of the fan cultures around *The Archers* which take the traditional form of membership of the official fan club, and activities such as penfriend networks. In discussing feminist subcultural capital, however, a rather complex relationship with cultural capital per se emerges. Since academic feminism is a significant offshoot of feminisms as a political movement, and now constitutes one of its most significant manifestations, there is likely to be a close relationship between feminist subcultural capitals and cultural capital in the more classic sense, as defined by Bourdieu. Academic feminism is perhaps one of the few aspects of feminist identities or subcultures which *has* been explored. In the early 1990s Charlotte Brunsdon commented on the impact of academic feminism, both as a body of literature and as the presence of a feminist teacher in the classroom, on women students' responses to popular media texts. Her analysis indicates how responses and identities are modified by this feminist presence, and how 'feminism begins to function as the politically correct form of femininity' (Brunsdon, 1991: 376). She traces this back to early manifestations of second-wave feminism and their hostility to popular femininities: 'because ... the identity "feminist" has historically been constructed partly in contrast with "ordinary women", this opposition is always potentially present in the classroom' (ibid.: 373). More recently Brunsdon has investigated the persona of the feminist intellectual in more depth, in a study of feminist research on soap opera between 1975 and 1986 (Brunsdon, 2000). Here I aim to look at the impact of feminist presence and cultural capital in non-pedagogic contexts, and to explore how such influences operate in 'everyday' talk about media texts. Clearly, some of these research events, which were semi-structured, but nonetheless led by a researcher with a set of prepared questions, may in some ways be closer to the classroom context than to other social interactions. Academic feminism is also represented by my principal respondent in Chapter 6. However, this is not the case for all of the interviews and focus groups discussed here, and the project can claim to have looked at instances of relations between feminisms, audiences and media texts outside the Academy.

Methodologically, I was anxious to avoid a situation in which my audience research would fall into the trap of 'othering' the audience. Again, Charlotte Brunsdon has charted the growing awareness among feminist researchers of the split between the researching feminist subject and the 'ordinary women' who are the objects of her study (1991: 380 and 2000; see Chapter 3). The relationship between researcher and researched is an extremely complex issue, and it is one which I shall return to in the empirical chapters and in my conclusion. An element of the research design, however, specifically addresses this issue. Rather than studying, for instance, youth culture from which I am separated by age, or the female fans of romantic fiction which I rarely read, I have chosen to study audiences and fan cultures which I myself am part of. Inevitably, in making this choice, I am raising questions about the role of the researcher in such a project. What happens when the researcher is also part of the audience being researched, and when the power differential, and the dynamic between researcher and researched, are transformed by this shared belonging? How are the research context and the data generated changed by the researcher's dual, or split, role – partly objective observer, partly member of the group, sharing anecdotes and experiences? The fact that many of these respondents are highly articulate and capable of analysing their own responses to the programmes further questions the role of the researcher, who is no longer the sole holder of the power of interpretation and knowledge. Is it possible to create a feminist audience research project where the researched are in some way involved in the production of knowledge, rather than the 'objects of study', passive recipients of the researcher's analysis?

Barker and Brooks comment: 'The danger is that the ambiguities concealed in the notion of being "on the side of" the audience can lead us to researching only "safe" audiences, people we like who like materials we also like. That is very dele-terious' (1998: 25). This is an important warning, but does not necessarily lead to the conclusion that we should positively and permanently avoid such topics, in favour of the study of people and materials we have little empathy with. As a keen listener/viewer of *The Archers* and *Morse* I am certainly 'on the side of' the programmes, though this does not entail the automatic suspension of my critical faculties. Being 'on the side of' the audience is a claim I would not make, since it is both vague and potentially patronising. However, I have been concerned to try to 'open up' the research in the ways I have described above, and to explore the issues which this raises in my conclusion (Chapter 7). Furthermore, it is important to note here that although I would define myself as a fan of both series, I do not automatically participate in every aspect of the fan cultures surrounding the programmes. The question of the role of the researcher can therefore be exam-ined in different contexts: in some I am as close as possible to the culture under study, in others I am both connected to it, and separate from it. In drawing conclu-sions from my audience study I will inevitably make comparisons between these positions and comment on their effect on the conduct of the research, and its outcomes.

An important aspect of this study is the empirical exploration of the theory of cultural taste developed by Bourdieu in *Distinction*. A more detailed discussion of Bourdieu's work is therefore required, and this follows in Chapter 1. If the rela-tionship between feminisms and identities is also to be explored empirically, feminist theories of identity must be considered: this discussion completes the theoretical background of the study presented in Chapter 1. In Chapter 2 I focus on the texts themselves, relating them to the discourse of 'quality' in contemporary British media, and to academic work on the heritage text, its negotiation of tradi-tion and modernity. Representations of gender, class, 'race' and ethnicity are also discussed. Chapter 3 introduces the methodological reflection which is an impor-tant theme throughout, as well as describing the parameters and processes of the audience study, itself the subject of Chapters 4–6. In Chapter 7 I look back on the research and return to the questions raised in this introduction. My own conclu-sions are enriched by my respondents' comments on my analysis of their talk about *The Archers*.

Chapter One

Bourdieu, Butler and Beyond: Theoretical Background to the Study

Bourdieu: Cultural Habitus, Capital and Games

A consideration of some elements of the work of Pierre Bourdieu is demanded by this study's concern with questions of taste in relation to 'quality' media texts, and with the processes of self-definition which talk about these texts involves. One of the inevitable focuses of analysis of this talk is the ways in which participants individually and collectively differentiate themselves from others, and thus lay claim to a particular social identity. The social and to a lesser extent psychic benefits which seem to be derived from these differentiations within a particular social interaction form part of the analysis, since they result from appropriations of media texts, and are crucial to the discussion of the interaction itself and the context for talk about texts which it provides. Bourdieu's *Distinction* ([1979] 1984) devotes a lengthy analysis of surveys and questionnaire-based interviews to the relationship between cultural and 'life-style' tastes and social class. The basis of this analysis – the contention that 'taste classifies, and it classifies the classifier' (Bourdieu, 1984: 6) – is clearly relevant to the study of the research events discussed in Chapters 4–6, where the participants were asked to talk about a favourite radio or television programme. In the first section of this chapter I will therefore provide a brief account of Bourdieu's achievement in *Distinction*, and of some of the critiques of his work, in order to situate my own study and to extrapolate the most useful insights from Bourdieu.

As Mary Mander has commented, the concept of the 'habitus' is fundamental to Bourdieu's work (1987: 428). In *Distinction* Bourdieu refers back to this concept, which he describes as 'the generative formula which makes it possible to account both for the classifiable practices and products and for the judgements, themselves classified, which make these practices and works into a system of distinctive signs' (Bourdieu, 1984: 170). In his view the habitus is a matrix of dispositions (Mander defines 'disposition' as 'a way of being, an habitual state or a predisposed inclination'; 1987: 429) which results directly from the material conditions of existence, and hence practices, of a class or class fraction. The image of the matrix brings to mind the plastic maps of France that French schoolchildren are equipped with – each of which reveals a particular aspect of the country, such as its geography or administrative boundaries. These perspex diagrams provide a transparent window both onto geographical fact and onto the ideology of the French nation, through their reproduction of the image of the perfectly balanced hexagon. In a similar manner, the habitus provides a way of seeing the world, a structure which organises and interprets experience, and a generative framework for actions (or, in Bourdieu's terms, practices). As Terry Lovell points out, however, the habitus is not based on conscious knowledge or learning, but on 'the ability to function effectively within a given social field' (2000: 12). Although some of the dispositions of a particular habitus may be based on ideological beliefs, the habitus cannot be described as an ideology. It affects the body as much as the mind, and in Lovell's words is to be found in 'the bearing of the body (hexis), and in deeply ingrained habits of behaviour, feeling and thought' (ibid.: 12). The habitus is uniquely adapted to a particular class, and one of its principal functions is indeed to render that class-specific experience acceptable, to make a virtue of necessity by generating a match between material conditions and structures of perception: 'The habitus is by necessity internalised and converted into a disposition that generates meaningful practices and meaning-giving perceptions' (Bourdieu, 1984: 170). According to Bourdieu, the habitus is internalised in early childhood so that the family and later the school play a crucial role in this process (see Bourdieu and Passeron, 1977). However, subsequent experiences can also shape the habitus, and at some points in *Distinction* Bourdieu emphasises the importance of trajectory, as well as class of origin (e.g. 1984: 110). Like the maps of France, it seems that layers of habitus can be superimposed, one on another – so that the early versions are not entircly effaced, but merely enriched by subsequent refigurings.

It is in this area that an important critique of the concept of habitus has been made:

> We are told that the initial habitus is durable but, since it is also transformable, we are never sure just what difference this durability makes, or under what circumstances it makes a difference for what phenomena. This question, that of the stability and plasticity of personality, is one about which Bourdieu has little concrete to say.
>
> (DiMaggio, 1979: 1468)

The habitus is an ambitious notion in that it attempts to explain the relationship between structure and agency, and to account for the acceptance by the dominated classes of hierarchies of value by which they are negatively defined. However, the unexplained functioning of its durability/transformability indicated by DiMaggio is problematic, as is the rather reductive rigidity of the correlation made by Bourdieu between social class and cultural taste. The fact that individuals can be culturally in one class and economically in another, or that their cultural tastes might be more complex and contradictory than survey data can reveal, as well as the relative lack of attention to factors such as gender and ethnicity in *Distinction*, are further problems (though gender is the topic of a later work – discussed below).

In *Distinction* Bourdieu is in effect exploring the effects of habitus in terms of lifestyle and cultural choices. He argues that cultural differences between classes contribute to the reproduction of the economic and cultural inequalities of the existing social order. This argument hinges both on the concept of habitus and on the notions of cultural and economic capital. The idea of cultural capital, and the attempt to conceptualise the relationship between economic and cultural inequalities, can be seen as one of the important contributions of Bourdieu's work, although some commentators have argued that his use of the term and the proliferation of different types of capital – symbolic, linguistic, academic and so on – in his writing render it imprecise and variable (DiMaggio, 1979: 1468–9). Frow finds the relationship between economic and cultural capital to be inadequately theorised in Bourdieu's work, and disagrees with Bourdieu's notion of the mutual convertibility of the two capitals (Frow, 1987). I would agree with Frow that the two capitals are not equivalent; as he says, they imply very different relationships to the means of production, and hence very different forms of social power (ibid.: 70). However, lack of equivalence does not necessarily imply inconvertibility, and in my view, Bourdieu's insistence on the links between economic and cultural capitals is more convincing than Frow suggests. Bourdieu points to the crucial role played by the education system both in permitting the conversion of cultural into economic capital through the value in the job market of qualifications, and also, precisely, vice versa:

> It can immediately be seen that the link between economic and cultural capital is established through the mediation of the time needed for acquisition ... the length of time for which a given individual can prolong his acquisition process depends on the length of time for which his family can provide him with the free time, i.e., time free from economic necessity, which is the precondition for the initial accumulation.
>
> (Bourdieu, 1986: 246)

Bourdieu aims to avoid both the denial of such links, for instance, through the ideology of natural ability, and economism, 'which, on the grounds that every type of capital is reducible in the last analysis to economic capital, ignores what makes the specific efficacy of the other types of capital' (ibid.: 253). Thus the capitals are not reducible, one to another, but they are linked, and at different levels, and in specific contexts convertible:

> So it has to be posited simultaneously that economic capital is at the root of all the other types of capital and that these transformed, disguised forms of economic capital, never entirely reducible to that definition, produce their most specific effects only to the extent that they conceal (not least from their possessors) the fact that economic capital is at their root, in other words – but only in the last analysis – at the root of their effects.
>
> (ibid.: 252)

In the first chapter of *Distinction*, 'The Aristocracy of Culture', Bourdieu attempts to demonstrate how differing relationships to art and high culture are expressive (as well as reproductive) of the class-based hierarchy of French society. He identifies three forms of cultural and artistic taste which are broadly linked to social classes: the legitimate taste of the dominant classes, the middle-brow taste of the lower middle classes (*classes moyennes*) and the popular taste of the working classes (*classes populaires*; Bourdieu, 1984: 16). He associates the first of these with the 'aesthetic disposition' (ibid.: 28–30) and the 'pure gaze' (ibid.: 3) which can be summarised as a tendency to prioritise form over content, and which, as a result, are capable of categorising art according to period, style and artist, thus fully mobilising and displaying significant amounts of cultural capital. The 'popular aesthetic' (ibid.: 32–4), 'naïve gaze' (ibid.: 32) or 'barbarous taste' (ibid.: 130–2), on the other hand, have no interest in artistic forms, or knowledge of their history or significance. Instead, in a rapprochement of 'art' and 'life', art works are judged according to their content: 'Popular taste applies the schemes of the ethos, which pertain in the ordinary circumstances of life, to legitimate works of art, and so performs a systematic reduction of the things of art to the things of life' (ibid.: 5). This also results in judgements which are based on ethics rather than aesthetics, and in a working-class rejection of modern or avant-garde art which foregrounds formal experimentation. Immediate sensual pleasure is preferred to the more distanced mode of appreciation of the aesthete

> who, as is seen whenever he appropriates one of the objects of popular taste (e.g., Westerns or strip cartoons), introduces a gap – the measure of his distinct distinction – vis-à-vis 'first degree' perception, by displacing the interest from the 'content', characters, plot etc. to the form, to the specifically artistic effects which are only appreciated relationally, through a comparison with other works.
>
> (ibid.: 34)

A further element in these hierarchies of distinction which Bourdieu is particularly concerned with is the difference between two elements of the dominant class – the bourgeoisie (who enjoy both economic and cultural capital, though more of the former) and the intellectuals, who are richer in cultural than economic capital, and who are described by Bourdieu as 'the dominated fractions of the dominant class' (ibid.: 170). The intellectual approach to art represents a heightened version of the pure gaze and aesthetic disposition described above in its particular penchant for the avant-garde. If the interest in formal and stylistic properties and the rejection of sensual pleasure (which in its more refined form, e.g. impressionist paintings, even the bourgeois is attached to) characterise the intellectual approach, the taste for social critique which it also encapsulates is seen by Bourdieu as the result of a habitus based on low economic capital:

> So the contrast which is usually drawn between 'intellectual' or 'left-bank' taste and 'bourgeois' or 'right-bank' taste is not only an opposition

between the preference for contemporary works ... and the taste for older more consecrated works ... it is also an opposition between two world views, two philosophies of life, symbolised, for example, by Renoir and Goya (or Maurois and Kafka), the centres of two constellations of choices, *la vie en rose* and *la vie en noir*, rose-coloured spectacles and dark thoughts, boulevard theatre and avant-garde theatre, the social optimism of people without problems and the anti-bourgeois pessimism of people with problems.

(ibid.: 292)

Several commentators have identified a hostility to the intellectual class in Bourdieu's writing. For Garnham and Williams, this 'frontal assault' on the intelligentsia is a positive achievement (1980: 210). They also see in Bourdieu's work a positive valuation of working-class culture which 'never lapses into naive populism or workerism' (Garnham and Williams, 1980: 222). Other writers are, however, less sanguine on both counts. Frow finds that Bourdieu fails to account for the specificity of the intelligentsia, and is unconvinced, given the very different constitution of capitals of each, by the merging of intelligentsia and bourgeoisie into a single dominant class. According to Frow, Bourdieu's attribution of intellectuals and bourgeoisie to the same dominant class is undermined by his own analysis of the differences between the cultures of the two groups (see quotation from Bourdieu above). It also leads him to 'neglect the potential for contradiction in the role of the intelligentsia' (Frow, 1987: 70) and to oversimplify the intelligentsia's class location, which is in fact 'unstable and not in itself unified' (ibid.: 71).

Mary Mander also questions Bourdieu's views on intellectuals and on human nature generally. In relation to the former she is unconvinced by the economic or at least self-interested motivation which Bourdieu ascribes to the intellectual's perpetual pursuit of cultural capital: 'since there are, indeed, far greater profits to be had outside the academy – at least in the USA' (Mander, 1987: 445). This raises the broader question of human motivation: 'At rock bottom, Bourdieu's metaphorical preferences deny the moral dimension of human pursuits and refuse to recognise the ludic and expressive quality of human experience' (ibid.: 445). Mander rejects Bourdieu's metaphor of the 'games of culture' (Bourdieu, 1984: 54) on the grounds, first, that such games are in fact a reflection of his image of a 'dog-eat-dog world in which human beings engage in ploys, artifices, strategies, bluffs and disguises to increase their own social and cultural capital to the disadvantage of others' (Mander, 1987: 443). Presumably for Mander the ludic might include practices which cannot be reduced to such struggles for ascendancy, and Bourdieu's view of society is in this sense both too grim, and too reductive. Second, she notes his use of the term 'game' to indicate that the activities concerned, which tend to be those of intellectuals, are something of a sham. Again, she questions his negative picture of intellectuals.

These kinds of questions also inform Mander's critique of Bourdieu's analysis of the dominated classes, which, unlike Garnham and Williams, she sees as being 'from the point of view of the elite' (Mander, 1987: 436). She questions Bourdieu's assumption that working-class people accept the hierarchy of cultural value which excludes them: 'I can find nothing in his work to indicate that he has actually tested whether or not members of the working class *do believe* in the inherent supe-riority of the so-called dominant culture' (ibid.: 436). Frow is also critical in this respect, and sees a regressive binarism in Bourdieu's portrayal of the oppositions between high and popular culture. Like Mander, he questions Bourdieu's appar-ently unshakeable belief in the dominance of high culture:

> Cultural disadvantage is, in fact, operative only *on the ground of high culture.* Bourdieu assumes that the legitimacy of this ground is still imposed on the dominated classes; but it may well be the case, particularly since the massive growth of a television culture in which working-class people tend to be fully competent, that it has become largely irrelevant.
>
> (Frow, 1987: 65)

Mander finds the universal acceptance of the legitimacy of high culture particu-larly unlikely in the British and American contexts, and thus highlights what is in my view one of the salient features of Bourdieu's work in *Distinction* – that is, its specificity to France, and even to the France of the period in the 1960s when the survey work was carried out. This is particularly true in relation to his analysis of the role of the intellectual class, which it is arguably much easier to conceive of as a class in the French context, where intellectual brilliance is more highly respected than it is, for instance, in the UK, and has its own social niche, particularly in Parisian society. The figures of Sartre and Beauvoir are a significant presence in French culture, and it can be argued that they have legitimised an intellectual lifestyle which has no equivalent in anglophone countries.[1] The conversion of cultural into economic capital is a more convincing notion in the context of an education system where teachers' pay and hours are differentiated according to level of qualification; as Bourdieu's translator points out, pay is related to academic qualifications in the whole civil service (Bourdieu, 1986: 256, note 10). Bourdieu's comments on intellectuals have to be seen in this context, and do not necessarily transfer to other cultures. To some extent, the privileged position of intellectuals in French society accounts for his sense of the widespread belief in the legitimacy of high culture even in the dominated classes. He is not alone among French writers in recognising feelings of inferiority and shame among working-class people when they are confronted with middle-class or intellectual culture (see Ernaux, 1997). However, the theory is weak on this point and, as Frow indicates, it fails to take into account the impact of mass cultural forms such as television on these hierarchies.

After this discussion, what is left of Bourdieu's analysis, and how does it relate to this study? The primary legacy of Bourdieu's *Distinction* here is probably the concept of cultural capital, which is closely linked to educational qualifications.[2] First, this is clearly relevant to the analysis of the texts themselves, where, particu-larly in the case of *Morse*, the inscription of various forms of cultural capital in the text, such as classical music, becomes a marker of the claim to 'quality'. The implication of this, and one of the questions posed by this study, is that Bourdieuian systems of distinction are at work in the fields of radio and television, rather than questioned by them, as Frow suggests. The notion of cultural capital will also be useful in the analysis of talk about these texts, where it seems highly likely, particularly in view of their 'quality' label, that participants will draw on the cultural capital at their disposal. This is likely to affect *how* the texts are talked about as much as the content of the discussion. It remains to be seen whether the kinds of differences attributed by Bourdieu to the 'pure gaze' and the 'naïve gaze' will emerge here. Will the discussions and interviews be characterised by the dominance of formal analysis on the one hand, and ethical considerations stemming from a rapprochement of 'art' and life on the other? Will Bourdieu's split between middle-class distance and popular involvement, between analysis of the text as cultural artefact and as 'slice of life', emerge as significant differentiations here? Will it be possible to observe in these events the claiming of cultural distinction, and hence of power, which Bourdieu sees as fundamental social processes?

By extension, the notion of subcultural capital developed by Sarah Thornton is also likely to be relevant in the discussion of fan cultures around *Morse* and *The Archers*. The extent to which this term can also be applied to feminist talk about media texts, and the overlaps between cultural and subcultural capitals in social identities informed by feminisms, will also be areas of discussion which clearly rely on Bourdieuian terminology. How does a feminist, of whatever precise political persuasion, distinguish herself as such in talk about media texts? This question seems particularly relevant given the absence of a single 'politically correct' line on popular media texts in contemporary feminisms.Will the distinguishing marks of feminist talk which I may identify here bear any similarity to Bourdieu's depiction of intellectual culture? Bourdieu's view of the cultural game played by the dominant class is that it must be played with 'playful seriousness'. He comments:

> This is clearly seen when by an accident of social genetics, into the well-policed world of intellectual games there comes one of those people (one thinks of Rousseau or Chernyshevsky) who brings inappropriate stakes and interests into the games of culture; who gets so involved in the game that they abandon the margin of neutralising distance that the *illusio* (belief in the game) demands; who treat intellectual struggles, the object of so many pathetic manifestos, as a simple question of right and wrong, life and death. This is why the logic of the game has already assigned them rôles – eccentric or boor – which they will *play* despite themselves in the eyes of those who know how to stay within the bound of the intellectual illusion and who cannot see them any other way.
>
> (Bourdieu, 1984: 54)

This quotation raises a number of points which may well be relevant to the analysis of some of these research events, particularly those where an intellectual feminist persona emerges. The first is the whole concept of play, and the 'neutralising distance' on which it depends. If one accepts that in some intellectual talk a distanced and to varying degrees playful mode can be adopted in order to emphasise academic detachment and precisely the ability to *play* with ideas, then Bourdieu may have a point, at least in some instances. This combination of distance and play would be one possible mode of talk about these texts, and this mode would also replicate Bourdieu's description of intellectual appropriations of popular culture, which rely on the establishment of a gap between the pleasures of the text (immediately available to all) and theorisation about its formal properties (the distinguishing mark of the intellectual). The question of whether such talk can be associated with Mander's more generous notion of the ludic, or whether in fact it can be seen as a further manifestation of the kind of grim struggle for domination and the inauthenticity which Bourdieu ascribes to intellectuals, can only be determined in the detailed analysis of each sample of talk.

This leads to a second question raised by the quotation, and Bourdieu's ideas generally: what happens when there is a clash of dispositions, cultures or different levels of cultural capital in one interaction? Does the dominant class inevitably dominate? Are those who do not fit in categorised as eccentric or boors? Is the recognition of the struggle for dominance in fact the only way of analysing social interactions? In the end, Bourdieu's theory of cultural capital as dominance will in some modest way be put to empirical test here, and it is a test which, despite the enormous detail of his own surveys, his theories were not subjected to, since nowhere does he analyse the functioning of social hierarchies of distinction in actual social interactions. In Bourdieu's own words:

> When endeavouring to grasp systems of tastes, a survey by closed questionnaire is never more than a second best, imposed by the need to obtain a large amount of comparable data on a sample large enough to be treated statistically. It leaves out almost everything to do with the modality of practices; but in an area which is that of art, in the sense of a personal way of being and doing, as in 'art of living', the way things are done and the way they are talked about, blasé or off-hand, serious or fervent, often makes all the difference (at least when dealing with *common* practices, such as viewing TV or cinema).
>
> (Bourdieu, 1984: 506)

Feminisms, Gender and Identity

As the account given above illustrates, Bourdieu's theories in *Distinction* are mainly concerned with social and cultural hierarchies based on class. The relationship between class, education and cultural taste is a significant dimension of this project, but other socially constructed forms of difference, such as gender and national or ethnic identity, are equally important. Furthermore, as I have already indicated, one domain of this study is the social construction of feminist identities. In order to underpin these aspects of the empirical work, I will focus here on theories of gender and on the divergent approaches to the question of identity in general which they reveal. Inevitably this discussion raises underlying issues which are far from resolved in contemporary cultural and social theory: the relationship between structure and agency, materialism and idealism, discourse and reality. Such large and complex questions are unlikely to be resolved here, but a path through the arguments needs to be hacked out, in order to make clear the theoretical basis of the audience study which forms the main body of this work.

First, in part as a corrective to the partial account of Bourdieu's work given above, some discussion of his views on gender is called for. In *Masculine Domination*, published in France in 1998, Bourdieu has provided some of the analysis which is missing from *Distinction*. Here he describes the role of gender in the construction of the habitus, going so far as to describe genders as themselves 'sexually characterised habitus' (Bourdieu, [1998] 2001: 3). Basing his analysis on his earlier ethnographic study of the Berbers of Kabylia, Bourdieu argues that the dispositions of which the habitus is composed are inseparable from the social structures 'that produce and reproduce them in both men and women, and in particular from the whole structure of technical and ritual activities that is ultimately grounded in the structure of the market in symbolic goods' (ibid.: 42). Bourdieu's emphasis on the symbolic in his discussion of gender is important since he sees women playing a specific role as objects of exchange between men in Kabylia, where male systems of honour depend on the virtue of their female relatives. In contemporary France this phenomenon takes a less obvious form, with women (particularly, though not exclusively, in bourgeois families) functioning as carriers of symbolic capital through their work in the home and family. Bourdieu argues that this relational and aesthetic work is often unrecognised and generally undervalued and unrewarded (ibid.: 42–9, 96–102). Terry Lovell has pointed to the difficulty which this aspect of Bourdieu's theory poses for feminist analysts. She refers to the body of feminist work, particularly in the field of psychoanalysis, which suggests that women do not unproblematically accept and assume femininity, or their positioning as objects of exchange between men. Lovell asks how we might conceptualise the complex negotiation of identity required by female subjects who, as well as being positioned as the repositories of capital for others, themselves aspire to 'existence as capital-accumulating subjects' (Lovell, 2000: 22).

Bourdieu's emphasis on the symbolic role of women does not preclude a strong sense of the importance of material structures and institutions in his analysis of gender inequalities. In this text Bourdieu also makes it clear that he sees gender differences and specifically the power differential between men and women as socially constructed, but nonetheless deeply embedded and embodied, practices: 'Symbolic force is a form of power that is exerted on bodies, directly and as if by magic, without any physical constraint; but this magic works only on the basis of the dispositions deposited, like springs, at the deepest level of the body' (Bourdieu,

2001: 38). Given this emphasis on the profound roots of practices based on gender inequality, some feminists, such as Lovell, have commented that Bourdieu's work results in 'a strong sense of political paralysis' (Lovell, 2000: 17). She remarks that when questioned on the subject of agency, Bourdieu's answer ran to four pages (Lovell, 2000: 16). However, Bourdieu is not alone in struggling between the sense of the power of social structures which their analysis must inevitably convey and a political commitment to the importance of collective and individual political agency. In the next section of this chapter I will consider similar tensions in feminist writing on the topics of gender and identity.

Chris Weedon's discussion of the relationship between feminism and poststructuralism emphasises the significance of the latter for an understanding of gendered subjectivity: 'For poststructuralism, femininity and masculinity are constantly in process, and subjectivity, which most discourses seek to fix, is constantly subject to dispersal' ([1987] 1997: 96). While on the one hand 'a poststructuralist position on subjectivity and consciousness relativizes the individual's sense of herself by making it an effect of discourse', Weedon goes on to argue that:

> to see subjectivity as a process, open to change, is not to deny the importance of particular forms of individual subjective investment which have all the force of apparently full subjectivity to the individual and which are necessary for our participation in social processes and practices.
>
> (1997: 102)

Here, the threat to agency is less the sense of the fixity of the habitus and the social and material structures which produce and reproduce it, but the instability or dispersal of the subject. As a political movement aiming to bring about social change, feminisms cannot easily relinquish the notion of agency, and yet there is a tension between this and post-structuralist theories of the subject as an effect of discourse. This tension is reflected in much feminist writing, and Weedon's text is no exception. Her phrase 'particular forms of individual subjective investment which have all the force of apparently full subjectivity to the individual' suggests a tension between theory and practice or lived experience. Here, rather than being liberated by the awareness of the construction of her subjectivity in discourse, the feminist activist might need to retain a more traditional notion of identity if she is to be politically effective. Weedon reinforces this point later, in a discussion of identity politics and postmodernism:

> While there may be strategic needs for identity politics, defined by shared forms of oppression and political objectives, postmodern feminists argue that it is important to recognise the nature and limitations of the essentialist foundations of many forms of identity politics. They propose a theory of identity which sees it as discursively produced, necessary but always contingent and strategic.
>
> (1997: 176)

The relationship between discourse and material reality is a significant dimension of the feminist debate. Weedon emphasises the material location of discourses: 'In order to be effective and powerful, a discourse needs a material base in established social institutions and practices' (ibid.: 96). It follows then that political intervention at the discursive level will not suffice: 'Discursive practices are embedded in material power relationships which also require transformation for change to be realised' (ibid.: 103). The discussion of the work of Judith Butler is one of the areas of feminist theorising where the tension between the post-structuralist emphasis on discourse and materialist feminisms has been articulated (see *Feminist Review* 64, Spring 2000). In Butler's view, the binaries of gender identity are maintained by repeated performance within the discursive framework of compulsory reproductive heterosexuality. According to Lovell, Butler distinguishes between 'performatives' which are performances that reinforce the social status quo and enhance social status (such as marriage) and 'mere performances' which lack this authority (Lovell, 2000: 15). The constant repetition of performances which are also *performative* succeeds in making them appear 'natural' and in reinforcing the myth that gender identity is the expression of an inner core of difference. In reality, according to Butler, gender and biological sex are cultural constructions; although identities are in fact fluid and unstable, heterosexual coherence is maintained by the imposition of stability. Gender performance is thus 'a strategy of survival within compulsory systems' (Butler, 1990: 139).

Despite these hegemonic forces, 'the construction of coherence conceals the gender discontinuities that run rampant within heterosexual, bisexual, and gay and lesbian contexts in which gender does not necessarily follow from sex, and desire, or sexuality generally, does not seem to follow from gender' (ibid.: 138). Butler concludes that the parody of gender which underlies practices such as drag has subversive potential: 'Just as bodily surfaces are enacted *as* the natural, so these surfaces can become the site of a dissonant and denaturalised performance that reveals the performative status of the natural itself' (ibid.: 146). For Butler, this opens up, rather than closes down, the possibility of political agency:

> the critical task is, rather, to locate strategies of subversive repetition enabled by those constructions, to affirm the local possibilities of intervention through participating in precisely those practices of repetition that constitute identity and, therefore, present the immanent possibility of contesting them.
>
> (ibid.: 147)

However, in a significant paragraph Butler states the important proviso that 'parody by itself is not subversive'. While some repetitions are 'effectively disruptive, truly troubling', others 'become domesticated' and merely confirm hegemonic structures. The implication, though it is not developed, is that contexts of reception and production of the performance are significant factors: 'What performance where will invert the inner/outer distinction and compel a radical rethinking of the psychological presuppositions of gender identity and sexuality?'

(ibid.: 139). Elisa Glick (2000) has argued that Butler's emphasis on discourse leads to an evacuation of the material, or, more precisely, to a lack of theorisation of the relationship between representations and social and economic realities. In other words, Butler does not explain how the transgressive performances she valorises will work to transform oppressive political, economic and social conditions. As a result, the claim for their subversive potential may be less convincing than it appears at first. Glick goes on to argue that in fact Butler's theory is consistent with post-Fordist consumerism, agreeing with Rosemary Hennessy that postmodernism is 'the cultural commonsense of post-industrial capitalism' (Hennessy, 1996: 232–3, cited in Glick, 2000: 34). Glick also recounts how since the publication of her book *Gender Trouble* Butler has sought to distance herself from those 'bad readers' who have taken up her claims for the subversive potential of transgressive gender identities with enthusiasm, and for whom, in Butler's words, the idea that 'I can get up in the morning, look in my closet and decide which gender I want to be today' has led to their 'taking on gender as a kind of consumerism' (Butler, 1992: 83, quoted in Glick, 2000: 35).

Butler's attempt to distance herself from some readings of *Gender Trouble* was also noted by Bourdieu, and interpreted as a rejection of the 'voluntaristic' version of gender put forward in that work (Bourdieu, 2001: 103, note 37). Needless to say, he is sceptical about Butler's theories of the transgressive performance of gender, which he describes as 'spuriously revolutionary redefinitions of subversive voluntarism' (ibid.: 103).[3] Terry Lovell provides an interesting overview of the two theorists, where she argues that one can provide a useful corrective to the other. She sees Bourdieu's theory as salutary for postmodern feminisms because of its stress on the importance of social class. If Bourdieu fails to account for those social spaces where resistance to gender norms can occur, or where at least they can be exposed, Butler's and other postmodernists' emphasis on masquerade and play sits uneasily with the emphasis on the power and solidity of the binaries of gender (Lovell, 2000: 16–17). In my view Butler's theory of gender is ground-breaking; nonetheless it does not fully explain how *in practice* certain kinds of performance can subvert the strong forces of 'compulsory systems' and 'politically enforced performativity' which she identifies (Butler, 1990: 139, 146). In this sense Butler may have more in common with Bourdieu than at first appears.

In their introduction to a collection of articles based on empirical work on identity, Sasha Roseneil and Julie Seymour identify two main approaches to identity in contemporary academic work: the post-structuralist deconstruction of identity, of which Butler would be a leading proponent, and social constructionist theories of identity. The former tends to be based in cultural studies and to argue that the fluid and constantly fluctuating subject is constituted in and through discourse. Roseneil and Seymour point to the problem in relation to agency which this poses (and which emerges in different ways in discussions of both Bourdieu and Butler): 'post-structuralist theories of identity tend to emphasise processes of subjectivization in which human beings have little agency against the power of discourse, to resist or transform dominant discourses and therefore to produce new identities' (1999: 4–5). They cite Butler's theory of performativity as an instance of this, arguing that the emphasis on the performance of gender as an effect of discourse removes any notion of choice or intentionality (ibid.: 5). Like post-structuralist deconstruction, social constructionist theory is concerned to question earlier versions of the unitary, stable subject based on Enlightenment philosophy, but retains the idea that individuals actively and consciously construct their identities. The restoration of reflexivity and conscious agency into the process is perhaps particularly attractive to those engaged in empirical work; Roseneil and Seymour comment that their collection, which like social constructionist theory is located in the field of sociology and consists mainly of accounts of empirical research, generally 'sees identities as actively constructed, chosen, created and performed by people in their daily lives' (ibid.: 5). Roseneil and Seymour's account constructs a binary opposition of post-structuralist evacuation and social constructionist reclaiming of agency which does not fully reflect the complexity of arguments on both sides. As my discussion of the work of Weedon suggests, many feminist post-structuralists emphasise the importance of agency, and/or of the embeddedness of discourses in material structures. However, the split which Roseneil and Seymour identify between social science and cultural studies approaches to gender formation and identity is problematic. Celia Lury argues that there is a need for a feminist methodology 'that is sensitive to both social and cultural specificity' and to the relationship between the two (1995: 43). If, in its anxiety to avoid interpreting representations as reflections of social reality, feminist cultural analysis has failed to link the cultural and the social, then, as Lury implies, work which focuses not only on textual analysis, but also on audience readings and appropriations, may be well placed to make the crucial links (ibid.: 37).

Beverley Skeggs, whose work is also discussed by Lovell, seems exemplary in this respect. Skeggs warns that

> the individualism which is assumed in a great deal of theorising on subjectivity is the product of, and in the interests of, privileged groups in very specific historical and national circumstances. The project of the self is a Western bourgeois project.
>
> (1997: 163)

Skeggs' study of white working-class women led her to question the individualism of contemporary theories of identity; she questioned the level of agency which the women she researched were able to employ in their construction of identity, emphasising the class- and gender-based constraints within which they were operating: 'This book is not an account of how individuals make themselves but how they cannot fail to make themselves in particular ways' (ibid.: 162). If Skeggs' observations seem to question the notion of agency, or at least the degree of agency associated with social constructionist and some post-structuralist theories, she is equally critical of some aspects of the post-structuralist or postmodern deconstruction of identity, where she sees a similar individualism:

many postmodern theories and theories of performativity assume that people can traverse the boundaries in which they are located, and many feminists have assumed that all women have equal access to ways of being (be it feminist, gendered, sexed, etc.).

(ibid.: 19–20)

On the basis of her own ethnographic study Skeggs concluded that discourses of individualism were largely irrelevant or even inaccessible to the women she studied, for whom public discourses such as respectability were more significant, and who sought to avoid drawing negative attention to themselves: 'the women's ontological security was found precisely in not being an "individual" but in "fitting in"' (ibid.: 163). Skeggs' comments are an important warning to academic researchers steeped in contemporary Western middle-class notions of self-image, personal space and therapeutic self-revelation. The contradiction between the prevalent post-structuralist deconstruction of the subject and the 'real-life' preoccupation with self-development in some contemporary intellectual milieus seems ripe for Bourdieuian analysis.

Conclusion: Empirical Research and Post-structuralist Accounts of Identity

For the purposes of this study identity is a key concept, although my use of the term is imbued with the critiques of it made by feminist post-structuralist thought, and is close to Weedon's formulation: while on one level recognising the theoretical limitations of the term, my contention is that it may well be a strategic and necessary notion in people's everyday experience and talk. The idea that individuals construct their identity or present versions of themselves within available discourses and the material constraints imposed by their social location is fundamental to this research. In some ways this position is a combination of the theories referred to above: I have retained the sense that identity construction is an active and self-aware process; from poststructuralism I have acquired the awareness that this construction takes place within a discursive framework, and that identity is not fixed, stable or permanent, but constantly in process. Butler's notions of 'performance' and 'performativity' also seem relevant to the analysis of social interaction: while the subversive potential she claims for some performances may not be fulfilled, the idea that the maintenance of gender, and perhaps other forms of identity, requires constant and repeated acts of performance seems suggestive. The talk which I analyse in Chapters 4–6 may well illustrate the constant work which identity of various kinds requires, thus belying any essentialist notions of gender.

Perhaps the most clearly post-structuralist element of the use of the term 'identity' in this study is the strong sense of its limitations. The meaning of the term identity in the context of the analysis of talk about media texts is often very limited indeed: identity as momentarily constructed within a specific social context is often the appropriate sense. While to varying degrees individuals construct coherent biographical narratives which are often underpinned by an illusory sense of a stable and developing self, the identities constructed or subject positions assumed in talk about media or anything else may have much shorter-term functions and resonances. In this they converge with post-structuralist accounts of the unstable and discursively constructed subject.

For this reason, discourse analysis will provide a significant method of analysing identity construction in talk. In the words of Potter and Wetherell:

> Not only do we need to be able to describe the content of representations of people in different contexts or the sheer range of self-images available in ordinary talk, but we also need to ask how these images are used and to what end, and thus what they achieve for the speaker immediately, inter-personally, and then in terms of wider social implications.
>
> (1987: 110)

As Skeggs has emphasised, questions of access, or lack of access, to certain discourses are crucial and should be taken into account in the analysis. Lury has also pointed to the common assumption in recent academic work that 'identities are universally available as resources, that identities are constituted as the cultural property of the individual which all individuals are equally free to exchange' (1996: 41). The emphasis on the individual critiqued by Skeggs and Lury may to some extent be attenuated here by posing Potter and Wetherell's questions in rela-tion to the focus group as a whole, since it is quite possible that the construction of identities in these contexts may be a collective, rather than, or as well as, an indi-vidual, act or performance.

Bourdieu's concept of cultural capitals will be particularly useful here since it is likely that talk about media texts will reveal different kinds and levels of cultural capital. The linking of these variations to educational level or social class may at times seem evident, and at others of necessity more tentative. While individuals may well exercise choice in the way they present themselves or their relation to the texts being discussed, these choices will be exercised within the limitations imposed by the discourses available in the wider society and the particular social interac-tion, as well as the individual's social location and resulting cultural capitals. In Lury's words:

> The ability to be an individual, including the ability to own an identity as a resource, to display it as a performance, is thus necessarily gendered. But how it is gendered, and how this process of gendering is also raced and classed, can only be determined through investigation.
>
> (1996: 42)

This question is highly relevant to all of the empirical research presented in Chapters 4–7. However, along with Butler's notion of performance it is particu-larly pertinent to the part of this research which is concerned with feminist cultural identities (Chapter 6). Can we speak of a performance of feminism, rather than of femininity? If so how would such performances be different from gender identities less informed by feminisms, and how, following Lury's formulation, would they be gendered, raced and classed? Could self-conscious performance of gender identity be part of the 'resource' available to those enjoying feminist cultural capital? Will we find such 'bad' (or maybe very good) readers of Butler in this sample? What will it mean if they are heterosexual couples in unisex jeans rather than leather-clad SM dykes, or drag queens in gold lamé? To repeat Butler's own words: 'What performance where will invert the inner/outer distinction and compel a radical rethinking of the psychological presuppositions of gender identity and sexuality?' (1990: 139).

Empirical audience research faces the difficult task of avoiding essentialism or determinism in the use of the categories of gender, 'race' and class, while at the same time retaining a constant awareness and sensitivity to the limitations and constraints within which respondents operate, the wider social context for their talk. In practice, the avoidance of unsubstantiated generalisation or assumptions of causality ('this group spoke in this way because they are working class') needs to be balanced against an excessive emphasis on the individual and individual interpretations which reproduce Western humanist notions of the centrality of the unitary subject. Pam Alldred (1998) has discussed the dilemmas facing researchers influenced by poststructuralism and feminism who would question the objectivist stance of much empirical research. When the objectivist or realist warrant for the validity of the research findings is rejected, how can research 'findings' be presented? Is post-structuralist empirical research a contradiction in terms? Clearly, the kind of claims for truth made in the presentation of research are fundamental. Alldred makes a number of important points in response to this question. She argues that the traditional language of research, the use of specular imagery, for instance, indicates its epistemological basis in objectivism, and that such language can and should be avoided in post-structuralist-influenced accounts.

For feminist researchers a particular dilemma is the conflict between the politically motivated desire to represent the voices of respondents (especially when they belong to oppressed groups) and post-structuralist questioning of the conception of identity as reified and fixed and of the notion of 'authentic' experience (both of which may be implied by the term 'voice'). In Alldred's view it is crucial to emphasise the socially constructed nature both of respondents' accounts and of the researcher's own analysis:

> In poststructuralist informed discourse analytic research, representations of interviewees' accounts are made without a realist, objectivist warrant. Research is recognized to be a practice of re-presentation, and 'findings' a re/presentation[4] through a particular lens. The participant's 'voice' is seen as produced from what was culturally available to her/him, rather than a private reserve of meaning. The fantasy of the authentic subject, one whose subjectivity is imagined to be independent of, or prior to, culture is rejected.
>
> (1998: 155)

She also cautions against any automatic notion of research as empowerment for the researched:

> Recognizing the fact that in providing a research voice for a particular group we may simultaneously reinforce their construction as Other, and concurrently our own perspective or the dominant cultural perspective as central, prevents us from assuming that our work is bound to be liberatory.
>
> (ibid.: 154)

Alldred suggests that in some contexts the notion of 'voice' might be considered as a discourse itself, and that in general a discourse analytic approach which is sensitive to the broader social context of power relations in which the research takes place can help resolve some of these issues. A crucial aspect of this is the treatment of both researcher and researched as occupying (changing) subject positions rather than 'owning' fixed identities, and the researcher's own reflexivity, both in the process of data collection and in presentation of the analysis. A balance needs to be struck between allowing one's account to collapse into relativism and recognising and avowing its partiality.

While attempting to integrate Alldred's feminist and post-structuralist cautions into my research, I am also aware that the decision to conduct empirical research does imply a belief in some resulting greater knowledge of the social world, however limited and partial it may be. The 'turn to language' in empirical work should not have the result of completely undermining its validity. Research which engages with people outside the Academy is obliged to face the kind of ethical and epistemological questions indicated in this discussion. It seems important for empirical research to retain the qualities of self-questioning and reflexivity without colluding with the suspicion it sometimes generates among predominantly textual researchers. Lorraine Code's description of the tension between postmodern and post-structuralist notions of the fragmented self and the need to retain the concept of the person both in everyday relationships and in research is very relevant here:

> The contention that people are *knowable* may sit uneasily with psychoanalytic decentring of conscious subjectivity and postmodern critiques of the unified subject of Enlightenment humanism. But I think it is a tension that has to be acknowledged and maintained. In practice, people often know one another well enough to make good decisions about who can be counted on and who cannot, who makes a good ally and who does not. Yet precisely because of the fluctuations and contradictions of subjectivity, this process is ongoing, communicative and interpretive. It is never fixed or complete; any fixity claimed for 'the self' will be a fixity in flux. Nevertheless, I argue that something must be fixed to 'contain' the flux even enough to permit references to and ongoing relationship with 'this person'. Knowing people always occurs within the terms of this tension.
>
> (Code, 1993: 34)

This kind of tension underlies this project. Its aim was never to give an accurate or full account of the respondents' personalities or subjectivities, and in many ways the use of pseudonyms emphasises the fact that I am evoking subject positions adopted in a particular research event, rather than 'people'. Nonetheless, as Code says, 'something must be fixed', to make sense of the clusters of subject positions identified. Just as we read and categorise others in everyday social life, here, the respondents' comments are connected and related to their gender, age and ethnicity, as well as other variables. To deny this and treat the talk as instances of free-floating discourses would be to deny the wider social context of the interactions. It is probably the case that in practice an everyday, functional notion of 'the person' creeps in the presentation of the research, particularly given the importance I have attached to the relationship between researcher and researched. As Code suggests, one has a relationship with a person, not a fluctuating subject position. The tension between this and a feminist and post-structuralist theoretical position is difficult to resolve in practice, but it is important that it should be declared. An interesting further dimension is provided by the final stage of *The Archers* research when respondents were given the opportunity to comment on drafts of Chapters 5 and 6. The question of identity seemed to take on an enormous importance in the responses I received, many of which were concerned about biographical inaccuracies in my representation of them as individuals. This underlines the discrepancy between theory and lived experience, and implies some ethical problems in the abandonment of the concept of the subject in empirical research. If identity politics still matters to the participants, can identity be rejected as an outmoded concept by researchers? I will return to these questions in my conclusion (Chapter 7). In the meantime, I will temporarily set aside the question of audience readings in order to focus on the texts themselves, and their particular combinations of socially validated performatives and subversive performances.

Chapter Two

'Quality' Media: Critical Debates, Texts and Contexts

Critical Debates

Introduction

The publication in 1988 of the British Government's White Paper – *Broadcasting in the '90s – Competition, Choice and Quality* – generated much debate about definitions of quality in the media. The broader content of these debates is less my concern here than the analysis of the textual features and critical discourses associated with a body of texts which have become 'shorthand for quality' (Brunsdon, 1990; Corner *et al.*, 1994; Mulgan, 1990). My interest is in the relationship of two texts which are generically outside the corpus usually cited to this 'shorthand', and the kinds of textual features and critical discussion which it promotes. These are marked by a set of binary oppositions: between modernity and tradition, and between enterprise and heritage – which have been presented as fundamental features of the *Zeitgeist* of contemporary Britain (Corner and Harvey, 1991a). How, if at all, are these oppositions represented in *Inspector Morse* and *The Archers*? How do a radio soap opera and a TV crime series participate in the construction of these tensions in contemporary British culture? My discussion not only extends the canon of media texts aspiring to the 'quality' label, but also highlights a further tension – between 'quality' and 'the popular' – which runs through both the academic and journalistic writing on the subject.

Most of the critical work in this area has focused on texts concerned with the 'tradition' or 'pastness' pole of the opposition, and this has resulted in the definition of a whole area of popular culture as 'heritage', and in the invention of new genres, such as the 'heritage film'. It has also involved discussion of definitions of 'quality' in popular culture: Brunsdon, for instance, describes how 'quality' is defined as a combination of a literary source, well-known actors, high production values (and corresponding outlay of money) and 'a certain image of England and Englishness' (1990: 86). This association of 'quality' with the highly exportable 'heritage text' has had far-reaching repercussions, with the result that even texts such as *Morse*, which are not strictly speaking 'heritage dramas', are profoundly affected by it.

These repercussions may be less immediately obvious in the case of *The Archers*, and yet a soap opera broadcast on Radio 4 is an interesting site of tensions in relation to 'quality'. The 1997/8 BBC Director General's Report quoted an independent advice panel: 'Radio 4 continues to be a standard-bearer of excellence for the BBC, both in terms of authority and programme quality. The network is also a genuine national voice.' This comment, intended to epitomise the 'quality' image of Radio 4 and its role in the construction of national identity, clearly has implications for *The Archers*, one of its most successful programmes in terms of audience size: the figure of 4.5 million listeners was quoted by the Editor, Vanessa Whitburn, on Radio 4's *Straw Poll* on 7 September 2001. The significance of this figure is underlined when we read in the *Listener Report*, published in 1999, that the Radio 4 audience as a whole is 9.2 million. The *Listener Report* also makes clear that the changes in the Radio 4 schedule of April 1998 attempted to use *The Archers* as a means of attracting listeners to other 'quality' programmes:

> The move of *The Archers* to 2.02pm has led more people to listen after lunch, and many are staying for the daily 2.15pm *Afternoon Play*. And, in the evening, *The Archers* is now followed at 7.15pm by the award-winning arts magazine *Front Row*.
>
> (*Listener Report*, 1999: 4; see also Hendy, 2000: 105)

Institutionally, therefore, despite the low status genre it belongs to, *The Archers* has a pivotal position in Radio 4's careful balancing of 'quality' and popularity: in one sense *The Archers* is the popular 'hook' into more clearly high culture broadcasts, yet, in another, it is clear that *Archers* listeners are viewed as a 'quality' audience, likely to be equally attracted by an 'award-winning arts magazine'. The concern with 'quality' manifested at institutional or production level is mirrored in the critical literature; significantly, judgements of the series are often based on the writer's interpretation of the programmes' balance of modern and traditional elements.

In this chapter I am positing the 'canon' of texts associated with discourses of 'quality' and 'heritage/tradition' as a cultural context in which both *The Archers* and *Inspector Morse* can usefully be read, and I am arguing that this is at least as fruitful as comparisons with other crime fiction, or other soap opera. My primary justification for the introduction of these debates here is the fact that both the texts themselves, and the literature surrounding them, are imbued with these oppositions of tradition and modernity, enterprise and heritage. However, my interest extends beyond my two case studies to the whole question of relations between popular culture and the Academy. This literature is particularly interesting in that respect, since the heritage text, deemed redolent of Thatcherite values, seems to have become the *bête noire* of academics in the 1980s and 1990s. Raphael Samuel has defined this trend as 'heritage-baiting' which he describes as 'the favourite sport of the metropolitan intelligentsia' (1994: 259). I will return to Samuel's arguments later in my discussion.

Cairns Craig, for example, has commented negatively on the ideological underpinnings of the particular version of Englishness promulgated by Merchant–Ivory films of the 1980s, such as *A Room with a View*. Craig linked such images of Englishness to a national crisis of identity and to the materialism of the Thatcher years, reading them as both a search for stability in a period of radical and destructive change, and as 'conspicuous consumption' colluding with Thatcherite values (1991: 10). If Craig can see only ideological harm in the films, after a brief plea for the role of the spectator and the plurality of possible readings, Tana Wollen (1991) also concludes that the films are part of 'a deeper sickness'. In an important article on British heritage films of the 1980s and early 1990s Higson (1993) interprets the films as re-affirming an upper-class English identity, which is still useful to contemporary Conservatism. However, Higson's position is more nuanced than that of Craig, or even Wollen. He seems more aware of the ambiguities in the texts, and like Light, in her reply to Craig, sees their liberal-humanist narratives and social satire as critical responses to Thatcherism (Light, 1991b). Nonetheless, Higson concludes that the visual pleasures of the films ideologically collude with the conservative values which the films' narratives critique:

> Even those films that develop an ironic *narrative* of the past end up celebrating and legitimating the *spectacle* of one class and one cultural tradition and identity at the expense of others through the discourse of authenticity, and the obsession with the visual splendours of period detail.
>
> (1993: 119)

Dyer provides a detailed analysis of the liberal content of *The Jewel in the Crown*. Here a heritage drama is no longer read as the cultural manifestation of a new Conservative era, but as a form of liberalism whose villains are 'those who speak in the language of Thatcherism' (Dyer, 1996: 229). Dyer does not find any politically progressive content in heritage texts of this kind, but at the same time he is prepared to discuss them in terms of the pleasures they provide, rather than simply castigating their reproduction of Thatcherite values and politics (Dyer, 1992). It is to these pleasures, and to the characteristics of the texts which provide them, that I will turn next.

The Pleasures of 'Quality'

Many of the writers discussed above see flight not only from modernity but also from the urban as a fundamental characteristic of the heritage text. Corner and Harvey discuss this predilection for the rural in the context of the leisure industry around museums and country houses (1991b: 51–3). They also identify the presence of discourses of community and common ownership as a significant feature of heritage culture; National Trust houses, for example, provide a social space, an opportunity to escape the isolation of the home and to imagine oneself as proprietor of a shared inheritance. For Wollen, the notion of England as an imaginary rural community is a striking characteristic of the British films of the 1980s which she is analysing:

> The nostalgia here is a sickening for a homeland where there is endless cricket, fair play with bent rules, fumbled sex, village teas and punting

through long green summers. British identities have been subsumed under a particular version of Englishness.

(1991: 182)

Higson describes how the heritage films turn their backs on 'the industrialized, chaotic present' in favour of 'an essentially pastoral national identity' (1993: 110). Wollen interprets this nostalgia for an imagined rural English past as a symptom of a lack of confidence in the future. For Higson, nostalgia for the absent past is a way of creating a comforting presence: 'Nostalgia is then a narrative of loss, charting an imaginary historical trajectory from stability to instability, and at the same time a narrative of recovery, projecting the subject back into a comfortably closed past' (1993: 124). It would be difficult to argue with the notion that nostalgia is based on an entirely constructed narrative of the past, and that it may often be expressive of a certain discomfort in relation to the present moment. One might, however, question the suggestions of moral cowardice and decadence which are connected with the pleasures of nostalgia in some of these accounts, as well as the implication that this is a peculiarly British phenomenon. I would argue that this vision of nostalgia as 'the English disease' is too narrow and moralistic an interpretation. Like Wheeler, we might ask whether nostalgia is always 'nasty' (Wheeler, 1994).

The association of national identity with a country's rural roots is not confined to Britain, and may be connected to the cultural homogenisation which is one of the outcomes of globalisation. Higson places his discussion of the British heritage film in the wider context of postmodernism, which in its reaction against modernism is concerned with the past, even if it is a very particular version, a 'flat depthless pastiche' of the past, which is represented (1993: 112). The idea that these images are associated not merely with the national malaise, but with a cultural context common to many Western countries, would seem to be supported by the existence of similar representations elsewhere. In Ireland, and in Irish culture in Britain, it is not difficult to observe a struggle to represent an authentic national identity, resulting perhaps in this case from the experience of colonisation, rather than the loss of empire so often referred to in the discussion of the British texts. Despite the diametrically opposed historical backgrounds to these phenomena in Britain and Ireland, an element of Irish culture too is concerned with a predomi- nantly rural and nostalgic image of the cultural heritage, expressed, for example, in the popularisation of the traditional dance in *Riverdance*. In France the lost peasant communities of the rural provinces are still one of the most common images of the country in advertising, while the existence of the French heritage film has been acknowledged and analysed (Esposito, 2001; Vincendeau, 1995). Such examples seem to suggest that this phenomenon is not merely the result of the specificities of the British political and historical conjuncture, but a general feature of Western postcoloniality. In their reinforcement of national cultures they are a reaction against homogenised global culture and, through their similarity, an instance of it. These shared tendencies perhaps in part explain the international success of a programme like *Morse*, whose images of traditional Englishness may resonate in other cultures with similarly nostalgic iconographies of a rural past concealing deep historical and political differences. Televisual representations of Englishness may indeed function in a wide variety of cultures, as an appropriated iconography, 'capable of representing what is lost in the experience of enlightenment modernity' (Wheeler, 1994: 95). If these images are in part a reaction against globalised modernity, it is ironic that they have become the archetypal global product, sold to an audience of one billion world-wide (*The Last Morse*, Carlton, November 2000).[1]

Higson, however, provides a useful and detailed discussion of the British heritage films of the 1980s, which do give the impression of a closed world. He remarks on the self-referentiality of the films, in which the same quite small group of actors constantly reappear, and on an emphasis on spectacle rather than narrative, which leads to the creation of 'heritage space' rather than narrative space (Higson, 1993: 117). He defines the former as an almost obsessive interest in setting, props and costume which causes the camera to linger on visually spectacular scenes, rather than scenes which progress the narrative, or provide emotional intensity. As a result he finds in the films 'a typically postmodern loss of emotional affect' (ibid.: 118). This argument seems reminiscent of Dyer's reading of *The Jewel in the Crown*, where he emphasises the serial's lack of momentum, resulting from the use of symbols, flashbacks and repetition, the absence of 'cliffhanger' endings, and a generally slow pace. It is these formal qualities which, in Dyer's view, give a sense of apathy and inaction, whether in the face of the imperial past, or 'the onrush of Thatcherism' (Dyer, 1996: 238).

It is significant that both Dyer and Higson comment on the emphasis on spectacle in heritage films, and that Dyer makes the link between the loss of narrative pace and the exploration of passive femininity in *The Jewel in the Crown*. He also links the 'femininity' of the text with the emphasis on costume and setting typical of 'quality' drama: 'To this we may add the contribution to *Jewel*'s success of costumes and domestic settings, also areas in which women tend to acquire more expertise, and amplified here by the vogue for retro fashion in the early 1980s' (Dyer, 1996: 227). Elsewhere Dyer has discussed the 'feminine' nature of the visual pleasures of 'quality' fiction more generally, with its emphasis on the domains of fashion and interior decoration, traditionally associated with women and gay men. The broadening of the discussion to include gay men is more implied by the camp tone of Dyer's discussion than overt:

> The pleasure of this well-done density is partly sensuous – *Fortunes of War* would have been worth it for Harriet's cardigans and teacups alone; or as a friend of mine puts it, the trouble with the qualities is that the actors will keep standing in front of the furniture.
>
> (1992: 36)

This quotation from Dyer is significant, not only because of the irreverent designation of heritage drama as 'the qualities', but also because of its introduction of the possibility of pleasurably subversive readings of these texts to what has generally been a particularly serious political and moral discussion by academics.

35

Higson also refers to the camp qualities of the heritage film, drawing on Sontag's description of camp as 'decorative art, emphasising texture, sensuous surface, and style at the expense of content' (Sontag, quoted in Higson, 1993: 126). This description seems to correspond to Dyer's appreciation of the sensuous aspect of the 'quality'/heritage text, the pleasures provided by images of rooms embellished by rich textiles, carefully colour-coded floral arrangements, and luxurious furniture, on which the occasional actor is allowed to recline. Higson develops the idea of camp less in relation to this indulgence in the pleasures of colour and texture, and more in terms of Sontag's definition of camp as 'the theatricalisation of experience' (Sontag, [1964] 1999: 62). He identifies a self-conscious gaze in the films, and sees their concern for authenticity pushed to such an extreme that the films become almost a parody of themselves, a pastiche of the past.

Raphael Samuel turns the argument away from textual qualities, and onto the audience, commenting on the misogynistic aspect of the general academic distrust of the pleasures provided by heritage culture:

> Heritage-baiting is an exclusively male sport, and one way – it might be suggested – in which literary men can prove themselves manly. It is remarkable how often it is the pot-pourri and toiletries side of 'heritage' which is singled out for ridicule. Is it that the manifestation of femininity compounds the offence, or was it in some ways the original cause of disgust?
>
> (1994: 272, note 27)

Samuel describes an exhibition at the Photographers Gallery – *'Flogging a Dead Horse'* – as 'a sustained essay in disgust' with 'ordinary people, Northerners especially – as the grotesques rather than midgets or freaks' (ibid.: 263). He observes here a general suspiciousness in relation to pleasure itself – 'the unspoken and unargued-for assumption that pleasure is almost by definition mindless' as well as a particular horror of the spectators of heritage (ibid.: 271). In her work on the audiences of heritage film Claire Monk notes the wide appeal of such films to a mainstream rather than art-house audience, but also the older profile and 'femininity' of the heritage audience (1999: 36). If Bourdieu is to be believed, this audience profile may also contribute to academic suspicion of the genre, which fatally combines both the feminine and the 'middle-brow'. In the context of critical work on heritage culture, Samuel and Monk are almost alone in discussing the audience; the assumption is often that audiences are beguiled by the powerful representations of class and Englishness on offer. This view is sometimes betrayed by the kind of language used to describe the pleasures of the heritage text. Higson, for example, talks of figures and space '*seductively* laid out' (Higson, 1993: 122, my italics), or again: 'The theatricality of the Raj, and the epic sweep of the camera over an equally epic landscape and social class is *utterly seductive*' (ibid.: 124, my italics). These films are seen as inviting a less than 'pure gaze', and this analysis betrays a desire to resist the pleasures of texts which are not straightforwardly 'highbrow', and whose visual pleasures do not correspond to the formal asceticism of true art, identified by Bourdieu.

Since the early 1980s audiences have been viewed more as active participants in the process of meaning production than as victims of ideological seduction. However, it is clear from much of the above that audiences of mainstream 'quality' media texts containing representations of heritage or tradition are no more immune to the negative view of their activities than fans of *Coronation Street* or of a Hollywood star. My aim here is to investigate the responses of audience members, rather than extrapolating them hypothetically from the analysis of the ideological power of the text. In this investigation, the recognition of the pleasures offered by the texts will not automatically assume that audience members are completely beguiled by them, nor that they are ideologically immune. I am interested in the visual pleasures identified by Dyer, and the potential for camp readings which he points to. Whether my respondents share these interests is another matter. For the time being, the relationship of this discussion to *Morse* and *The Archers* must be explored.

Inspector Morse

Audience ratings are not enough to give cultural status to a television programme, as the fate of any number of soap operas will attest. However, *Morse* has succeeded both in terms of audience size and as a cultural icon which can be invoked to illustrate and epitomise the term 'quality television'. The discourse of quality, despite its literary background, has always been prevalent in discussion of television, which as a medium still struggles for respectability. It could indeed be argued that the definition of certain programmes as quality productions has played a vital role in increasing the cultural status of television, and in countering arguments about its nefarious influence. Charlotte Brunsdon has described the impact of the White Paper of 1988 on definitions of 'quality' television: the quality discourse, for example, in newspaper previews can comprise traditional aesthetic criteria, professional codes, realist paradigms, entertainment and leisure codes and moral paradigms, though in the White Paper, significantly, mainly moral and realist criteria are used (Brunsdon, 1990). In her work on the American organisation 'Viewers for Quality Television', Sue Brower has similarly identified a combination of aesthetic concerns and moral values in the organisation's definitions of quality; she describes the moral values as '"enlightened", middle-class, liberal, feminist', and argues that the members of the organisation use quality as a mask for fan behaviour, and as a way of acquiring status by association (Brower, 1992: 172).

In Britain, both the aesthetic and moral aspects of the discourse are given a particular inflection by the association of 'quality' with Englishness, which is diametrically opposed to all things American (see Mulgan, 1990: 18). In the context of crime fiction, this differentiation seems to hinge on factors such as the absence of violent struggles or car-chases, a detective who uses his or her intellect rather than physical strength in the fight against crime, and a rural or small-town, rather than big-city, setting. Even before the first broadcast in January 1987 *Morse* was described in a *Sight and Sound* preview as part of a crusade to reclaim a quintessentially English tradition: 'With this crew, one feels that the English detective story is safe on its home ground with no hankering to convert the middle-aged, edgy maverick of the Thames Valley force into something more chic and Californian' (Kockenlocker, 1986: 240). In her use of the term 'Brideshead/Jewel' to define a particular type of quality TV, characterised by its 'heritage export value', Charlotte Brunsdon describes this association of nostalgic nationalism with cultural quality (1990: 86). *Morse* shares with the two programmes cited by Brunsdon an iconography of Englishness which became a commonplace of film and television culture in the 1980s, and which can be seen in part as a response to the pressures on British broadcasters to produce exportable television. This visual expression of Englishness requires village greens and gardens, medieval lanes and churches, and wood-panelled interiors where log fires burn even in high summer. In *Morse* none of this is denied us; the tragedy and violence of English middle-class life are revealed and deplored by Morse, and yet the secure routines of tea and dinner, the aesthetic pleasures of a country residence, remain undisturbed. Even Morse's own collapse, in the last episode, *The Remorseful Day*, is transferred from his North Oxford flat where it takes place in the novel, to a college quadrangle, so that the dreaming spires are Morse's last vision of the world (Carlton, 2000).

The reviewers frequently seem to have absorbed this aspect of the series so completely that its pleasures are described using the same cosy and domestic imagery of Englishness which the programmes themselves abound in: 'The plots have a nice comfortable ring to them like Agatha Christie stories re-written by Iris Murdoch. They remind one of sensible shoes and unchilled sherry, toasted crumpets and the triumph of good over evil' (Naughton, 1987: 36). The narrative structure of *Morse* certainly seems typical of the crime genre in its playing out and eventual containment of political and psychic anxieties (Neale, 1980). However, Craig's reading of the Thatcherite values implicit in Merchant–Ivory should not be grafted onto *Morse*. While there is no denying the nostalgic nationalism identified by Brunsdon, the very size of the *Morse* audience suggests an appeal to a wider political and social spectrum, and the feminine and domestic tone of the programmes can be seen as out of tune with the more bellicose utterances of Thatcherism.

In general, characters who seem to represent the 'enterprise' culture of the 1980s receive short shrift from Morse and from the plots in which they are enmeshed. The yuppie Maguire in *Last Seen Wearing* (Zenith, 1988) may not be implicated in any crime but he is guilty of working as a 'negotiator' for a Docklands luxury development, and of owning a flat whose black, white and chrome decor and car-shaped telephone are sufficient grounds for arrest as far as Morse is concerned. Almost inevitably a house with a swimming pool indicates foul play or, at the very least, an unhappy marriage. Yet the conditions of production of *Inspector Morse* seem ironically typical of contemporary privatised industry; it is made by Zenith, a company originally owned by Central, who initiated the project, and subsequently taken over by Carlton Communications and Paramount (Sanderson, 1991: 26). In series six, the credits announced that *Morse* was now 'in association' with Beamish Stout, thus making an uncomfortable link between the textual resistance to enterprise, and the reality of the text as commercial product.

If *Morse* has succeeded commercially without completely espousing the political ethos of its times, it seems relevant to ask whether the depiction of the private sphere maintains a similarly delicate balance between conservative and radical elements. *Morse* does not belong to a 'women's' genre, the main characters are men, and with some exceptions such as script writer, Alma Cullen, and producer, Deirdre Keir, the production team was predominantly male. If in this sense *Morse* does not belong to the category of text usually subjected to feminist scrutiny, it is all the more significant that the gender politics of the original novels were not thought suitable for 'quality' television. The analysis of feminist elements within the programmes which follows may therefore provide a case-study of the influence of feminisms on a series which, with audiences of around 15 million, was one of the most resounding television successes of the late 1980s and 1990s.

The principal difference between the six *Morse* programmes closely based on the novels by Colin Dexter and the original texts is the relative absence of sexual objectification in the portrayal of the women characters in the TV version. The requirements of 'quality' television clearly demanded a more subtle approach, and Morse's character has been substantially changed so that the sexually predatory element is replaced by romantic yearning. In *Last Bus to Woodstock* (Zenith, 1988), for example, the television Morse reprimands his sergeant, Lewis, for his use of sexist and proprietorial language about his wife and children, while in the novel, Morse leers at the barmaid in the pub where the murder has taken place, and eventually succumbs to the charms of the murderer herself. Whereas in the television version Sylvia Kane's death results from an accidental combination of circumstances, in which both the don, Crowther, and his mistress are implicated, in the novel, Sylvia's death is caused by a vicious blow from the jealous woman. A similar pattern can be observed in *Last Seen Wearing*; in Dexter's original version the Headmaster is guilty of no major crime, the Deputy Head, Baines, is not even female, let alone lesbian, and the murderer is Valerie, the missing girl herself. In the television version the Headmaster is indirectly responsible for Valerie's disappearance, and directly responsible for the death of Baines, while Valerie is guilty only of adolescent confusion.

The effect of these reversals may be to return women to the traditional status of victim, but Dexter's image of women using their sexuality against men, and showing no qualms in resorting to violence, would be more likely to cause offence. The positive representation of a lesbian character in the TV version of *Last Seen Wearing* is only marginally useful to the plot and seems to emphasise the corruption and emptiness of the heterosexual relationships around her. Although the representation of women generally in the television series is far from radical, characters such as Baines do indicate some acknowledgement that if the television Morse is a reformed character, the women he encounters need to be more than objects of desire. However, the feminist agenda is perhaps most apparent in those programmes which were written for television. In *Fat Chance* (Zenith, 1991), scripted, significantly, by a woman, Alma Cullen, we see a narrative based on feminist concerns: the ordination of women in the Church of England, and the impact of oppressive stereotypes of female beauty on adolescent girls. Zoe Wanamaker plays a character exemplifying the conventionally irreconcilable – a penchant for Italian designer suits and feminist politics. When Morse receives her seal of approval, having championed the feminist cause throughout, we are inclined to agree with her that he really is 'one of the good guys'.

All around Morse, heterosexuality, particularly of the married kind, wreaks havoc. It is unremarkable that *Morse*, along with a great deal of crime fiction, should manifest the deeply rooted cultural association of death and sexuality, but the repeated castigation of the morals of married men lends added significance to the emotional purity of Morse's single life, or even, though to a lesser extent, to Lewis's cosily asexual conjugal bliss. With Lewis as the notable exception, married men deceive their bored and frustrated wives and exploit the vulnerability of the single women they seduce, sometimes, as in *The Dead of Jericho* (Zenith, 1987), leading them to degradation, despair and death. Morse oscillates between the generic requirement for celibacy (see Wilson, 1988) and the strong romantic tendencies of the character and the plots. His singleness is obsessively referred to in lines such as: 'Chastity and continence, when did I ever have anything else?' (*Service of All the Dead*, Zenith, 1987). The contrast between Morse and the happily married Lewis is fundamental to the structure of the programmes. Murderers, potential victims and the relatives of victims all take the opportunity, on encountering Morse, to enquire after his marital status, and to contrast his singleness with their own entanglements. In general, the family is a vipers' nest, and symbols of affluence almost always guarantee the deadliness of its occupants.

It is presumably safe to assume, nonetheless, that the writers and producers of the television series were not *engagés* in the fight against Thatcherite family values, and that these negative images of married and family life have come to perform some crucial function in the development of the character and charisma of Morse. If Morse is surrounded by examples of male perfidy, they serve to highlight the idealised masculinity he represents, which can be seen as one of the linchpins of the programmes' claim to 'quality'. Lewis also has his part to play in the depiction of an acceptable masculinity, but while his ability to cope with the modern demands of companionate marriage, shared childcare and DIY are admirable, unlike our hero, he cannot sustain the emotional limelight. In the first instance Morse is deeply moral; he plays the traditional role of the detective as representative and upholder of the Law and is always on the right side in the universal battle between good and evil, which the crimes of passion he investigates often seem to invoke. As in many heritage films, a moral crusade is under way, and the spectator is left in no doubt about the rights and wrongs of the case. Morse expresses righteous anger on the victims' behalf, and the programmes frequently end with a soliloquy on the wicked ways of men, which may include a quotation from a work of literature, and is often set against shots of Oxford's awe-inspiring architectural beauty. Morse's moral struggles are thus represented visually as part of the 'quality' package. Morse can never resist the opportunity to point out who is the real villain of the piece, and as, for example, in *Deadly Slumber* (Zenith, 1993), is particularly enraged by the prioritisation of money-making over human life. In this sense Morse is out of tune with the times, simultaneously liberal rebel and avenging patriarch, but above all passionate in his pursuit of justice. Like the 'qualities' themselves, he harks back to a bygone era, and is himself an embodiment of nostalgia.

The difference between Morse and ordinary men does not, however, lie solely in his stern righteousness, and there are indeed times when his involvement with a guilty party clouds his judgement. Perhaps it is the combination of the traditionally paternal qualities described above with an ability to nurture which makes Morse blessed among men. Morse willingly provides a shoulder to cry on and is a sensitive and perceptive listener. At times the tasks of nurturing others and punishing crime are in conflict, as in *Deadly Slumber*, where Morse's sensitivity to the tragedy of Michael Steppings' daughter makes him rather too willing to cross Steppings off the list of suspects. If this ability to give emotionally renders Morse a less effective policeman, it may do a lot for the audience ratings. In her analysis of the appeal of romantic fiction, based on Freud, Amal Treacher (1988) has argued that the romantic hero nurtures as well as dominates the heroine, and that it is in this representation of a hero who is both ideal mother and ideal father that the emotional satisfactions of such works lie for their largely female readership. Something of this kind may be in play here; without doubt parenting is a theme in *Morse*, and it is a theme which was not present in the original novels. If the 1980s' 'new man' of the advertisements has failed as an icon of anything more than a hollow self-sufficiency, perhaps Morse's attempts to father and mother are a more resonant fantasy for male and female viewers.

But what of Morse's own needs? We return again to romance, and to the appeal of Morse's own vulnerability. Morse, like the operas he immerses himself in, is a vehicle for the expression of grand emotion. Unlike other male detectives, or for that matter the Morse of the Dexter novels, emotion rather than intellect is his true medium. Although the Inspector goes through the motions of thinking, it is increasingly Lewis who has the brainwaves, while Morse relies on that most feminine of skills, intuition. In this sense Morse, despite his traditional appearance, is breaking through boundaries, both of gender and genre. In *Dead on Time* (Zenith, 1992) Morse's new/old masculinity may have strayed even beyond its own parameters; the sight of Morse sobbing over the corpse of his former fiancée and the provision of an 'explanation' for his moodiness were dangerous developments. But *Dead on Time* allowed Lewis to make his contribution to the image of caring manhood, and it seemed fortunate that a sensitive soul such as Morse should have Lewis to watch over him. While the programmes continually depict the secure and civilised pleasures of Morse's home-life – the music, good wine and tranquil lounging on the sofa – an encounter with an attractive woman '*d'un certain âge*' inevitably rekindles a poignant and disorientating longing for intimacy. Morse does all those old-fashioned things which are eschewed by the new man or irrelevant in the more prosaic world of Lewis; he sends flowers, asks women out and pays touching if clumsy compliments. The fact that this rarely leads to anything remotely resembling a relationship is a further enhancement of his charms. Morse remains the ideal lover, always more involved than the woman in question, and not afraid to admit it. Detection and romance thus combine admirably, since the requirement for celibacy in the former creates an enticing lack, the ultimate romance narrative where the threat of satisfaction, and thence of the loss of desire, is removed (Neale, 1980).

In all of this, *Morse* can be seen as re-defining the crime fiction genre, or developing a sub-genre dominated by TV adaptations of Agatha Christie, by inscribing some of the pleasures of the heritage text in a contemporary setting. The narrative is crucial in *Morse*, but the complexity of the plots and slowness of pace constitute a form of narrative pleasure which is at times more akin to the heritage film than to a fast-moving crime series. The frequent pauses to allow the viewer the opportunity to revel in the visual delights provided by shots of Oxford colleges or country pubs and the accompanying classical soundtrack are a further similarity. Setting is as crucial to *Morse* as it is to the heritage film or classic serial, and the positive representation of Morse's single life owes much to the images of his elegant, classically furnished flat, with just a hint of self-indulgence (lying on the sofa, surrounded by unwashed plates, and so on …). As this example suggests, the depiction of Morse's refined tastes, the pleasures of spectacle and classical music, and the nuanced representations of gender, are crucial components of the textual construction of 'quality', and they are all inextricably linked. Morse's new/old masculinity is representative of the programmes' engagement with concerns about tradition and modernity, as is the contrast between Morse and Lewis. As in Merchant–Ivory Forster adaptations such as *A Room with a View*, there is an implied critique of the materialism of contemporary society, a nostalgia for an earlier form of Englishness, based on eccentricity, rather than enterprise. There is a resistance to American-style managerialism and cultural homogenisation in this celebration of the English past. Yet at the same time, modernity is far from banished. The women in Morse's life may always be 'ladies' in the old-fashioned sense, but they are also prison chiefs, headteachers, pathologists, or even detectives. The representation of the dilemmas and limitations of contemporary heterosexuality is the principal mode of modernity in *Morse*, and it is more in evidence than the technological trappings of contemporary policing. The fact that it is also the expression of nostalgia for old-fashioned romance indicates the extent to which the programmes' claim to 'quality' is dependent on the careful balancing of tradition and modernity, past and present.

The Archers

If *Inspector Morse* is an exceptionally successful piece of television, *The Archers* (BBC Radio, 1951–) is in many ways a still more unusual cultural phenomenon. A successful soap opera on radio in an age dominated by television, and one of the world's longest-running fiction serials, it has recently spawned a fan club of thousands, a company producing a catalogue of associated products with a member of the cast as Managing Director, its own website, and ongoing media attention. Interestingly, much of this attention has focused on representations of gender and 'race' in the programmes, while tensions between tradition and modernity in contemporary British culture are also played out. Two recent spin-off books on *The Archers* participate in these debates: the first, by the current producer, Vanessa Whitburn, defends the recent modernisation of the programmes, while the second, by a former producer, William Smethurst, claims that the scripts have deteriorated as a result of an issues-based editorial policy (Smethurst, 1996; Whitburn, 1996). Smethurst's book expresses a desire to return to a vision of England undisturbed by any awareness of the inequalities of gender, class and 'race'. In the final chapter he imagines 'people out for a Sunday afternoon drive', passing through the only *apparently* peaceful village of Ambridge (the village in the fictional county of Borsetshire where the soap opera is set):

> And they would go on their way remarking what a sleepy place Ambridge is – a bit of England where time has stood still – and would not realize for a moment what a ferment of greed, sexual passion, family discord, racial hatred, and rampant radical feminism they were leaving behind them.
>
> (Smethurst, 1996: 243)

As this extract indicates, Smethurst's writing pushes the polarities of tradition and modernity to their most extreme version: modernity becomes a highly dangerous state in which men become the victims of powerful and ruthless feminists, while England's rural past is part of a hallowed, blissful and benignly patriarchal tradition. Smethurst's view may be extreme, but he is in fact merely deploying the oppositions which have become a commonplace in media discussions of *The Archers*. Thus in a *Radio Times* interview, Allison Pearson concluded that Whitburn had achieved the right balance between contemporary social concerns and the more traditional elements of the programmes:

> Whitburn's skilful blending of contemporary dilemmas – abortion, squatters, jailing Susan Carter for helping her armed-robber brother – with more traditional ingredients like progress in milk marketing and Lynda Snell's doomed Euro-panto, has won her many new listeners in their 20s and 30s, without alienating the old guard.
>
> (1994: 36)

However, unlike Pearson's article, much of the recent discussion of *The Archers* in the print and broadcast media sees the modernity of the series as controversial, an ideological attack on the programmes' faithful audience. Significantly, a feminist political agenda is seen as one of the most striking features of this threatening contemporaneity.

These vehement debates suggest that *The Archers* has a cultural significance in Britain which (outside academic analysis) is not generally attributed to soap opera. Scannell, and more recently Morley, have argued that broadcasting, in creating a shared public sphere, plays a crucial role in the construction of national identity.

Drawing on the work of Scannell (1996) in Britain, and Lofgren (1995) in Sweden, Morley comments:

> National broadcasting can thus create a sense of unity – and of corresponding boundaries around the nation; it can link the peripheral to the centre; turn previously social events into mass experiences; and above all, it penetrates the domestic sphere, linking the national public into the private lives of its citizens, through the creation of both sacred and quotidian moments of national communion.
>
> (2000: 107)

Morley cites Chandler's commentary on the Shipping Forecast, which although incomprehensible to the majority of listeners unites the nation through its very familiarity and the image of the storm-rocked British Isles which it conjures (Chandler, 1996). *The Archers* seems to perform a similar function in constructing the nation: it is quotidian both in content and form, and the endless repetition of the same theme tune, the same voices, at the same time each day, symbolically (if not actually) unites the national family around the radio set. The imagined listening family is replicated in the text whose lead family also, it can be argued, symbolises the nation. Like the Royal family, they go to church, celebrate Christmas, Easter, christenings, weddings and funerals. The public and the private are integrated by this public sharing of private lives, and by references to contemporary news in the scripts: important national events are included by means of last-minute additions to the programme, known as 'topical inserts'. In the spring of 2001 the whole script for several weeks had to be re-written because of the outbreak of foot and mouth disease in the British countryside: Ambridge was preserved from the devastation represented by images of burning funeral pyres on the national news, but the decision to isolate Brookfield farm from the rest of the village reflected the gravity of the crisis. Even the Radio 4 schedule, with *The Archers* always immediately following the news, reinforces the programme's role as a national broadcast, which provides an emotional, feminised and private link with the public sphere.

In the rest of this chapter, and in the account of the audience research which follows it, this apparent 'socialisation of the public sphere' will be examined further, and interrogated (Scannell, 1988: 28). If the images of Englishness in *Morse* have become international currency, in *The Archers* they are confined to a national role and significance, though the availability of national radio on the Internet may eventually modify this. The precise nature of this significance is my concern here. My aim is to argue that a series which is often referred to as a quaint anachronism is in fact at the cutting edge of contemporary British popular culture. Despite its extraordinary longevity, the current incarnation of *The Archers* is profoundly of its time, less because of the programme-makers' determination to be topical, than in its simultaneous looking forward and looking back, so typical of the present moment.

The Archers as Heritage Text

The Archers can be seen as the ultimate heritage text, since it has its own past and its own traditions. An immediate sense of pastness is conveyed by the familiarity over time of many of the actors' voices. Jill and Phil Archer, the couple currently 'heading' the Archer family and who replaced Dan and Doris as the main parent figures of the programme, are still played by Norman Painting and Patricia Greene, who joined the cast in 1951 and 1956 respectively. To the familiarity of these voices one might add those of Lesley Saweard (Christine Barford) and June Spencer (Peggy Archer) who have also been in the cast since the 1950s.[2] The actors playing Sid Perks (the landlord of the village pub, 'The Bull'), Jennifer Aldrige (née Archer) and Tony Archer were originally cast in the 1960s, while current stars of the show, Shula Archer and Eddie Grundy, have been played by Judy Bennett and Trevor Harrison since the 1970s. Christine Geraghty (1991) has commented on the importance of the diegetic past to the construction of a sense of community in soap. Community, as I will suggest later in this chapter, is a crucial feature of *The Archers*, as it is in British TV soaps.

Here, however, the medium, itself a relic of the past, the relatively high number of long-term characters and the strong emphasis on tradition add a further dimension. It is not necessary to be a fan, or anything more than an accidental or casual listener, to be familiar with these voices, and to associate them with daily rituals such as listening to the news or doing the washing up. Arguably, they have formed the background to so many people's domestic lives for so long, that in themselves alone they evoke a comforting sense of continuity. As Scannell comments: 'In the course of many years, over generations, broadcast output has become sedimented in memory as traces both of a common past and of the biography of individuals' (1988: 19). A recurrent theme in the literature on radio is the particular affective quality of sound, which, it is claimed, plays an important role in constituting 'a person's sense of time and place' (Hendy, 2000: 117). This Proustian quality results in part from the fact that radio accompanies everyday tasks and becomes embedded in particular routines, the memory of which, triggered by a familiar theme tune, can evoke a whole phase of life. It is also argued that the necessity of creating our own images which the medium imposes, and the active imaginative participation that this implies, give radio a particular evocative power (Crisell, [1986] 1994; Douglas, 1999; see Chapters 5 and 6 in this book).

These features of the medium are particularly strong in a programme which is broadcast twice daily and enjoys such exceptional longevity. The impression of 'pastness' is textually inscribed in references to the programme's long history in contemporary scripts. Thus, in 1994 when Shula's husband Mark is killed in a car crash, her father Phil talks to his youngest daughter Elizabeth about his own feelings when, in 1955, his first wife Grace was killed in a fire in the stables (Whitburn, 1996: 43). As the focus groups analysed in Chapter 6 make clear, some fans have been listening for long enough to remember the drama of Grace's death, so that this kind of reference is particularly evocative for a faithful core of the audience. For those whose enthusiasm for the series is more recent, the fan club sells 'Vintage

Archers' tapes, which allow listeners to catch up on the dramatic highlights, as well as the clipped speech of the 1950s. Since the 1980s David Archer has presented the case for modern farming methods in the face of some resistance from his father Phil, who ironically had himself played exactly the same role in relation to Dan Archer. David's role in the dramatised history of Ambridge therefore represents a link between present and past, a reminder of the long history of the programme, and of its characters.

The past which the contemporary programmes are able to draw on is, of course, profoundly rural, and it is not surprising to find that a series whose original purpose was to give advice to farmers shares with the heritage texts discussed earlier a pastoral vision of English life. Higson's notion of 'heritage space', with its implied tension between narrative and spectacle, may not be entirely applicable to a radio soap opera, where the nature of the genre requires constant narrative development. However, there is a tension within *The Archers* between different kinds of narrative: the intensely dramatic and the 'everyday story'. The balance of these elements in the programmes is the subject of some controversy, with drama associated with modernity, and the stories based on the routines of farming and village life with tradition. Without attaching to these polarities the moral and political values which the journalistic writing abounds in, I would merely comment that *The Archers* has its own particular version of the tension between stasis and 'unlimited process' identified by Stephen Neale (1980: 26). For a soap opera to lack a strong narrative drive is unthinkable, and the series would probably not have lasted fifty years if this had been the case. At the same time, I would argue that the pleasures of *The Archers* are to some extent the pleasures of repetition, and of comforting familiarity. Dialogues regularly contain descriptions of the beautiful rural surroundings enjoyed by the characters, which temporarily suspend the narrative and invite the listener to imagine the scene, just as lingering shots of parks and countryside provide moments of spectacle in the heritage film.[3] The attempt to modernise the programmes has not, in fact, resulted in the abandonment of this aspect of the series, and the background of rural setting, annual cycles of events and stories based on trivial, but humorous plots is still a crucial part of the programmes. These aspects of *The Archers* could be said to constitute the radio equivalent of 'heritage space'.

One of the participants in the '*Archers* Addicts' weekend discussed in Chapter 5 commented, paradoxically, on the strong *visual* quality of the programmes. In the same discussion it was pointed out that radio's lack of visuals in fact leaves the listener free to generate images of his or her own choice, images which can be particularly pleasurable to the individual concerned (see Hendy, 2000: 118–19). The programmes' ability to evoke the images of rural life associated with visual media such as the heritage film through sound alone is of particular interest here. As well as the familiarity of the actors' voices, the combination of sound effects and traditional-sounding place names provides the necessary material for the imaginary construction by the listener of a range of rural scenes. The farming stories may refer to 'modern' problems such as milk quotas, BSE and complex new machinery, but the animal sounds provide a reassuring continuity. Lambing is as significant, and noisy, in the twenty-first century as it was in the 1950s. Birdsong, the sound of digging and conversation between the gardener, and various other characters 'passing by', can suggest a fine summer's evening, and a cottage garden worthy of the BBC's own book on the subject (Hamilton, 1995). The knowledge that the scene has taken place in the garden of Blossom Hill, Honeysuckle or Glebe Cottage can only add to the effect.

The environs of Ambridge enjoy equally picturesque appellations: Penny Hassett is a nearby village, and Borchester is immediately associated with images of a county town and, until recently, relative urban sophistication, in the form of Nelson's Wine Bar. Forays into Borchester allow the inhabitants of Ambridge to indulge in the milder pleasures of urbanity, without leaving the heritage diegesis of Borsetshire, whereas trips to Birmingham remain either peripheral or threatening. It seemed quite appropriate that a Birmingham hotel room was the scene for the sexual fiasco between Caroline Bone, and her unlikely fiancé, Robin, then vicar of Ambridge, or that Hayley's attempt to organise a night out in Brum for John Archer's twenty-first was thwarted by the latter's failure to materialise as a result of trouble with pigs at Grange Farm. Occasionally, villagers go for bracing walks on Lakey Hill, which, complete with whistling wind, trudging footsteps and more birdsong, has often been the scene of moments of philosophical wisdom or intense emotion.

The big houses, such as Ambridge Hall, Grey Gables and Lower Loxley, are almost as abundant in the village as the cottages; the latter two represent the combination of heritage and enterprise which in real life has become the bane of some cultural historians. The presence of these country mansions in such abundance in the village links the programmes to the experience of the countryside doubtless shared by many of the listeners – the day out at a National Trust or English Heritage property, and to the images of country house life predominant in the heritage film or TV series such as *Brideshead Revisited*. A number of the writers referred to in the first part of this chapter see the country house experience as a fundamental aspect of heritage culture. Corner and Harvey comment on this and similar leisure sites as projecting 'a common and shared inheritance, available to all for the price of a ticket on a Sunday outing' (1991a: 11). *The Archers* provides a similarly 'behind the scenes' view of the country house; Lower Loxley is still inhabited by its upper-class owners, the Pargetters, whose family tree 'can be traced as far back as the seventeenth century' (Greene *et al.*, 1994: 205). The commercialisation of Lower Loxley has on several occasions, such as the regular point-to-point races, fairs, or the opening of the tree-top walk in the spring of 2000, opened the house and gardens to the villagers, providing a fictional version of the accessibility of a common heritage discussed by Corner and Harvey. The new teashop in the Orangery, shop and art gallery complete the auditory day out provided by Lower Loxley. The country houses thus combine with the 'chocolate-box' cottages of Ambridge to complete the range of heritage settings which listeners can visualise, with all their connotations of tradition, Englishness and nostalgia.

As a result of the scripts' development of a range of precise locations and the relationships between them, listeners probably do develop their own personal sense of the geography of Ambridge. Should they fail to do this, or require more concrete confirmation, they can buy the Ambridge map, marketed by the fan club and a small publishing company specialising in 'English heritage' material, *Old House Books*. The existence of this product indicates the vital importance of a sense of place in this particular soap opera. Arguably, because of the medium, *The Archers* has to work harder at this than television soap. However, it is also clear that the rural setting carries with it connotations of a particular kind of nostalgic Englishness which Brookside Close will never evoke. Comparison with *Coronation Street* and *EastEnders* is more complex, since both texts contain archetypal images of Englishness in the form of northerners and cockneys respectively. Both Richard Dyer and Christine Geraghty have commented on the significance of the fact that the characters in both of these series live mainly in Victorian buildings (Dyer, 1981; Geraghty, 1991). In *The Archers*, nostalgia is played out in a different way; it is associated more with middle-class culture and the programmes construct, through sound alone, the same kind of imagery of rural Englishness as the heritage text. In this sense, *The Archers* thus contributes a different dimension to the representations of traditional Englishness which bind together the communities of British soap; these particular features of the Ambridge community will be my next theme.

The Ideal Community: 'Race', Ethnicity and Sexuality

As Christine Geraghty has pointed out, setting is the basis of the soap opera community; in relation to representations of cockneys and northerners she comments: 'What is significant is that soaps have used such assumptions as a means of presenting the viewer with a community in which difference from outsiders is asserted not by money or ambition or power but by qualities which can be shared by virtue of living in the same place' (1991: 92). The sense of place created by the textual features enumerated above similarly contributes to the construction of the ideal community in *The Archers*. As we have seen, travel outside the boundaries of Borsetshire seems to carry an inherent threat, and yet, as I will argue, culturally and socially disparate characters within those boundaries share an extraordinary level of communication and communion. Much of this is built on the sense of belonging to the village space, or its immediate environs. An interesting and daring development in relation to this took place in spring 2000, when another, more urban dimension was given to the image of Borchester with the Grundys' move to a high-rise council flat in the town. Scenes were played in the flat to a background of sirens wailing, more reminiscent of *NYPD Blue* than the habitual soundscape of *The Archers*. The potential dangers of this move, both within the diegesis – the disintegration of the family, isolation and loneliness for Joe Grundy, and teenage vandalism and petty crime for Edward – and as a threat to narrative coherence, were contained by the Grundys' frequent visits (and eventual return) to Ambridge, and the equally frequent expressions of concern about them. They were sutured back into the village community by interventions such as the vicar of Ambridge, Janet Fisher, arranging for Joe to attend a pensioners' lunch club in Borchester or by the Carters looking after Edward after school.

If the place and house names indicate that Ambridge, with its village green, shop, church and cottages, is everything an English village should be in terms of architecture and geography, the scripts ensure that the seasonal patterns of traditional rural life are observed. As in the TV soaps, rituals of this kind are used to bring the community together in one space, and to represent it symbolically (see Geraghty, 1991: 87). However, in the case of *The Archers*, the rural context gives a particular heritage twist to these moments of bonding. The annual repetition of these events is linked to the heritage text's representation of nature and the seasons, as well as its attempt to convey an impression of stability and continuity. *The Archers* may be listened to by city dwellers, for whom November and February may not seem very different, but the programmes depict a world where changes of season are fundamental aspects of individual experience, and social and working life. If farming, in the form of lambing, dominates the spring, most summers feature a cricket story and a village fête. In the autumn there is the Flower and Produce show, swiftly followed by preparations for the Christmas pantomime, which usually provide light relief between October and December. Some of these events contribute to the creation of a feminine culture which, as well as being traditionally associated with soaps, also bears some relation to the concern with interior decoration and the pleasures of domesticity which Dyer has identified as characteristic of the heritage text, and which Higson sees as a concern with surface rather than emotional depth. This 'embroidery and flowers for the church' aspect of *The Archers* is reminiscent of Samuel's discussion of the much maligned feminine aspects of some heritage culture, and it may constitute one of the 'heritage pleasures' of *The Archers*.

Despite the squabbles and long-running disputes which are the stuff of soap opera, Ambridge is still a kind of rural utopia, where private tragedy becomes a matter for public concern, and grief and hard times are shared. Death itself can be tolerated in such a setting, and is often idealised by the bucolic context. In 1995, a grieving Tom Forrest described how Martha Woodford had been found dead in her garden, clutching a bunch of snowdrops – the latter doubtless symbolising the purity of a soul which had never really adapted to the 1990s. An earlier death in rural idyll was that of Dan Archer, who died heroically trying to rescue a sheep, in the presence of his granddaughter Elizabeth. The controversial and sudden death in a car crash of Mark Hebden was rather less idyllic, but the village rallying round to support the widow Shula was a strong feature of subsequent scripts, culminating in her presentation of a trophy in memory of Mark to the cricket club. Thus this 'tragedy', which seemed to threaten a diegesis based largely on the 'everyday' to the extent that it prompted some fans to protest to the BBC, was sutured back into the succession of community events, the calendar of village life.

Another dramatic story developed in late 1996 when the Grundys were threatened with eviction from Grange Farm by their landlord Simon Pemberton. This event became a significant vehicle for the expression of the ideal community discourse, with the whole village making every effort to support the Grundys, buying them drinks, offering them lifts and endless sympathy. This scenario was repeated in spring 2000 when the Grundys finally did go bankrupt, and lost their farm; Caroline Bone took in the eldest son, William, so that he would be able to live in Ambridge and keep on his job as assistant gamekeeper, and David Archer organised a petition against the eviction of the Grundys by 'Borchester Land'. This utopian vision of a small community rallying round to support its most vulnerable members at times seems to challenge the programmes' own codes of social realism: in 1996, for example, the upper middle-class (and recently widowed) Caroline invited the not quite respectable working-class Grundys for Christmas. The rather forced good spirits, and occasional lapse into sentimentality of this very disparate company, may have challenged the suspension of disbelief of the most avid listener, but the fiction that in village England no-one can be lonely at Christmas was primarily maintained. Similarly, in 2000, Roy and Hayley shared their first Christmas together with the elderly widow Marjorie Antrobus.

The controversial 'modernisation' of the programmes by the current editor of the series has also called into question the utopian community described above, as well as providing challenges to the boundaries of the community, which, as Geraghty has argued, are typical narrative devices of soap opera. In 1995, Usha Gupta, an Asian woman lawyer who had moved into the village in 1991, was subjected to racist attacks by fascist youths who had involved one of the village boys, Roy Tucker, in their activities. The attacks seemed to confirm the line taken by Usha's family in Wolverhampton, that she had no place in a community like Ambridge. The issue was explored, but in the end contained. The youths were outsiders, and Roy's involvement was presented as weakness in the face of intimidation, rather than racism. Usha is currently presented as fully integrated into village life, with a strong friendship with Ruth (see below), and well-attended Diwali parties. Despite this Usha remains a marginal character. Early in 2001, Usha's isolation as the only black character in Ambridge ended when Kate Aldridge returned from South Africa, and gave birth to a child, whose father, Lucas Madikane, became the first character of African origin in *The Archers*. Before Lucas's arrival in Ambridge, Kate's father Brian asked 'he's not black is he?', but apart from that, there were only covert references to 'race'. Commentary has ranged from suggestions that this is unrealistic political correctness to an article in *The Guardian* which argued that 'In leaving Lucas's colour unspecified, the programme forces listeners to confront their prejudices' (Lawson, 2001: 3).

However, a similar silence in relation to a recently introduced Irish character, Siobhàn Hathaway, perhaps questions this sanguine view. Here difference seems to have been made invisible, in a manner which has been identified as typical of the mode of 'integration' of the Irish in Britain (Hickman, 1995). Siobhàn's Irishness is rarely referred to, and Siobhàn has thrown herself into English village life despite differences of religion and culture. In this way Englishness itself is not treated as an ethnicity, but represents a neutral and universal culture which everyone can belong to (see Hall, 1992). In late 2000 there was a mutual attraction between Siobhàn's husband Tim and, ironically, the village's Church of England woman vicar. When Lynda Snell forced Siobhàn to take this seriously in February

2001, Siobhàn's reaction caused Lynda to comment on her 'fiery temper', a phrase which conjured stereotypical images of the passionate, flame-haired Irish colleen.[4] A few episodes later, when Tim and Siobhàn appeared at church in the village, Susan Carter asked why Siobhàn, as a Catholic, was there. Shula, in slightly shocked tones, 'corrected' her, commenting that people from all denominations are welcome in church (*The Archers*, 25 February 2001). This was only the second time that Siobhàn's religion had been mentioned since her arrival in Ambridge in early 1999, and the fact that the first hint of anti-Catholicism came from one of the working-class characters is significant.

Similarly, while the middle-class characters made no comments on cultural differences in relation to Lucas, Eddie Grundy expressed surprise that he was not wearing robes, or more used to walking everywhere. One can therefore see a combination of invisibilisation of difference – both Lucas and Siobhàn are assimilated into the village, and hence into white Englishness, with few conflicts or difficulties – and an association of racist or narrow-minded attitutes with working-class culture and characters (Roy, Eddie, Susan), while the middle classes maintain polite silences on these subjects. Lucas's participation in a Radio Borsetshire special on the theme 'Is Britain a Multicultural Society?' seems to epitomise the problem the scriptwriters and production team are trying to address. By broadening the discussion beyond 'black/white dichotomies' (Hickman, 1995: 250), and relating it to the representation of class, it is possible to identify the current limitations of the 'ideal community'. Nonetheless, the presence of an Irish character and of a black South African playing major roles does significantly alter the white English soundscape of Ambridge (and indeed of Radio 4 as a whole).[5] The future development of the narratives around these characters will determine whether the ideal community is really to be redefined.

If there has been some progress in relation to 'race' and ethnicity, the dominant heterosexuality of Ambridge has remained intact. Sean, the landlord of 'The Bull's' rival pub, 'The Cat and Fiddle', came out as a gay man, despite the awkward and homophobic response of the landlord of 'The Bull', Sid Perks. This story was discussed in detail by the first focus group at *The Archers* weekend who questioned the realism of Sid's homophobia (see Chapter 5). The question of Sean's integration in the village was an issue for some time, but his election to captain of the cricket team suggested that the Ambridge community would again provide evidence of mythical English hospitality and openness. On 7 February 1997 Sean was heard discussing the question with Jill Archer, the matriarch of Ambridge. Jill's traditional offer of a cup of coffee and generally sympathetic response implied that whatever the short-term problems might be, in the longer term Sean would be accepted. In his own words: 'But getting elected cricket captain, well, it probably sounds daft to say it, but it really feels like I belong here.' Unfortunately in 2000 Sean and Peter sold up and left the village, leaving Ambridge without even a token gay person.

Adrian Mellor, in his discussion of the pleasures provided by an outing to Liverpool's renovated Docks, has argued that a leisure/heritage site such as the Docks provides a social space, an antidote for the loss of community in late twentieth-century Britain (1991: 115). The emphasis on community in British soap opera suggests a similar function (Geraghty, 1991). *The Archers* seems to offer a particular version of this pleasure – characteristic of the genre, but embedded in images of rural Englishness associated more with the heritage film than soap. The feeling of belonging to a community expressed by the newcomer to Ambridge, Sean, may perhaps be one of the attractions of 'visiting' Ambridge on a daily basis, despite the community's limitations and boundaries. I will return to this theme when discussing the views of some regular listeners in Chapters 5 and 6. First, I would like to turn to those aspects of *The Archers* which cannot be subsumed under the 'heritage culture' label.

The Modern Village of Ambridge

Gender

Changes in the representation of gender in *The Archers* are associated with the programmes' new claim to modernity, whether in a positive sense by the producers and some supportive journalists, or in a negative sense by the critics of the series' current form and style. William Smethurst, for instance, has accused the current producer of a radical feminist take-over of Ambridge, and in his recent book has expressed nostalgia for a time when 'the word feminist had scarcely been heard in Ambridge, and its first exponent had yet to sneak across the Am' (1996: 248). Despite the accusations of a radical feminist revolution in Ambridge, *The Archers* is still predominantly traditional in at least one aspect of its representation of femininity: the female characters are depicted as primarily responsible for nurturing and caring for others.

Jill, who in many ways continues the tradition of the maternal farmer's wife, established by Doris Archer in the 1950s, is the universal confidante, always ready to offer help and support to the inhabitants of the village, as well as her own family. Jill endlessly produces cakes, cups of coffee and casseroles, which are the physical symbols of her nurturing and empathetic presence. Jill's daughter, Shula, though less attached to hearth (or Aga) and home than Jill, in some ways maintains the tradition of caring femininity: she is active in the local church, and always supportive of others at times of crisis. Working-class women in Ambridge appear to be similarly tied to the caring role, with rather more drudgery, and less free time to devote to good works than their middle-class counterparts. For these women, constant domestic labour combined with a range of part-time jobs seems to be the norm. Clarrie Grundy is almost enslaved by her all-male family's perpetual requirements for food and domestic servicing, and her production of meals was a significant element of the scenes at Grange Farm. Betty Tucker has been required to patiently support her difficult husband Mike through various stages of mental breakdown, while simultaneously taking on cleaning jobs and working in the village shop. These images of female fortitude are presented against a backdrop of women in the village consistently expressing concern for others. This caring attitude is not confined to the female characters, but it seems nonetheless to be the case that women are the pillars of the ideal community of Ambridge.

In a programme which is trying hard to be modern, it is, however, not surprising that this conventional image of caring femininity is not the whole picture. Jill and Pat Archer and Jennifer Aldridge can in some ways be regarded as a generation of women in transition, who to varying degrees have occasionally stepped outside the traditional role. Of the three, it is Pat Archer who in Smethurst's terms was the first feminist to 'sneak across the Am'. Pat attended Women's Studies classes in Borchester in the early 1980s, and argued with her husband Tony over her decision to take the children on a CND march (Greene *et al.*, 1994: 43). Despite the stereotypically humourless version of feminism which Pat Archer has at times represented and the fact that these days she is more likely to be heard discussing her latest business venture – an organic shop in Borchester – than the politics of the nuclear family, her business achievements in recent years confirm that she has successfully realised her own project. The fact that she has continued to be wife and mother in quite a conventional way also confirms her place in the 'transitional' generation, albeit at the helm. There is, however, a whole generation of 'new women' in Ambridge, for whom the pursuit of a career is a matter of course. Young or youngish women such as Elizabeth Archer, her sister Shula, her sister-in law Ruth and cousin Debbie, as well as the lawyer Usha Gupta, the manager of Grey Gables, Caroline Bone, and Siobhàn Hathaway, a translator who is married to the village doctor, are all determinedly pursuing careers. All of these women are in some way juggling relationships, with partner, child, family of origin or even bereavement, with their careers. All of them do so in more privileged circumstances than the working-class women of their generation, Clarrie, Betty and Susan Carter, for whom feminism has mainly meant the freedom to work the double shift.

One area of changing gender representations in *The Archers* is the friendships between women. It is possible to 'pair off' many of the Ambridge women. Thus, Caroline and Shula remain close friends, Elizabeth and Debbie also confide in each other, and Ruth, a newcomer to the village herself, quickly befriended Usha Gupta. In July 2000, scenes between Usha and Ruth, who was about to go into hospital for a mastectomy, were almost textbook accounts of supportive female friendship, with Usha persuading Ruth (like the L'Oréal ads) that she was 'worth' the expensive nightdress. Pat has been loyal and supportive to a number of women in the village, and in 2000 offered a home to Kathy Perks, when her marriage to Sid ended. Clarrie and Susan Carter are also good friends, and were able to make up after a row over the conflict between Susan's job in the estate office and loyalty to Clarrie. A friendship across the generations existed for a while between Jennifer's problem daughter, Kate, and Lynda Snell, a woman whose over-zealous efforts to be a pillar of the community are doomed to failure. In general, though, it is striking that it is the 'new women' of Ambridge who have close women friends, while the old guard – Jill, Jennifer, Peggy – remain ensconced in their families and heterosexual relationships.

LIVERPOOL JOHN MOORES UNIVERSITY
LEARNING SERVICES

The representation of masculinity in *The Archers* has perhaps undergone fewer sea changes, but Ambridge abounds in men who are able and willing to talk about their feelings, and be supportive to women. David is supportive of Ruth's career, and quite happy to live on take-aways, while a comic storyline had Phil learning to cook, and throwing Jill's kitchen into chaos in his search for limes and coriander and other Delia Smith requisites. More recently the comic element has disappeared and Dad cooking Sunday lunch for the family has become a commonplace. Mike Tucker advised Pat on dealing with her depression, while his son Roy cheerfully took on full responsibility for his small daughter Phoebe after her mother's flight to Morocco. Julia Pargetter's new 'friend', the architect, Lewis, showed Julia how to take care of her twin grandchildren and even the sex-crazed Sid Perks is a caring father to his son Jamie.[6] As is the case for *Inspector Morse*, the imagined requirements of a middle-class audience seem to have fostered this plethora of new masculinities, with the dominance of the feminist-influenced middle classes in Ambridge allowing them to remain within the codes of realism.

Perhaps, however, the most interesting man in Ambridge was the now permanently vanished Nelson Gabriel, who will serve to introduce the topic, and company, of camp characters in Ambridge, and whose 'new man' tendencies were confined to perpetual offers of quiche at his wine bar in Borchester. Nelson was a complete mystery: in the 1960s he was implicated in a robbery, and acquitted, but shady deals and louche associations are very much part of his image. Nelson's urbane sophistication, world-weary tones and the occasional suggestion of an interesting private life, if only through his acquisition of black silk sheets, made him stand out in the wholesomely rural context of Borsetshire. His sexuality was perhaps the most profound mystery of all, since he remained outrageously camp, despite his overtly expressed affection for Julia Pargetter. His relationship with the creator of the quiches, Shane, was the subject of speculation, and his involvement in the antiques business introduced a further slightly camp element. His relationship with Julia, however, was a case in point, since it was an example of Nelson's unquestionable place in the 'feminine' side of the programme: for years Nelson stood in his wine bar receiving the confidences of his female customers, and dispensing a more cynical *sagesse* than Jill would be capable of. A moment of high camp occurred during the preparation for the 1996 Christmas pantomime, when Julia discovered a pair of red high heel shoes in Nelson's wardrobe, and was seriously worried. Nelson's rendering of his role of 'ugly sister' was, of course, most convincing.[7]

However, camp in Ambridge is not confined to this male character. Julia herself is an entirely camp creation, staggering from one gin and tonic, and one scheme for self-aggrandisement, to the next. If the Sontag definition of camp as the 'theatricalisation of experience', referred to earlier, is applied, then Julia, who has created an entirely fictitious persona for herself, and whose responses are always excessive, is a case in point. Other camp characters are Marjorie Antrobus, who is also fond of a gin and even fonder of her Afghan hounds, and Lynda Snell, whose pretentions include her dramatic and organisational ability, two goats called Persephone and Demeter, and in 1988, the 'upstaging' of Dame Edna Everage

(Dame Edna made a celebrity appearance when Lynda and Robert Snell went to her show and Lynda 'found herself' on stage, expounding her views on interior decoration). Jean-Paul, the chef at Grey Gables, is another camp character. Always ready to fly into a rage, especially when anyone interferes with his cooking, Jean-Paul has an accent which is so exaggeratedly French that listeners have complained – only to be told that the actor, Yves Aubert, really is French. As well as providing the pleasures of camp humour, these excessive characters, who consistently break the codes of psychological realism predominant in the programme as a whole, inhabit and create a space for ambiguous representations of gender and sexuality in a programme otherwise dominated by conventional heterosexual couples and families. They provide a link with some other soaps (the exaggerated femininity of characters such as Bet Lynch in *Coronation Street*, for instance), but are also an unusually noticeable feature of *The Archers*. In my analysis of readings of *The Archers*, responses to the camp elements of the programmes will be of particular interest.

The Enterprise Culture in Ambridge

The enterprise pole of the couplet described by Corner and Harvey is a significant aspect of the modernity of *The Archers*. In Ambridge, business is omnipresent, and, in general, thriving. As previously mentioned, Lower Loxley represents precisely the combination of enterprise and heritage analysed by Corner and Harvey. Its owner, Nigel Pargetter, transformed his family's ancestral home into a business as a conference centre, and is now about to open to the public as a stately home. The Victorian gothic mansion, Grey Gables, has functioned as a country club since the early days of *The Archers*, and since 1962 has been further developed as a hotel and restaurant by Jack Woolley, a self-made man from Birmingham. The village pub has opened a restaurant, the Hassett Room, and Nelson's wine bar was refurbished as a trendy café in late 1996. In 1992, Brian Aldridge decided to expand his already thriving farm business by developing the leisure potential of his land in the form of a fishing lake and off-road riding course. More recently he threw in his lot with the company 'Borchester Land'. This enumeration of activities might give the impression that the whole village of Ambridge has become a 'heritage' leisure site, thus reflecting, and even exaggerating, contemporary trends.

The farming activity in Ambridge is a major enterprise zone, and no-one in modern Ambridge would argue with the notion that a farm is a business. This represents a significant change from the 1950s, when the BBC and the Ministry of Agriculture worked as a team in the production of a programme designed to help farmers feed the nation. Farming as a form of service to the nation has been replaced by the need to make profit. Awareness of market trends is portrayed as part and parcel of the work of farming: Pat and Tony have successfully developed their farm on an organic basis, cashing in on recent food scares; their son John, who was portrayed as a typical product of the 1980s in his unthinking enthusiasm for enterprise, seized the opportunity presented by the BSE crisis to develop his sales of organic pork. In early 2001 the younger Archers are all aware of the need to sell to the heritage meat market in order to survive: Tom Archer has taken over

John's pork business, Debbie Aldridge is developing 'Hassett Hills lamb', and Ruth and David have bought in a new herd of Hereford beef cattle.

Since most of the population of the village are involved in business activity of some kind, it is interesting that the enterprise culture is still represented negatively. In a major storyline in the mid-1990s Simon Pemberton decided to evict the Grundys from Grange Farm. On 9 December 1996 Shula commented wryly that 'morality doesn't figure very highly on Simon's list of business activities'. As a representative of the enterprise culture Simon was shown to be lacking in emotional depth, human warmth and morality. His sidekick, Graham Ryder, brought in to do Shula's job when it became clear that she would have moral qualms, does little to redress the balance in this representation of enterprise; when Graham arrived in the estate office, he regaled Shula and Susan with patronising 'new management speak', combining insincerity with the all too obvious clichés probably acquired at a course on human resource management. If Graham and Simon represented the worst excesses of enterprise, more recently the 'Borchester Land' executive Matt Crawford has taken up the role; Matt completed Simon's unfinished business in evicting the Grundys, and like Simon, though on a less violent and aggressive scale, behaved in an oppressive manner towards Debbie Archer. With his mobile phone, estuary English and complete lack of any ethical principles, Matt Crawford resembles the enterprise characters in *Morse* and is unlike any of the Ambridge villagers.

In his work on *EastEnders*, David Buckingham analysed the narrative structure of soap opera as 'similar to that of many Westerns: threats to the community, often deriving from sources outside it, serve to disrupt the basic equilibrium, which then has to be reasserted by the forces of law and order' (Buckingham, 1987: 91). As Buckingham points out, this is where the similarity ends, since the serial structure of the soap opera renders closure, and thus any final removal of the threat, impossible. He also comments that the latter is just as likely to come from within, as from outside the soap opera community. In the case of the Pemberton versus Grundy story, the threat came from outside, in that Simon always remained an outsider in Ambridge, a fact which he expressed painful awareness of at times. However, the real threat to the Grundys, which Simon merely symbolised, was the enterprise culture itself. While a benign, or relatively benign, form of enterprise is repre- sented by the business activities of the villagers (characters such as John or more recently Helen Archer may at times appear excessively business-oriented, but they retain a human side), the outsiders, epitomised by the corporate presence of 'Borchester Land', pose the real threat.

On the day when the auctioneers assessed the farm buildings and the Grundys' property, they confirmed that old farming implements, which had 'been in the Grundy family for generations', were of value since they could be sold to 'heritage style' pubs. If the programme was clearly on the side of Eddie Grundy in his rail- ings against this, the recent development of a business around the fan club, the '*Archers* Addicts', seems more ambiguous. The textual ambivalence in relation to enterprise marks a sharp contrast with the determined marketing of *Archers* spin-off products, ranging from the Grey Gables umbrella to regular *Archers* cruises with entertainment provided by members of the cast. The fan club, and the 'Village Voice Company' which runs it, were set up in April 1990, and are managed by Hedli Niklaus, the actress who plays Kathy Perks. The marketing of Ambridge has become significantly more sophisticated since the early days. The simple list of products printed in two colours on one side of A4 of the early years was replaced recently by a glossy brochure, which for Christmas 1996 offered a 'hand-crafted sculpture' of 'The Bull', 'The World of Eddie Grundy Album' on CD or cassette, as well as the traditional range of T-shirts, mugs, tea towels, pens and 'herb wellies'. Two of the spin-off books have already been discussed; they are both marketed by a publishing company specialising in English 'heritage' products – *Old House Books* – in a leaflet inviting us to 'celebrate the genius of Britain', and are advertised along-side works such as *The English Companion: An Idiosyncratic A–Z of England and Englishness* or *The Country Sportsman's Record Book and Journal*. As their nature and the context of their marketing suggest, these products represent precisely the marriage of enterprise and heritage discussed in the first part of this chapter. However 'modern' the production team strives to make the programmes themselves, the commercial venture which they have spawned remains firmly rooted in heritage culture. In Chapter 5, I will discuss the response of at least some fans to the culture around the text, and particularly to the access to the cast which it provides.

Conclusion

This analysis of *Morse* and *The Archers* has demonstrated that, despite the obvious differences of genre and medium, the programmes share representations of Englishness reminiscent of Merchant–Ivory adaptations of Forster or *Brideshead Revisited*, combined with a rejection of the more aggressively nationalistic culture of enterprise associated with the 1980s and with Thatcher. While the ironies of the programmes' own production and spin-off products are significant, these represen-tations seem to question the association of heritage-style Englishness with right-wing politics in much critical writing. They indicate the complexity of popular culture, even at textual level, and the need for a recognition of this complexity in ideological deconstructions. The still greater complexity revealed by empirical audience study will be the subject of Chapters 3–7.

In the area of gender, differences of medium and genre are significant. Despite changes made in adapting the original novels for TV, women characters in *Morse* remain predominantly objects of desire for the Inspector. Ambridge clearly has its femmes fatales, but the soap opera genre permits the exploration of a much wider range of roles for women, while the medium makes it difficult to focus on femi-ninity as spectacle.[8] Arguably, the dominance of middle-class characters in *The Archers* leads to an emphasis on the problems of professional women as well as the strong mother figures common in British TV soap (see Geraghty, 1991). In the representation of masculinity, however, there are more similarities, in that both *Morse* and *The Archers* have to some extent explored 'feminised' masculinities. Humour, in both cases, is a vital ingredient of the representation of changing masculinities, at times diffusing anxieties which may be generated.

Representations of Englishness in *Morse* have become a global product; the nostalgia and tradition they connote are clearly relevant and resonant in a range of cultural contexts. *The Archers*, on the contrary, portrays a utopian rural community, with the emphasis firmly placed on the local and the national. The formula can be reproduced in other national contexts, but national specificity is important. This specificity derives in part from the programme's long history, but also from its place in radio schedules, and from the cultural (as opposed to merely visual) Englishness which it epitomises. Characters from other cultures and ethnicities are now included, and although I have discussed the limitations of these representations, they do offer scope for development and for a more multicultural Ambridge.

This all-pervasive Englishness of *The Archers* is clearly more problematic in the twenty-first century than it was in the 1950s. Irony and camp humour may be both an aspect of the programmes' cultural Englishness, and a way of diffusing the discomfiture which it generates. The self-consciously camp elements of *The Archers* indicate an occasionally ironic mode in the programmes' production, as if the contradiction in terms of the phrase 'quality soap' sometimes threatens the realism required of the genre. A similarly ironic tone is evidenced in my discussion of both of these texts at several points in this chapter. Academic 'objectivity' is temporarily abandoned in favour of a reading position which I would describe as ironic fandom. Could this be an instance of the critical distance identified by Bourdieu as typical of the intellectual relationship to popular culture? It remains to be seen, in the empirical chapters, whether this mode of reading is a personal quirk or a facet of some fan cultures around these 'quality' texts, and whether Bourdieu's hierarchy of tastes is applicable here. My discussion of the texts has already introduced elements – such as the femininity of the 'qualities' or the pleasures of camp – which Bourdieu's class-based theory would not encompass, though one could argue that these elements relegate the texts discussed here to the zone of the middle- rather than high-brow. I would argue that texts such as the heritage film occupy a middle place in Bourdieu's cultural hierarchy – their aspiration to 'quality' and reference to high culture can only take them so far, since, like impressionist paintings, and unlike avant-garde art, they are 'easy on the eye'. The issue is still more complex in the case of a popular soap and a crime drama: these complexities will be unravelled further in the audience study.

Chapter Three

Introducing the Audience Study

Feminisms and Audience Research

This project can be seen as part of the turn to empirical audience study pioneered by David Morley in the early 1980s. It is based on the premise that empirical audience work does have something significant to tell us about the place of media texts in contemporary culture, and that this 'something' is different from the insights created by academic analysis of texts. It also follows on from a now established tradition of feminist audience research which has included Dorothy Hobson on *Crossroads* (Hobson, 1982), Janice Radway on readers of romantic fiction (Radway, 1984), Ien Ang's work on *Dallas* (Ang, 1985), Seiter *et al.*'s study of women soap opera viewers and more recently her research on parents, teachers and fundamentalist Christians (Seiter *et al.*, 1989; Seiter, 1999), Jacqueline Bobo on *The Color Purple* and *Daughters of the Dust* (Bobo, 1995) and Stacey's and Walkerdine's very different work on film spectators (Stacey, 1994; Walkerdine, 1986).

These projects illustrate in different ways the tensions in the role of feminist researcher, and in her relationship with the subjects of her research. Various negotiations of these tensions ranging from strong autobiographical identification (Taylor, 1989), political validation of female audiences and 'feminine' texts (Bobo, 1995; Hobson, 1982; Stacey, 1994) or combinations of this with ideological critique or distance (Ang, 1985; Heide, 1995; Radway, 1984) can be identified. Methodologically, it is striking that written data are the dominant research method in a number of these projects (Ang, Stacey and, to some extent, Radway) but that the interview and focus group are increasingly favoured (Bobo, 1995; Seiter, 1999). In the case of the latter two methods, although the position and identity of the researcher are increasingly discussed in detail (e.g. Press and Cole, 1999), the analysis of relations between the researched, of the subject positions they adopt in the research context and of group dynamics, is still relatively rare in feminist research on audiences. In this respect Seiter's recent work is exemplary, strengthened by a combination of different research methods: focus group, correspondence, individual interview – and by the longevity of the project (Seiter, 1999). As Geraghty (1997) has noted, the desire to draw general conclusions from audience studies is perhaps inevitable, but caution needs to be exercised. The desire to address 'big questions' – such as the relationship of oppressive ideologies of femininity and women's pleasures, or the reading strategies of black or older women – has perhaps at times led to a neglect of the necessary level of detail in the analysis of qualitative data, and attention to specificity of context in the analysis.

The question of the distinctive qualities of feminist research remains problematic. Brunsdon identifies three broad stages in feminist research: the 'transparent' stage or approach, where the woman researcher has no qualms in speaking as a woman and on behalf of women. In the second, 'hegemonic' approach, the researcher differentiates between femininity and feminism:

> What we find, over and over again, in early feminist television criticism, is the complicated negotiation of the position from which the author writes. There is a fleeting and fluctuating identification with a gender group (the residue of 'we women') which is at the same time a disavowal of many of the attributes of conventional femininity, crossed with the contradictory demands of intellectual credibility, which is of course conventionally ungendered.
>
> (Brunsdon, 1993: 314)

In the third, most recent approach which Brunsdon describes as 'fragmented', the categories of both 'woman' and 'feminist' are problematised: the impossibility of speaking on behalf of other women leads, in Brunsdon's view, to autobiographical approaches and to a reaction against the earlier concentration on gender and neglect of variables such as ethnicity and class. Clearly, there is no specifically feminist approach to methodology in audience research, and if the widening of the research agenda proposed by Van Zoonen (1994) is adopted, definitions based on choice of women's texts or female audiences also fail to encompass the field, though they may well validate the claims to feminist politics of particular projects. Perhaps this can be seen as a positive aspect of the 'fragmented' moment: feminist concerns may, and should, inform all audience research, rather than being the preserve of women academics identifying as feminists.

All the projects discussed here form the background to this study. However, it is different from them in a number of ways. Like Radway and Seiter I have used a range of research methods: telephone interview, focus group and questionnaire. The *Archers* research contains the most 'ethnographic' element – participation in a fan club weekend, and some longer-term contact (focus groups in 1997 at the weekend, followed by telephone interviews and correspondence in 1999). However, the research is not as close to ethnography as Seiter's, since it is less sustained over time, and my participation in the *Archers* weekend was primarily dictated by the research. In the analysis of the data, there is a very detailed discussion, both of my own position and of the relationships between participants and the particularities of each interaction. In this sense this research can be seen as a methodological development of some of the work reported here. I am also strongly influenced by the level of detail of analysis found in Buckingham's work on *EastEnders* and on children as a media audience (for example, Buckingham, 1987 and 1993d).

My project did not originate from the desire to critique or validate a 'women's' genre/text/audience, though the cultural place of feminism and its relation to media texts and audiences are clearly a fundamental preoccupation, linking this research to its predecessors. The desire to validate a disparaged 'women's' genre such as soap opera was not my motivation in choosing *The Archers*; *Morse*, as I have suggested, clearly does not fit into the dominant paradigm of feminist research. Similarly, women are not the focus of my audience study; even in attempting to identify and research feminist readings, I was equally interested in those produced by men. Social class, age, sexuality and ethnicity are introduced into the discussion as well as gender, even if, like those of most white feminist audience researchers to date, these samples do not contain black listeners and viewers (Bobo and Seiter, 1997; see below). This project could thus be said to respond to some, though not all, of the recent calls for a wider agenda for feminist audience research (Brunsdon, 2000; Seiter, 1999; Van Zoonen, 1994). At the same time, one of its main centres of interest is feminism as an element of cultural and social identity, however unstable and fleeting. The identity of the researcher is a key defining factor of audience research claiming feminist credentials. One element of my research questions the dichotomy between feminist researcher and 'ordinary women' found in some of this work, by choosing to study audience members who identify as feminists. This study can thus claim to be about feminisms both within and outside academia, and on the boundaries.

Sampling and Recruitment

An answer to the question of how to contact *Morse* fans was provided by the National Film Theatre's decision to screen a John Thaw season in September 1991, including one episode of *Morse* (*The Dead of Jericho*). I distributed questionnaires at the screening which asked people who might be willing to participate in a discussion group or telephone interview to give their name, address, occupation, age-group, and reason for attending the screening. From an audience of about 100, 30 completed questionnaires were collected.[1] Some months later, in April 1992, while a new series of *Morse* was being screened on television, this sample of 30 were contacted again, and asked whether they would be willing to participate in a telephone interview; thirteen responded positively and nine interviews (with six men and three women) ranging from 10 to 40 minutes in length were carried out. The thirteen respondents were then invited to attend a focus group at the then Polytechnic of North London, with the possibility of bringing a friend with them. One evening was arranged for a friendship group, consisting in the end of a couple and a single man, while the second group, who had not met before, consisted of two pairs of female friends and a single man.

The first stage in the research on the *Archers* audience was my attendance at an *Archers* fan club ('*Archers* Addicts') weekend in January 1997. This seemed an excellent opportunity to make contact with some keen listeners to the programme. In preparation for the weekend I arranged for a hand-out introducing me and my research to be put in each participant's room. I also negotiated two slots for focus groups during the weekend which the hand-out invited people to. In order to do this, I contacted the organiser of the fan club, Hedli Niklaus (alias Kathy Perks in *The Archers*), and the staff at Wood Norton Hall (the BBC training centre/hotel where the weekend was held). Initially Hedli Niklaus expressed some reservations about the appropriateness of a weekend aiming to be light-hearted and fun being used for academic research. Eventually she agreed, swayed perhaps by my argument that the discussions would be enjoyable, and that *Archers* fans would probably appreciate the opportunity to talk about the programmes. Eight of the twenty participants in the weekend agreed to take part in the discussions, one of which, involving five participants, took place over tea on the Saturday afternoon, and the other, with just three people, after breakfast on the Sunday morning. The groups reflected the social composition of the whole group in that they were predominantly female and older: in group 1 there were four women and one man, and in group 2, two women and one man. In group 1 the youngest person was in her forties and in group 2 in her fifties (see Appendix 2 and Chapter 5 for details).

Whereas in the *Morse* research telephone interviews were carried out before the focus groups, in this instance the method of recruitment made this impossible. The fact that I took a break from the research also introduced a further difference in that there was a long time lapse (of two years) between the fan club weekend and the telephone interviews. In some ways this turned out to be an advantage, since the pretext of 'updating' my knowledge of their views on the programmes made sense as a re-introduction. The continuous nature of soap opera made the timing of the research less crucial than it had been for *Morse* where it was important to conduct the interviews and focus groups during, and slightly after, the broadcast of a series. It also means that the *Archers* research, unlike the work on *Morse*, acquires a longitudinal element. Originally I had planned to contact exactly 50 per cent of the focus group sample again, thus replicating the *Morse* research where I had carried out telephone interviews with four of the eight participants in the focus groups (two from each group). In fact, here I contacted five, since two of the three members of group 2 were a married couple. I was also anticipating that given the two-year time lapse all might not respond – though in the event they all did. Tim and Janet (the married couple) themselves suggested using their second phone so that they could both talk to me in a joint interview. In total therefore four interviews were carried out with five respondents in March and April 1999.

In the second phase of the research on the *Archers* audience, which was also initiated in 1997 and completed in 1999, my aim was twofold. First, a theatre performance by members of the cast of *The Archers*, a scriptwriter and producer, entitled 'From Roots to Radio',[2] was an opportunity to contact a larger sample of *Archers* listeners, who were not necessarily involved in the official fan club. The questionnaire was therefore based on the principle of asking quite general, open questions on likes and dislikes, favourite characters, routines of listening and so on, in order to obtain a broader picture of *Archers* listeners than the qualitative methods used so far had permitted. A further, and very central, aim in this part of the *Archers* research was to explore independent instances of feminist fan cultures around *The Archers*. Thus, with the aim of identifying and eventually contacting feminist fans of *The Archers*, I included two questions on gender representation in the questionnaire. The event was part of an Arts Festival in a large town in the south of England in May 1997. I obtained permission to distribute forms requesting help with my research on the *Archers* audience at the door of the theatre as people arrived for the performance. The fact that the performance was sold out and that there was an audience of *circa* 900 is indicative of the popularity of *The Archers*. I gave out 300 forms, and 158 people returned completed forms at the end of the performance. The high response rate (just over 50 per cent) is also indicative of the strength of fan cultures around the programme and of its popularity. In the weeks following the performance I sent out questionnaires to my sample of 158. Some 110 completed questionnaires were returned; the exceptionally high response rate (70 per cent) is again indicative of regular listeners' commitment to the programme, but it is also perhaps linked to the class profile of the sample (see below and Appendix 2). In general in this research I had no difficulty in getting people to talk or write about *The Archers*: several commented that it had been a pleasure to fill in the questionnaire or said they would be keen to read my work. Broadly speaking, and with the exception of the higher numbers of retired, older people and people not in employment at Wood Norton, the samples are demographically similar, that is, middle class, middle aged and white.

The samples I was able to recruit in this research were doubtless determined as much by the venue where the initial contact was made as by the nature of the 'real' audience of the programmes. This is particularly the case in relation to the *Morse* research, where the sheer size of the audience and its transitoriness, given the irregular and unpredictable nature of the broadcasts, make any notion of a 'representative' sample difficult to imagine, let alone achieve. Although the National Film Theatre venue doubtless influenced the composition of the sample, particularly in terms of age, this was mitigated to some extent by the snowballing technique used for the focus groups, which were the most significant aspect of the *Morse* research. The audience of a soap opera is a more long-term entity than that of a crime fiction drama broadcast on television at irregular intervals, even if, clearly, it is also in a constant state of flux. There may well be differences between fan club members and the broader audience, but since information on the former cannot be released because of data protection laws, this is impossible to determine. The Arts Festival questionnaire sample certainly allowed me to contact a much larger group of *Archers* listeners, with a less atypical age and class profile than the Wood Norton group. It is also possible to say that this sample is broadly characteristic of the *Archers* audience as described by the BBC's own research.[3]

The result is samples in the *Archers* research which are older, more middle class and whiter than the general population of Britain. While the *Morse* groups were more diverse in terms of age, they are also predominantly middle class, and white. Of these three factors the age profile is both what I expected, and what I was interested in researching: older fan cultures and audiences which I myself could be part of, as opposed to youth cultures, were from the outset a feature of the research. The term middle class, as the research reveals, is extremely broad, and requires very considerable nuancing. I do not regard my research as restricted in this respect, particularly since I have attempted to be sensitive to the notion that class is both extremely difficult to determine, and far from being a fixed feature of identity. Where possible I have alluded to the significance of class trajectory.

The whiteness of the samples, as I have already indicated, is more problematic. It is difficult to judge whether it resulted from the choice of texts or the nature of the two main recruitment venues: the National Film Theatre in London and an Arts Festival event held in a theatre in a large town on the south coast. In the case of the *Morse* audience, its sheer size (*The Last Morse*, Carlton, 2000, claimed that 85 per cent of the national population had seen the programme) suggests a much greater ethnic and racial diversity than this research has discovered. The same may be true, though probably to a much lesser degree, of the *Archers* audience. It seems likely that the combination of the recruitment venues, particularly the south of England theatre, the noticeable 'whiteness' of the texts themselves and the invitation from a white researcher worked to reduce the possibility of recruiting black audience members. This does not necessarily mean that the texts do not attract black viewers or listeners.[4] There is clearly a difference between watching or listening to a media text, attending a performance related to it at a theatre or cinema, and still more, expressing willingness to participate in media-related research. The latter two factors are significant in determining the nature of these samples, and one of the particular effects may have been the recruitment of almost entirely white samples. Jacqueline Bobo and Ellen Seiter have highlighted this problem: 'In cultural studies work on audiences (as in much of the mass communications research it seeks to oppose), samples have tended to be overwhelmingly white' (1997: 171). Speaking from a US perspective, they argue that this results from the 'demographics of the academy', as well as sampling error and 'the failure of individual researchers to be sufficiently diligent in making contacts' (ibid.). While these are clearly important points, there are problems with attempts to pre-define samples in terms of politically significant variables, and with the privileging of 'race', rather than, say, physical impairment or sexuality in such choices. The dominant definition of 'race' in terms of the black/white dichotomy has also been questioned by some researchers who have investigated the experience of the Irish in Britain as a racialised group (Hickman and Walter, 1995). It would be true to say here that despite the absence of black respondents, questions of 'race', ethnicity and national identity emerged as significant issues in the final stage of research on *The Archers*. The respondents in the second phase of the research all had oppositional and complex relations to the dominant Englishness represented in the programmes, and this provided some opportunity for the deconstruction of whiteness which Hickman and Walter recommend.

The Research Methods: Telephone Interview, Focus Group and Questionnaire

The first point to make about this research is that it should not be described as 'ethnographic' since it is not based on the researcher spending long periods of time with respondents in the 'natural setting' of their homes. The text-based, rather than context-based, nature of the project would have made such an approach difficult, since research visits would have needed to coincide with broadcasts, and this may well have been inconvenient for respondents and difficult to arrange. Such an arrangement would also immediately have removed the spontaneity of the choice to watch or listen to these programmes. It is thus questionable whether there would have been any great gain in terms of the 'authenticity' of the data. As Silverman reminds us, even 'naturally occurring' research data are mediated by the researcher's and the respondents' reasoning (1993: 208). Walkerdine (1986) has also pointed out the impact of the researcher's presence on social dynamics, even in 'natural' settings. Visiting respondents in their homes over long periods of time seems just as artificial and far more intrusive than the methods I have adopted here, where the boundaries of the research events were clear and limited, and where respondents could leave, or end the conversation at any point. Although one of the interviews (with Mary and Ben) was carried out in the respondents' home, in general, a public setting seems to provide necessary safeguards for all parties, and to give the event a clearer structure. In the interview with Mary and Ben a more informal mode of conversation developed and this lent a particular richness to the interview. This resulted in part from the high level of compatibility between researcher and researched. Had this compatibility been absent, the intimacy of the domestic setting may have made the interview a difficult experience for all concerned. Such a strategy seems to hold many risks, and on the whole, I have favoured the more formal setting of the focus group held in a public venue, or the greater impersonality of the telephone – in order to protect both myself and my respondents from difficult or negative experiences.

My approach here is clearly a multi-method mode of research in that I have used focus groups (two in relation to each text), telephone interviews, one face-to-face interview,[5] and in the *Archers* research, a questionnaire. The initial contact with the *Morse* audience at the NFT was also based on a questionnaire, which asked about reasons for liking the programme as well as the possibility of further contact. All three elements are therefore present in the research on both texts, though the questionnaire is much more developed in the *Archers* research, and the order of events was different in each case (see above). There is also a different emphasis in the analysis of each element, which is partly determined by a decision to foreground the focus groups whenever possible. This decision resulted in part from the dilemma of finding that the modes of analysis of the data meant that a small amount went a very long way indeed, and that there was more data than I was able to write up in book form. However, it also became clear that the focus groups were particularly interesting and pertinent to my theme of the construction of identities in talk about media texts. The unpredictable combination of interests and personalities which occurred in the groups rendered this activity a significant aspect of the talk. While clearly not an instance of 'naturally occurring' talk, the focus group bears more resemblance to this than a one-to-one interview where the researcher's presence and questions inevitably play a dominant role. In the focus groups it was far more possible for me to minimise my own involvement, and to allow the group to determine many of the topics discussed. Although in each case the extent of my influence and participation varies, it is possible to say that each group had its own dynamic, ambience and agendas. Again, the level of struggle between group members in determining these agendas varies, but in each case dominant interests emerge, which are often quite independent of my line of questioning. Thus, in *Morse* group 2, feminist deconstruction of the representation of women was a major theme, while in group 1 the 'quality' aspects of the programmes were emphasised. In the *Archers* research, Wood Norton group 1 was very concerned with issues of social class, and with romance narratives, group 2 again with 'quality' and 'realism'. The interview with Mary and Ben differentiated itself from all of the focus groups in its concern to analyse the audience of *The Archers*, and its discussion of the soap opera as text.

All of the interviews and focus groups were semi-structured: that is, while in each case I had a schedule of prepared questions I did not stick to it rigidly, and I did follow up on points made by the participants. The list of questions prepared for the *Morse* telephone interviews included quite general issues such as favourite episodes, scenes, plots and characters as well as some questions which related to my interest in the representation of single people and couples. The interviews always took place shortly after a broadcast and always began with questions about the most recent episode and the series as a whole. In the *Morse* focus groups the use of extracts led to a rather different approach, and in general I introduced fewer topics (see Appendix 3 for description of extracts). My questions asked for general responses to the extract and sometimes followed this with quite detailed questions, for example, about their response to Morse or other characters in the scene. There were also some general questions about favourite episodes and scenes. In general, the 'question–answer' structure of the telephone interviews is replaced in the focus groups by a much freer and more unpredictable discussion where I exert less overt control. In the *Archers* research, since no extracts were used in the focus groups it was possible to develop a more consistent and general set of questions on likes and dislikes, favourite characters, memorable moments or scenes, as well as listening patterns, how long they had been listening and participation in fan club activities (or just talking about the programme with friends). As well as these quite general questions three questions addressed the issues identified by the textual analysis – gender representation and the representation of tradition and modernity. Questions about current storylines were also included, and indeed were always the first to be asked in the telephone interviews. Broadly speaking, in the *Archers* research the same ground was covered in the focus groups, the questionnaire and the telephone interviews, so that changes in response resulting from the different contexts can be identified, and responses can be compared across the groups, always bearing in mind the different contexts in which they were produced.

With the exception of the interviews analysed in Chapter 6, the telephone interviews are used mainly as a point of comparison in this research project. In some cases it was interesting to compare the kind of discourses present in a one-to-one interview with those of the focus group, and differences often indicated the ways in which individuals adapted and responded to the group dynamics. For instance, individual interests which were quite dominant in the telephone interviews were not always expressed or reflected in the group discussions, indicating the constraints imposed by the group. Similarly, the group context at times stimulated responses which the more neutral questioning by a researcher did not evoke. This is not to say that either the telephone interviews or the focus groups offer a more authentic expression of an individual's views, but merely to emphasise the impact of social context on talk about media texts. The telephone interview as a form of research on media texts is relatively innovative in British Cultural Studies. Although I have found the focus group particularly rich as a source of data, and a less obviously research-focused event, these interviews were fruitful, and there is scope for more analysis of them than space constraints permit here. The particular characteristic of the telephone interview seems to have been an intimate, almost confessional tone, which is surprising, given that these are dialogues between strangers or near strangers. The physical absence of the interlocutor seems to have had a liberating effect, and one can only refer to the long tradition of unburdening oneself to a stranger in Western societies, whether in the confessional, on the analyst's couch or an Internet chatroom.

While the telephone interviews lacked the social dynamic of the focus groups, they certainly provided more complex and richer data than the questionnaires. The *Morse* questionnaire was unlikely to evoke lengthy responses given the circumstances of its administration at a screening of a *Morse* episode. Understandably, most respondents simply scribbled their name, address and telephone number and were in haste to leave the cinema after the screening. This was both predicted and predictable, so that in this case the questionnaire was not a significant element of the research. The postal survey of *Archers* listeners was a much more detailed and purposeful enquiry. The questionnaire was quite long (twenty-one questions), but despite this a high response rate was achieved. However, the length of the questionnaire may have determined the preponderance of brief, often monosyllabic, replies to the questions. The questionnaire was useful as a way of collecting larger numbers of responses than is possible through qualitative methods, but without the latter, the kind of data produced would have been disappointingly superficial. For example, the questionnaire included two questions on the role of women and of men in *The Archers*. These questions were phrased in a bland and everyday manner, as it was thought that phrases such as 'gender representation' may be unfamiliar and alienating to some respondents. It also seemed important to avoid revealing my interest in feminism which, once revealed, might have pre-determined some responses. The aim here was thus to see whether, and how, the issue would emerge, and particularly, whether feminist fan cultures similar to *Morse* group 2 could be identified. In the event, the questions inspired very few overt statements on the topic of feminism, and the majority of respondents commented either that both male and female characters were a good cross-section, or that in general the women characters were stronger than the men. It proved much more difficult to identify particular fan cultures through the questionnaire survey than it had been in focus groups, and this method of enquiry produced much more limited responses. The richness of social interaction was of course entirely lost, and the inevitable brevity of written answers, combined with the more rigid parameters created by a long list of questions, resulted in more paradigmatic and repetitious responses.

The multi-method approach is, as Silverman has argued, non-contentious. However, it is important to note its theoretical basis. I would agree with Silverman's critique of the claims of triangulation to produce a 'complete picture' by aggregating different kinds of data (1993: 157). The post-structuralist basis of this research would question the validity of such a claim, and as Silverman points out, data produced by different research techniques are qualitatively different and therefore cannot simply be amalgamated. Thus what is presented here are three very different kinds of data, which can usefully be compared, and may well in some ways complement each other, but which cannot be, and are not, combined to produce some sort of totality. As I have indicated in this chapter, any comparison must take into account the very different research contexts which the focus group, questionnaire and telephone interview methods represent. With this caution in mind, in the final section of this chapter I will turn to a question which is perhaps still more difficult than the collection of data itself – the analysis and presentation of 'results'.

Analysis of the Data

My position on this issue is accurately represented by Silverman, who points out how a quantitative element in the analysis can help to defend the research against the charge of subjective choice of examples:

> I shall try to show that simple counting techniques can offer a means to survey the whole corpus of data ordinarily lost in intensive, qualitative research. Instead of taking the researcher's word for it, the reader has a chance to gain a sense of the flavour of the data as a whole. In turn, researchers are able to test and revise their generalisations, removing nagging doubts about the accuracy of their impressions about the data.
>
> (1993: 163)

Murdock (1997) provides a similar argument for the integration of appropriate quantitative measures in the interpretation of qualitative data. Faced with a large amount of transcribed talk about *Inspector Morse* and *The Archers*, the employment of some more objective methods of analysis seemed a crucial first step in finding my way around the data. This was particularly important since all of the interviews and discussion groups apart from the two *Morse* focus groups were transcribed by employed transcribers rather than by myself. I employed three different transcribers at different stages of the project, and instructed them all to use the transcription conventions provided by Potter and Wetherell (1987: 188). In only one case, however, was the use of these conventions by the transcriber consistent. In all cases I checked and corrected the transcriptions against the tapes and my memory of the events, and I have used the Potter and Wetherell conventions in all quotations.

The first stage of the analysis was a line count of the number of lines spoken by each participant. This measure provided a quantifiable dimension to the discussion of dominant participants in the focus groups, although it was combined with my impressions of the dynamics, rather than being used as a simple measure of dominance (see Ellen Seiter's discussion of my use of this measure in the analysis of *Morse* group 2; Seiter, 1999: 54). The second process evolved during the course of the research: in the analysis of *Morse* group 2 which was undertaken first, I annotated the transcript using codes to describe the content developed by other media researchers: narrative, audience, modality (judgements about the realism of the programmes), agency (judgements about the programmes' producers and the production process) and character (Buckingham, 1993d). Further codes such as the representation of the personal, of women and of Englishness, and the 'quality' discourse, emerged from the repeated reading of the transcript. There was a further refinement and development of the '*Morse* specific' codes in the coding of *Morse* focus group 1, where I also produced a table or 'topic map'. The number of lines devoted to praise and criticism of the programmes in each focus group was also counted.

The codes developed for the *Morse* groups were then revised and refined in order to encompass the *Archers* data. The category 'agency', for instance, was subdivided in order to identify references to particular aspects of the production process. Some new codes, such as the representation of village life and country life, were necessitated by the material on *The Archers*. Narrative took on a rather different emphasis as a result of the difference in genre of the two texts; in the talk about *The Archers*, as one might expect in talk about a soap opera, prediction of future storylines was more significant. In relation to *Morse*, although there was a significant amount of retelling of the narrative of particular episodes, comments on narrative were often related to the 'quality' discourse in that they emphasised the intricacy of the plots. Using these codes, topic maps were made for the two *Archers* focus groups and eight interviews. Once a topic map had been produced for each event it was possible to determine how many new topics each respondent had introduced. This information was taken into account in the discussion of roles played by each participant in the focus groups and in the analysis of my role as researcher throughout. The topic maps were also crucial in that they provided a sense of the group's or individual's main preoccupations and interests and an outline of the moves made in the discussion from one area to another. Where relevant the number of lines or pages devoted to a particular topic was counted and if a topic was returned to repeatedly, this was also noted.

A further type of coding, which seemed particularly relevant to talk about soap opera, was developed at this stage: the number of lines where commentary was 'within the diegesis', that is, talk which 'pretended' the *Archers* are real people was also counted (approximately), and compared to the approximate number of lines where the programme was discussed as a constructed media text. Buckingham noted this combination, or slippage, in his research on *EastEnders*:

the speakers constantly shift back and forth between two positions – at certain points, they appear to be judging the programme and the characters from *outside* the fictional world, while at others they seem to accept the reality of that world, and make their judgements, as it were, from *inside* it.

(1987: 172)

These categories bear some resemblance to the terms 'referential' and 'critical' used by Liebes and Katz:

The referential connects the program and real life. Viewers relate to characters as real people and in turn relate these real people to their own real worlds. The critical (Jakobson's metalinguistic) frames discussion of the program as a fictional construction with aesthetic rules.

(1990: 100)

In their framework, discussions of modality which demonstrate awareness of realism as a set of codes would presumably fall into the 'critical' category; here such comments would certainly have been coded as outside the diegesis. However, their referential code includes comparisons with the real world (judgements relating to external modality) which I have also coded outside the diegesis, and hence 'critical', since they may also indicate awareness of the constructed nature of the programme. Lines were coded 'inside the diegesis' when they referred to characters or plots as if they were real. An example would be: 'When he and Shula were getting friendly there was that sympathetic side to him coming out. I thought Simon was going to be mellowed by Ambridge' (Group 2, Alice: 14–16). This is therefore a narrower code than Liebes and Katz' referential code, which also includes judgements of external modality. My framework is based more on attempting to analyse the extent to which it was possible to express involvement, and to speak as a fan of the programmes in these discussions. Talk 'within the diegesis', even if it is playful, would be a clear indication of this. For Liebes and Katz the codes, and the dimensions of 'hot' and 'cold' which they add to them, are designed to assess the audience's degree of 'protection' from the ideological messages in the text. An example of a statement which I have coded outside the diegesis, but which would fit into the Liebes and Katz referential code would be: 'I feel rather like Alice. I found them a sort of believable family and the issues they face a lot of families face. Obviously some of the [*inaudible*] are slightly over the top but things happen in life that are slightly over the top' (Group 2, Janet: 21–4). Because of the tendency to change from one mode to another in a single line, the counts are only ever approximate; nonetheless the technique does add a numerical dimension to the discussion of the level of critical distance displayed by respondents.

However, these analyses of the content of the discussions were only one feature of the research. Adopting the categories proposed by Fairclough (1989), and already applied to the analysis of children's talk about television by Buckingham (1993d), I analysed the discussions and interviews in terms of relations between group members and subject positions adopted, as well as content. This approach aims to avoid the danger of assuming that people say what they mean in any simple sense, and to counteract the tendency of some previous work in this area to divorce meaning from the social context in which it is produced:

> power in discourse is to do with powerful participants *controlling and constraining the contributions of non-powerful participants*. It is useful to distinguish broadly between three types of constraints on:
>
> *   *contents*, on what is said or done;
> *   *relations*, the social relations people enter into in discourse;
> *   *subjects*, or the 'subject positions' people can occupy.
>
> (Fairclough, 1989: 46)

In practice it was often difficult to separate subject positions from relations, since the adoption of the former is a crucial part of the latter. In the analysis of *Morse* focus group 2, for instance, a consideration of the group's relationships with each other leads into a discussion of subject positions adopted by group members, and the dividing line is inevitably blurred. The analysis of relations between participants involved attention to discursive and linguistic features, such as unsuccessful attempts to speak, repetition of the same words, finishing another person's sentence or rushed and excited delivery. The analysis of relations was not limited to Fairclough's notions of 'control' and 'constraint'; co-operative conversational moves, such as facilitation of another person, or of the group as a whole, were also considered significant.

Attention to linguistic detail was motivated and underpinned by the notion developed by discourse analysts that speech acts perform social and psychological functions as well as expressing meaning. As Potter and Wetherell note in their discussion of research on 'attitudes', the question for the discourse analyst is not what kind of attitude is being expressed, but *why* it is being expressed by this speaker in this context:

> If someone espouses attitude x on one occasion and the contradictory attitude y on another, the analyst clearly cannot treat the existence of attitude x or y as an unproblematic guide to what the person actually believes. But it is possible to treat the account containing the expression of an attitude as the focus itself, asking: on what occasions is attitude x rather than y espoused? How are these attitude accounts constructed? And what functions or purposes do they achieve?
>
> (1987: 35)

Throughout the analysis of respondents' interventions I aimed to put this approach into practice by emphasising and drawing out their function within the particular social context of the event, and the speaker's apparent relation to it. This took place both at an individual and at a collective level, since, frequently, the construction of a particular identity or mode of response to the text was a group, rather than individual, activity. I also played particular attention to my own role, and to the functions of my interventions, which ranged from 'affirming' the respondents by summarising/repeating what they had just said (or just saying mmm!), to silencing a respondent I perceived as potentially dominant, or participating in the discussion as a fellow fan. Significant differences emerged as a result of this analysis of the researcher's role: for example, in the interview with Mary and Ben, I intervened frequently as a fellow fan, whereas in the interview with Louise I remained more consistently in researcher mode, asking questions and following up on the interviewee's responses. The significance of such differences in terms of the kinds of identities and versions of fandom being constructed, and of the dynamics between researcher and researched, are analysed in detail in the empirical chapters.

The analysis of discursive and linguistic features of the interviews and focus groups was carried out by repeatedly reading the transcripts and listening to the tapes, and by comparison of these 'results' with impressions formed at the time, and with the numerical data and topic maps described above. Early readings of the focus group transcripts focused on 'flashpoints' – moments of disagreement, tension, or just high energy or excitement. These were identified by features such as interruptions, intonation, speed of delivery, respondents all speaking at once, breathlessness, stress on particular words, and so on. These moments of intense communication were subjected to detailed analysis, since it seemed likely that they were significant. Turn-taking generally, interruptions, and unsuccessful attempts to speak were also useful indicators of the relations between respondents and of particular dynamics – often suggestive of co-operative or more combative modes. For example, the tendency to complete each other's sentences in *Morse* group 1 was seen as indicative of the closeness of the participants, and their construction of a broadly similar version of *Morse* fandom, whereas the curtailing of Jim's attempts to speak, and his persistence despite this, were indicative of conflicting views and identities in group 2. Repetition was also found generally to be highly significant, both at the level of topics, and at times, in terms of particular words or narratives: the constant return to the theme of the representation of women in *Morse* group 2, or to romance in Wood Norton group 1, are examples of the former, while the language used to represent fandom (or its avoidance) would be instances of the latter. At times it is necessary to pay as much attention to what, it seems, cannot be said in a particular context as to what was said.

In all of this, it has to be noted that a written analysis cannot convey all of the nuances of meaning present in body language, intonation and facial expression. I have tried to take account of the material reality of these events whenever possible, for example by analysing the effect of the setting or lay-out of the room, but inevitably much of this level is lost. The discussion of irony and playfulness is particularly challenging in this sense. Distance between the speaker and a particular subject position may be conveyed almost entirely by tone of voice or facial expression. Thus Mary and Ben's 'within the diegesis' talk often uses a particular, knowing tone of voice, as well as exchanges of significant glances, and cannot be taken at face value as an expression of involvement. In the end, the whole context has to be borne in mind in the analysis of each moment of talk, and different modes such as 'straight' or ironic delivery taken into account.

In this chapter I have attempted to make transparent the processes of sampling, data collection and analysis of transcripts. A more detailed impression of my methods will, however, be conveyed by the three chapters which follow, which provide an account of each stage of the research.

Chapter Four

In Love with Inspector Morse

The popularity of *Morse*, and the amount of media attention which the audience itself has received, indicate that textual analysis in isolation would reduce to text alone a cultural phenomenon which also encompasses secondary literature, consumer goods such as audio and video tapes, experiences such as '*Morse* tours' of Oxford, and the fan cultures generated by, and generating, such ephemera. The *Morse* audience is variously represented in reviews as object of statistical analysis or as subject, with the reviewer identifying as a fan and meditating on the pleasures of the programmes. In the first case the audience tends to be described as middle class and middle aged, or more technically as 'ABC1 adults aged 35+' (MacArthur, 1990: 25). In the second, humour is a protection from the excesses of mindless fandom:

> *Morse* is back! There was, I think, a fresh spring in my step. I spent the day in anxious reverie. What would it be like? After months of youthful repeats, would the new series simply confirm that nothing stands the test of time? Or could the old red Jaguar still do two hours in what always seemed a mere 40 minutes?
>
> (Newnham, 1992: 29)

This self-reflective irony suggests that being a fan of a 'quality' series is not without its complexities. *Morse* aspires to cultural respectability, and to be a devotee of the series may therefore have altogether different connotations from those usually associated with TV fandom. My audience research was particularly concerned to investigate how these contradictions might be experienced and expressed by viewers of the series.

A second aim of this research was to explore how feminisms might inform talk about a 'quality' text, and how feminist elements in the text are taken up in particular social contexts. Although I did not attempt to recruit 'feminist fans' specifically, gender politics emerged as the main preoccupation in one of the focus groups (group 2), and some telephone interviews. As a result I was able to explore questions about the nature of a particular fan culture, the kinds of subject positions which were adopted within it and the reading strategies and discourses which it generated. I was also concerned with the paradox of an oppositional adoption of a conventional mainstream text. My analysis in the first part of this chapter will therefore focus on the *second* of the two focus groups, where these issues emerged.

In the second part of the chapter I will argue that the talk about *Morse* in focus group 1 was representative of a more 'mainstream' *Morse* fan culture. I will then go on to analyse the characteristics of the cultural identity expressed by this group. The telephone interviews with members of the groups will be referred to at relevant points. In my conclusion I will compare the two groups, in order to comment on audience/text relations in general, and on the role played by the social context in talk about media texts.

Morse as 'Lived Experience': Focus Group 2

The Social Context

The composition of the group was as follows:

Lisa, mid-twenties, white, postgraduate psychology student

Sarah, late twenties, white, postgraduate psychology student

Sue, late thirties, white, civil servant

Jane, late fifties, white, unemployed

Jim, early thirties, white, civil servant

An interested colleague, Karen, attended the second group as an observer; Karen and I were both lecturers at the then Polytechnic of North London, in our late thirties at the time, and Karen is German. At both discussion evenings food and wine were provided, and four extracts from *Inspector Morse* were screened with time for discussion after each one (see Appendix 3 for description of extracts). Despite the food and wine provided, the setting for the discussions was unmistakably educational, and it is possible to identify a tension between the 'party' connotations of the plentiful supplies of food and wine and the far from luxurious classroom setting. Analysis of my interventions shows that I was mainly in 'teacher' mode. Approximately 70 per cent of my interventions had functions such as:

- introducing new subjects/asking questions;
- addressing a named person;
- following up a point;
- summarising or reflecting back;
- giving information about the programmes;
- structuring/organising the event.

The fact that for about 30 per cent of the time I participated as a fan, recounting the plot, telling jokes or occasionally commenting on programmes, nonetheless indicates that I was split between my conscious intention to behave as a neutral facilitator of the discussion, and the desire to participate in the group, and switch to 'fellow fan' mode. The implications of this for the discussion are analysed more fully below. Here, it is sufficient to note that the combination of being both one of the group and in the powerful position of teacher/researcher means that the cultural agenda I set is likely to play a significant role in the development of the discussion.

The group dynamics in focus group 2 seem particularly influenced by gender difference. The fact of being the only man in the group elicited certain types of response from Jim, who seemed concerned to make an impression on the others and even to obtain a dominant position. This behaviour was met with opposition, at times verging on hostility, both from the group members and from myself. I certainly saw making sure that Jim did not dominate as an important part of my role as discussion facilitator. After the discussion Karen commented that it had been a women-dominated group, and I felt rather guilty about treating Jim unfairly. When part of the tape was played to a (mixed) group of fellow researchers they commented that Jim had had a hard time, and it was indeed the case that I silenced him on several occasions during this short extract. It is therefore interesting that counting the number of lines spoken by each person reveals that Jim spoke more than anyone other than Sarah, and that he introduced more new subjects than anyone other than myself. The fact that the representation of women in *Inspector Morse* became a major theme in this group, whereas this was not the case in the other focus group, has to be seen in the context of this gender-based power struggle.

However, one of the two telephone interviews carried out with members of this group (before the focus group took place) suggests that the emphasis on gender in this discussion was not only a result of Jim's presence. Very early in the interview with Sue, she introduced the topic of the representation of women:

> I also sort of dislike the standard woman who's sort of in her thirties and er (.) it's sort of patronising really, you know: 'Well, amazing that a woman should be able to do a job like this and she's good-looking as well.'
>
> (telephone interview with Sue: 33–9)

A little later in the interview I reintroduced the topic and she commented: 'There's no sort of woman character who's just doing a job in that and hasn't got a sexual role to play' (83–4). She also commented that the representation of women in Dexter's novels was still more one-dimensional and that this had prevented her from reading the books: 'I've read (.), I've tried to read one but I did not like it at all' (89). This theme is returned to at several points in the interview and there is some quite sustained discussion, involving comparisons with other crime dramas such as *Prime Suspect* (Granada, 1991–6). The dominance of this theme in the telephone interview with Sue suggests that in the focus group she met like minds, with a shared, feminist analysis of *Morse*, and was able to express ideas she had already worked out. In the telephone interview I carried out with Jim, on the contrary, gender was not mentioned at all; the conversation centred on comparison of *Morse* with other television detective series, and on the question of 'quality'. The fact that Jim expressed oppositional views on the issue of gender in the context of the focus group accounts for the energy of the discussion, but perhaps not for the dominance of the topic itself. Comparison with the telephone interview also suggests that he is responding to the agenda of the other group members rather than pursuing his own interests.

The line count of the focus group transcript revealed that the participant most involved in the representation of women theme, Sarah, is also the dominant member of the group. She introduces relatively few new topics, but she speaks most, is most responsible for the fact that certain areas are developed, and is most frequently the first to respond to questions which I asked. The fact that she was sitting opposite me and that empathy was expressed through eye contact and laughing loudly at each other's jokes meant that Sarah assumed a 'star pupil' role, and that to some extent a new and particularly powerful friendship pair was formed within the group. Given that Sarah and Lisa, and Jane and Sue had come as pairs of friends, it would be possible to comment that the all-female couple was a sub-text for the group, and that this provides an interesting context for the discussion of the images of heterosexual couples presented in the *Morse* extracts. The agenda set by these friendship pairs, and by my role, seemed to be that of educated, white, middle-class feminism. Sarah, Lisa, Sue, Karen and I were all in our twenties or thirties, and our class position was broadly similar, even if the trajectory we had followed to arrive at it may well have been different. The common culture which operated in this sub-group is perhaps most evident in the intertextual references, particularly to soap opera, where in the form of jokes there was a certain amount of feminist 'reclaiming' of apparently conventional texts such as, significantly, *The Archers*. The subject position which I and these group members adopted seemed to be that of critical reader, whose status in a feminist alternative culture gives her permission to enjoy 'ideologically unsound' popular texts.

Jim was excluded from this position by gender, and perhaps by educational background, and seemed more concerned to establish himself as critical reader in terms of knowledge of the programmes and the production process, and ability to evaluate 'quality'. Jane's position was more complex, in that she participated very little in the discussion and in that sense could be seen as far more excluded than Jim. This may be attributable to her age (over 55) and employment status, which differentiated her from the other women present. Perhaps because of these factors my attempts to bring her into the discussion were unsuccessful. Although Jane spoke very little, she introduced one entirely new area to the discussion (the theme of 'pastness' in *Morse*) and at times adopted an oppositional position in relation to Jim:

Jim: But the story is about a male detective and his male sidekick.

Sue: Yeah, but I bet the audience is mostly women.

Jim: Well, I mean, OK, you know, I don't go for middle-aged grey-haired men, I mean, I'm outnumbered here.

Jane: I might.

[*General laughter*]

(602–6)

As this extract shows, Jane is very much part of the oppositional 'women's culture' of the group, and here she introduces the topic of 'fancying' Morse which is developed later by other group members. At the same time she is perhaps differentiating herself from the younger women. Despite this, and the fact that the ages in this group range from early twenties to late fifties, some kind of a consensus emerged from the discussion of the representation of youth culture in *Cherubim and Seraphim* (Zenith, 1992); Sue was instrumental in this in referring to herself as 'an old fart' and thus making the only overt statement about age. The subject position adopted by Sue was clearly approved of by the women in the group, who laughed loudly at this point, and despite the presence of two very young women, being older and listening to Radio 4 rather than 'Acidhouse' seemed to form part of the feminist cultural identity being constructed in the discussion. This older identity may result from the fact that many 'second-wave' feminists are now in their late thirties or forties, and this may therefore be a more culturally established position than 'young feminist'.

The youth theme of *Cherubim and Seraphim* led to a heated discussion of class, as Jim's misrecognition of the youth subculture provoked an indignant response:

Jim: I think you can tell I'm middle class. I've never had any experience of that but from what I know and from what you read in the papers and what you hear, I think all that sort of underclass culture, I think it was toned down.

Lisa: I don't think it was underclass culture.

Lyn: They were middle class.

[*All talk at once.*]

Lisa: It was a youth culture.

Several voices: Yes.

(747–54)

The almost angry response of the other group members here perhaps denotes an anxiety in this area. Misrecognition of a middle-class person as working class may be particularly threatening to an insecure subject position resulting either from a move from working class to middle class, or from a middle-class person's political empathy with less privileged groups. In general, the subject position in relation to class adopted by Sarah, Lisa and Sue is certainly a long way from Jim's statement, and they refer repeatedly to the rich people on *Morse*, who are outside their normal experience. Another heated argument erupts when Lisa accuses the programme-makers of ignoring working-class Oxford, and Jim explains their financial motivations for this to her:

> *Jim*: But what the Oxford City Council or whoever it is wants to portray, they want to portray sort of dreaming spires and punting down the river, things like that, you know to get the tourists in …
>
> *Lisa*: [*angrily*] But I expect it's not the people who need the money that are getting it.

> (886–7; 896)

In this instance, and in the repeated distancing from wealthy characters, an oppositional position in relation to 'middle-classness' is being adopted as part of the alternative feminist culture which pervaded the discussion. It is therefore not surprising that Jim's more aspirational statement was met with disapproval.

Critical Reading and Emotional Involvement

Given this oppositional position in relation to 'middle-classness', the negotiation of the 'quality' aspect of *Morse* in this group was likely to be a complex matter. Although 'quality' was a less dominant theme than gender representation, it was referred to in the discussion which made conventional associations of 'quality' with high production values, realism, the intellectual challenge of the plots, and the character of Morse himself:

> *Sue*: It's supposed to be, you know, this is an intellectual.
>
> *Sarah*: It's extremely, he's not listening to 'Right Said Fred' and drinking brown ale here.
>
> *Lisa*: He can't possibly understand the wide real world …
>
> *Jim*: Good stuff that. I don't see why he shouldn't do that. I'm not a particular fan of classical music but a lot of what Morse listens to, is a darned sight better than what you get on television nowadays.
>
> *Sarah*: He is a sort of cultured man, he doesn't spend his evening with his feet up watching *EastEnders*. He is listening to that particularly good recording of Verdi with a nice bottle of wine or something. The way whenever he goes to a pub he doesn't just go to a pub he goes in one that's got good draught ale. It's always very quality.

> (1095–100)

As this extract shows, there are at least two kinds of relation to the concept of 'quality' in this discussion: while Jim is anxious to claim the ability to differentiate *Morse* from 'lower quality' texts, in this case popular, as opposed to classical music, Sarah and Sue are taking up a position of critical distance, able to appreciate the connotations of Morse's 'quality' tastes, without necessarily associating themselves with them. For them what is at stake is the demonstration of the ability to read the signs, rather than the capacity to be impressed by them. Jim, on the other hand, is anxious to affirm his middle-class status, by claiming the ability to appreciate classical music, which according to Pierre Bourdieu is a particularly significant cultural marker: 'For a bourgeois world which conceives its relation to the populace in terms of the relationship of the soul to the body, "insensitivity to music" doubtless represents a particularly unavowable form of materialist coarseness' (Bourdieu, 1984: 19).

Whereas Jim attempts to align himself with Morse's musical superiority, the other members of the group are reading off precisely the meaning defined by Bourdieu, and thus demonstrating their ability to interpret the significant elements of the Morse character, and hence to be aware of its constructed nature. Jim's attempts to claim 'cultural capital' in this context, where he does not belong to the critical culture being developed, consist partly, as here, in recognising the 'quality' aspects of the programmes, and partly in explaining *how* and *why* things are done. In the telephone interview he expressed a similar attachment to the notion of 'quality' and interest in evaluating *Morse* and other detective series in these terms:

> A good *Morse* is as good as a good *Miss Marple* or *Poirot* or whatever, and a bad *Morse* is as bad as anything else. You know I think all of them have high production values, and obviously, that they're made by people who care about them.
>
> (telephone interview with Jim, 111–14)

Ellen Seiter has described how in an interview with two men about soap opera, one of the men seemed most concerned to impress the 'high status' academics doing the interview by showing off his factual knowledge. Seiter uses Bourdieu to explain why such attempts are doomed to failure, and to position herself and her colleague as 'legitimate autodidacts' who have a stake in the maintenance of this particular cultural and social divide (Seiter, 1990: 65–6). Seiter's discussion seems particularly pertinent to the analysis of Jim's position in this group, where his knowledge is constantly rejected as illegitimate, or inappropriate to the academic setting and cultural agenda set by the other group members and myself. Jim's concern is to demonstrate that he knows how television programmes are put together, and while he expresses cynicism about the programme-makers' intentions, the tone of his discussion is one of acceptance, that this is how things of necessity have to be. In this again, he is at odds with the rest of the group, who are questioning precisely this inevitability:

Jim: You've got to remember that it's rich people that make sort of interesting characters. I mean, sort of people that do boring mundane jobs
and sort of come home in the evening and watch telly and go to bed,
I mean, where's the interest in that?

Sue: What about *Coronation Street?*

[*Laughter*]

(69–72)

Although the high production standards of *Morse* are referred to in this group, criticism is more prevalent than praise. This of course does not mean that the group
members are indifferent to this aspect of the programmes, merely that in this
context they feel that it is more appropriate to be critical:

Lisa: It's still compelling viewing, it really is. It's compelling sort of viewing. I
would do anything not to miss, I mean, most things I don't bother
videoing it if I'm going to be out, but *Morse* definitely, you know. I've even
learnt how to set the video to do it. But, yes, OK, you can be critical, but
then I think you're partly asking us to be critical.

(947–9)

This sense of being asked to be critical may be a response to the educational
setting, and it is significant that those most used to operating in this context felt
this. Jim was as concerned to be critical as the others, but his criticism took a very
different form. As we have seen, here, as in the telephone interview, rather than
questioning the ideological basis of representations, his aspirations to 'critical readership' involved displaying knowledge of the programmes and the ability to
discriminate between 'quality' television and 'rubbish'. In the telephone interview
he described himself as a discriminating viewer, thanks to the video-recorder: 'I
actually find that with the videos I watch more good stuff because you record the
stuff that you really want to see and you watch that. And then if you're in and
there's something rubbish on, well, you know, you don't bother watching it' (telephone interview with Jim, 297–300). Jim adopted a similar position in the focus
group, but because there it was contested, his utterances were more truncated, and
their tone argumentative rather than descriptive, as here.

The association of 'quality' with Englishness discussed in Chapter 2 was introduced here by the oldest participant, Jane, indicating perhaps that her silence may
be the result of a different range of interests from the rest of the group; at this
point there is a departure from the predominant feminist critique, and Sarah, who
is extremely active in the rest of the discussion, is significantly silent:

Jane: *Morse* to me never seems to be current. It seems to be in the past. I
don't know how far back in the past, not that far back …

Lisa: It's the whole thing about Oxford and the setting as well, isn't it?

Jane: Yes.

Lisa: I mean, it's a very sort of antiquated setting in a way and when you hear the word, sort of, Oxford, you assume that you're talking about, you know, the University and [the sort of buildings

Jim: [Too much dreaming spires and students on push bikes.

(375–86)

Lisa seems able to recognise and identify with what Jane is saying and she later returns to this theme in one of the rare moments where an emotional, as opposed to intellectual, pleasure is discussed:

Lisa: The trouble with all these little digressions into Australia and Italy and subcultures or whatever, I don't know, I actually like the old formula and the sort of almost the predictability of Oxford and the car and, you know, all these little things.

(765–7)

The sense of reassurance and security described here is reminiscent of the reviews, and may be an expression of the process of containment of anxiety by a television narrative. The satisfactions afforded by familiarity are, however, more frequently disavowed, displaced by critique of the repetitiveness of the plots or the stereo-typing of the characters, just as in general critical distance rather than emotional involvement is the predominant mode of talking about the programmes in this discussion.

Feminism and Popular Romance

It is in the area of romance that the tension between the expression of pleasure and the establishment of status as critical reader is most marked. The romance plot seems to be the aspect of the programmes which this group finds most fasci-nating, since it is introduced early in the discussion of each extract, and occupies more time than any other single topic. To some extent the choice of extracts set this particular agenda; however, in the other focus group the topic is not developed to the same extent. On the contrary, in several of the telephone interviews, which were of course independent of this screening, romance again emerged as a preoc-cupation. Although I chose the extracts because of their relevance to my own reading of the negative representation of the family and the heterosexual couple, this may not be obvious to spectators who are not specifically trained to be aware of issues of representation, as the first focus group would seem to attest. Even in this group, where the representation issue was addressed, the theme which I saw as the common thread linking the extracts did not emerge as significant, and it was the related but distinct question of the representation of women which became an almost obsessive concern. Here a great deal of critical energy was generated, as Sarah, Sue and Lisa poured scorn on the 'pathetic' women characters:

Lisa: They're very peripheral to the stories, I think, if they're not actually involved with Morse directly.

Jim: But the story is about a male detective and his male sidekick.

Sue: Yeah, but I would think its audience is mostly women.

(600–2)

This extract amply illustrates how critique is functioning as a way of acquiring and expressing solidarity as women, culminating in the view that 'we are the audience'. It is also interesting that the presence of the romance plot in the programmes and this group's preoccupation with it lead to a reversal of the conventional association of crime fiction with masculinity. It would, however, be wrong to conflate criticism of this kind with the absence of emotion, for while distance from the text is certainly expressed, usually in the form of irony, emotions such as anger, or indignation as here, do surface, indicating a passionate engagement with the programmes.

The more positive feelings usually associated with romance do nonetheless seem incompatible with the feminist persona who haunts this discussion. The talk about one of the most romantic episodes, *Dead on Time*, is dominated by criticism of the episode's implausibility, the cliché of the romantic dinner *à deux*, Morse's besotted-ness and the heroine's coy femininity, but immediately after the screening, before the critical mood gains momentum, Lisa expresses her feelings about the extract:

Lisa: It was so sort of touching, wasn't it, Lewis sort of protecting him from the knowledge right the way through to the end, and he never told him right at the end, and considering the hard time Morse always gives Lewis and, you know, the barking at him in the office and for getting things wrong and when he has actually got something right, he only, because it's too painful for Morse, he doesn't tell him. I thought that was such a sweet thing for Lewis to do.

(425–9)

The fact that this rare instance of emotional response to the text is focused on the Morse–Lewis relationship rather than on the romance plot seems to support the notion that there was an uneasiness in relation to romance here. Nonetheless, some of the identifications and readings proposed as possible sources of pleasure in Chapter 2 do seem to operate in some form. Early in the discussion awareness of the narrative necessity of Morse's unsuccessful romantic life was evident:

Jim: I mean, if he hadn't stuck his oar in or whatever, she'd still be alive and perhaps Morse would be enjoying a successful love life.

Sue: Can't have that.

[*Loud laughter*]

(85–7)

This was repeated later when Jim's suggestion – 'The Sergeant Lewis Show' – was greeted with horror, on the grounds that since Lewis is happily married, there could be 'no development'. The opportunities for identification provided by the gap in the text left by Morse's inconclusive affairs could not be embraced whole-heartedly in this context, but the use of irony did permit the expression of the fantasy. In this way it was possible simultaneously to remain outside the text, and to enter into it, by filling the gap in the narrative:

> *Sarah*: You imagine, you know, that he would say 'take off your glasses, why, Miss Smith, you're beautiful'.
>
> [*Loud laughter*]
>
> *Sarah*: He noticed me *yes*. I think that's the secret of it, he's so involved in his work, that if he does notice someone, it's something special.
>
> [*More laughter*]
>
> 644–9)

The energy of the female laughter here indicates partly that Sarah has achieved exactly the right balance – moderating the image of starry-eyed fan by her subtle and ironic intertextual reference, and partly it may be releasing any anxiety gener-ated by Sarah's crossing of the diegetic boundary. Immediately before this section, the fantasy of being the woman with whom Morse would at last be happy was linked to the combination of vulnerability and ability to nurture also discussed in Chapter 2:

> *Jim*: You know, do the women here (.) you know, do you like John Thaw?
>
> *Sue*:]Oh yes.
>
> *Lisa*:]He's terribly attractive.
>
> *Sue*: Yeah, you know, because the idea is that you're the person who under-stands him and he's had a really shitty life.
>
> *Sarah*: He's a sad man, who'd love you.
>
> [*Laughter*]
>
> (608–14)

Ann Rosalind Jones (1986) has discussed the impact of feminism on contemporary romantic fiction in terms of a transformed power relationship between hero and heroine, based on textual evidence of his vulnerability. Here Morse's vulnerability may be attractive to these feminist critical readers in a similar way, seeming to offer a reversal of the pattern common both in fiction and in women's experience of heterosexuality, where male emotional needs are often masked by projection onto the woman (see Hollway, 1992). This syndrome was already transparent to Simone de Beauvoir in the 1940s; in *Le Deuxième Sexe* she provides a detailed analysis of the

LIVERPOOL JOHN MOORES UNIVERSITY
LEARNING SERVICES

process whereby women's prioritisation of relationships leads them to a dependent role where they are forever trying to ensnare the man into spending more of his precious time with them, while he is anxious to escape in order to realise his many projects in life (Beauvoir, 1949). With Morse masculinity has come full circle, and the closing images of *Promised Land* (Zenith, 1991) demonstrate the penalties of the avoidance of intimacy: Morse stands alone and desolate on the steps of the Sydney opera house, while Lewis goes off to fill in time before the impending arrival of Mrs Lewis. Like Simone de Beauvoir, the women in this group feel that the problem of femininity, or at least of these representations of it, is the lack of projects, of something to do in life:

> *Sarah*: You know, if somewhere in Oxford it was not just entirely populated with attractive 45-year-old women.
>
> *Sue*: Blonde.
>
> [*Laughter*]
>
> *Sarah*: [*Laughs*] All blonde.
>
> *Jim*: Yeah but]
>
> *Lisa*:   ]They're incompetent. I mean, there are competent women around aren't there?]
>
> *Sarah*:]Yes and they're always]
>
> *Sue*:]Who do jobs rather than hanging around waiting to be screwed by Morse.
>
> (560–7)

However, unlike Beauvoir, they seem aware of the limitations of traditional masculinity; the appeal of *Morse* is that despite Morse's evident devotion to duty, the programmes present the inadequacies of a work-orientated existence. Morse's neediness, his constant pursuit of 'attractive 45-year-old women' seem here to be providing the beginnings of a feminist fantasy where female power can be combined with romance.

In this discussion, all of the participants were anxious to take up subject positions in relation to the programmes which emphasised the sophistication of their readings, and differentiated them from any common-sense notion of fan as undiscerning enthusiast (see conclusion of this chapter). The particular versions of this distanced position here were 'feminist critical reader' for most of the women present, and 'well-informed cynic about the media' in Jim's case. In the case of the former, the women in the group, including myself, were united by educational level, and by feminist politics, and middle-class, educated feminism became the dominant discourse. As a result of his inability to participate in this discourse, Jim became the least powerful member of the group. While recognising the small scale of this research, I would guess that the feminist culture expressed in this discussion is not an isolated phenomenon. It seems unlikely that the women in the group could have mobilised discourses such as critique of the representation of women with such alacrity if such discourses were not already well established in middle-class, educated circles. The complex position of feminisms as both oppositional and integrated into dominant cultures is indicated here by the group members' subtle negotiation of such issues as the conflict between feminist critique, and romance as a conventionally 'feminine' pleasure. Perhaps most significant are the sense of a feminist identity espousing the 'middle-aged' pleasures of Radio 4 or 'quality' television drama, and the role of irony in this identity. In Chapter 6, I will return to, and develop, these themes.

'Mainstream' Fandom: Focus Group 1

The Social Dynamics of Focus Group 1

The group was composed as follows:

Sandra, late thirties, white, secretary

Matthew, Sandra's partner, early thirties, white, commercial artist

Malcolm, early forties, white, commercial artist

One of the most striking features of the social context prevailing in the first focus group was that in contrast to focus group 2 the predominant mode of relating to each other was co-operative rather than competitive. Whereas in group 2 the difference in number of lines of speech between the person who spoke most and the person who spoke least was 355 lines, in this group it was 133 lines. The number of interventions was also more evenly distributed, in that the difference between the two participants who made the maximum and minimum number of interventions was 62 in this group and 155 in group 2. Quite apart from this numerical evidence, my own subjective impression of the discussion, both at the time and on listening to the tape on subsequent occasions, was that the group was much less in 'academic seminar' mode than the second group. There was a marked tendency to finish each other's sentences, as if all were striving towards the common aim of expression of enthusiasm; interruptions aiming to divert attention to oneself, to change the subject, or to gain control of the discussion were more rare. An example of this respectful and co-operative ethos is present in the extract below, when Malcolm expresses concern about 'spoiling' it for the other two:

Lyn: What do you remember about it and what do you like about it?

Malcolm: Well, I thought (.), it'll spoil it for you.

Sandra and Matthew: No, it's OK.

Malcolm: It was the twist that that's when they can't work out how he's shot hisself, isn't it?

Lyn: That's right, yeah.

(551–5)

The reasons for this are perhaps linked to the differences between the two groups. In group 1, it was less likely that the participants were used to the Higher Education context than in group 2, where two group members were postgraduate students. As a result they did not play the competitive game which often characterises discussions in that context. Since they came as an already established friendship group, one could also argue that they brought their own social context with them, and were less affected by the environment they found themselves in. The fact that the group was so small was also likely to contribute to a more intimate tone, and the lay-out of the room may also have played a role. While both focus groups took place in classrooms at the then Polytechnic of North London, the second group sat round a table with the television and tape-recorder at either end. The first group, however, were physically closer to each other and to me, since I had simply placed four chairs round the TV set and tape-recorder. Although all of this was unintentional, it may have contributed to the differences in atmosphere of the two evenings. At the very least it would be possible to say that I had inadvertently set the rooms up in a way that reflected the nature of the two groups.

The result of these differences seems to have been a very great contrast in tone between the two discussions. In group 1 it was much more possible to enthuse about the programmes. I counted around 38 instances of praise or positive comment, and only 8 instances of criticism, while in group 2 there were roughly 16 instances of praise, and 18 of criticism. This numerical evidence, though it supports the point being made, is in some ways less significant than subjective impression combined with analysis of the content of the discussions: in group 2 criticism is at times vehement, whereas in group 1 eulogy is equally intense. The nature of the language used indicates the unguarded expression of emotion in group 1. Adverbs such as 'really', 'incredibly' and 'very' were used frequently to intensify positive adjectives such as 'brilliant', 'fantastic', 'superb' and 'great'. The recurrence of phrases such as 'the other one I liked' ,'my favourite bit' or 'I loved that' also indicates the level of enthusiasm for the series being expressed here. This kind of language is also found in the two telephone interviews with members of this group: Malcolm and Sandra. Malcolm, particularly, described *Morse* as 'top-notch', 'marvellous', 'perfectly cast' and 'brilliantly done' in the interview, while Sandra was also consistently eulogistic. One of the relatively few criticisms was, however, made by Sandra, and she made the same point in the telephone interview (see below).

Even if talk among fans of any media text is in reality highly complex, and capable of adopting a wide variety of modes, tones and subject positions, the common-sense definition of the word 'fan' would involve the notion of unmitigated enthusiasm. While remaining aware of the many nuances of meaning present even in one social utterance, it is possible to observe that the general ethos of group 1 is more akin to the commonplace view of fandom as enthusiastic involvement with a particular text, star or activity (see discussion of fandom in Chapter 5). The absence of irony, combined with many moments where the pleasures and attributes of the series are being discussed very seriously, and at times emotionally, indicates that the readings made in this group are less subversive and critical than those of the second group. A mainstream text seems here to be taken to a great extent at face value; the values inscribed in the programmes are often reiterated in the discussion, and the value of the programmes is constantly reinforced.

Knowledgeable Readings

An area of discourse which was not only permitted, but positively encouraged, by this group was the display of detailed knowledge of the programmes and the surrounding texts. As well as demonstrating a thorough knowledge of the complexities of the plots of the television programmes, the group was also able to compare the programmes to the original novels:

Malcolm: I wonder, how it would have worked if they'd kept to the books.

Sandra: Well, it just seems unbelievable.

Matthew: It might be the same. If it was the other way round, you'd still have two characters, OK the roles would be reversed, but you'd still get the same patter.

Malcolm: I wonder why they changed that, I wonder why they did (.) because that's quite unusual, isn't it?

(820–6)

At one point there was also a detailed discussion of the music, which demonstrated not only an enthusiastic endorsement of the programmes' positive educational and cultural effects, but also evidence that information had been gleaned from secondary texts such as newspaper reviews and magazine articles:

Malcolm: And you know, I didn't know this (.) that in the first chords of each

Matthew: Is the Morse code.

Sandra: Yes, it is the Morse code.

Malcolm: Yes but

Matthew: And it spells out Morse.

Malcolm: Who did it.

Matthew: Oh. It spells out who did it?

Sandra: Oh [*surprised tone*]. What in every episode?

Malcolm: Yeah.

Matthew: I thought it just spells out Morse as in Morse code.

(123–32)

Information about the music written for the *Morse* series and its composer
Barrington Pheloung has been the topic of a number of articles and reviews,
notably an interview in *The Independent*.[1] It is clear that these fans have read and
absorbed this information, and that one of the social pleasures of 'fandom' is in its
exchange. Although there is evidence of 'background reading' in focus group 2,
most of the members of the group, with the exception of Jim, are more interested in
critical deconstruction than in exchange of information. The pleasure taken in the
collection and sharing of such facts here is also associated with the group dynamics.
At the beginning of the extract Matthew finishes Malcolm's sentence. This does not
seem to irritate Malcolm since individual dominance is less important than the
expression of shared enthusiasm for the series. The sentences in the whole extract
are short, as the excitement over the 'secret' of the music becomes almost breathless.
At the end Malcolm receives his reward, when the other two give him and his
second revelation their full attention in expressions of admiring astonishment.

The exchange of information includes not only that which has been gleaned
from the original novels, or from the secondary texts, but also from the
programmes themselves. Like group 2, this group showed themselves to be sophisticated readers of visual texts. The level of detail of their observations was
particularly striking:

Sandra: But I think you really got to know her because one minute she's at a
cocktail party with obviously something to hide, and he goes round for
coffee and says would you like to go out. That's it, and they've got a
wooden, she's got a really nice wooden, (.) sideboard or, you know, in the
kitchen.

Malcolm: How do you remember all that?

Matthew: A dresser.

Sandra: A dresser and, er, he has a mug of coffee.

(319–24)

In this discussion of *The Dead of Jericho* Sandra shows some awareness of the significance of sets and props in conveying character. Unlike the participants in the
second focus group, she does not make her analysis explicit, but her memory of
Anne Staveley's taste in furniture suggests that she has registered its connotations;
Staveley's slightly untidy, but tastefully middle-class interior is presumably designed
to depict her as a suitably educated and cultured partner for Morse. Later in the
discussion, after the third extract (from *Last Seen Wearing*), Matthew makes the kind

of reading of the connotations of visual and aural signs which abounds in focus group 2:

> *Matthew*: I found the soundtrack on that bit was the sleazy saxophone was implying sexual, and the way she's draped on that sofa.
>
> *Malcolm*: Which is nothing to do with the scene, really, was it?
>
> (491–3)

Despite the sophistication of this reading it is highly selective, and aware of only one of the levels of ambiguity in the scene. Matthew has observed the sexual connotations of the interlude, where Morse visits an attractive single woman late at night. Unlike at least one participant in group 2 (Sarah), he interprets the scene in purely heterosexual terms, and has not remembered that we are told quite clearly that the woman in question, Miss Baines, the Deputy Headmistress of a girls' school, 'doesn't get on with men'. Unlike Sarah, Matthew and the other two members of this group fail to notice the lesbian theme running through the plot, where one of the girls has a crush on Miss Baines, and where the latter's independence in relation to men is emphasised. This difference in reading one of the extracts shown seems to support my characterisation of group 1 as more 'mainstream'. Jim, the only member of group 2 who is excluded from that culture, has made a similar reading to Matthew, and he expresses his surprise when Sarah refers to the lesbian Deputy Headmistress: 'I've obviously missed a treat here, I mean, lesbian Deputy Headmistress' (focus group 2: 245). His reaction, in this and other instances, is far closer to the more conventional response of the first group, and suggests that he may have been at least more culturally at home in that ethos. His delight in expressing and discovering information about the series is also a point in common with the first group, and it is not difficult to imagine that he would have shared their pleasure in 'catching out' the programme makers:

> *Sandra*: No. But all the previous ones in his house always looked a bit more cramped, than there it looked a bit more spacious. I'm sure he lived in a house.
>
> *Lyn*: It's always been a house, I think earlier on, so that's a slip.
>
> *Sandra*: [*Laughs*]
>
> *Malcolm*: Have to write up about that.
>
> (546–50)

The 'Quality' Discourse

The relationship to the 'quality' discourse in this group was diametrically opposed to the subversive readings made by group 2. 'Quality' was one of the topics most frequently introduced in the discussion, second only, and albeit marginally, to the discussion of the representation of the personal. One aspect of the programmes which was particularly associated with the 'quality' discourse was the acting, and the appropriateness of particular actors for their role in *Morse*. The group seemed impressed by the number of well-known actors appearing in the programmes:

> *Malcolm*: Don't they say that they are queuing up to appear in *Morse*?
>
> *Lyn*: Yes, yeah.
>
> *Malcolm*: A lot of them are begging to.
>
> *Sandra*: Even if (.). There was one episode there were really about ten well-known names in it. I think that was the one about the family at the end.
>
> (725–30)

Validation of the identity of *Morse* fan is here obtained by the association of the famous with the programmes, who in behaving like fans themselves ('begging' and 'queuing up') confirm that 'fan' behaviour can be a high status activity, when it is in relation to a 'quality' text. In this claim for validity group 1 behaved like the 'Viewers for Quality Television' researched by Sue Brower, and like Jim in the second group.

This desire to associate being a 'fan' with social status can also be observed in the group's discussion of both the photography and the music. Like Jim in group 2, this group saw the music as a particularly important aspect of the programmes' quality. Bourdieu's comment on the role of classical music as a marker of cultural status is borne out here. Both diegetic and background music are associated with the character of Morse, who is the main guarantor of the programmes' aspirations to 'high' culture. The claim for their positive educational influence can be seen as a way of validating the pleasures of the programmes. In this, the group are participating in the Reithian tradition of combating the low status of television by referring to its role in educating the public:

> *Matthew*: Yeah, well, it's in a lot of things but especially in *Morse* cos it just sets a mood all the time and it, that's another consistent thing about it and it really goes well with his charac ... the opera sequence here is the actual soundtrack music, is it just it's his personality as well even though it's just moody half the time.
>
> *Sandra*: Yeah.
>
> *Malcolm*: And it suits.
>
> *Matthew*: A lot of it is just bass tones and stuff. That's what sets it apart from a lot of other series, I think.
>
> *Sandra*: I think it's actually been an introduction to classical music for an awful lot of people.
>
> (134–40)

As these examples illustrate, the ironic relation to the 'quality' discourse demonstrated by most of the participants in group 2 is here replaced by straightforward admiration. It is interesting that Sandra differentiates between herself and 'an awful lot of people' who have learnt about classical music from *Morse*. Her earlier comment that she has bought all the albums suggests that the music in *Morse* may in fact have played precisely this role for her. Yet even in a situation where she is defined as *Morse* fan, being 'researched' by an academic, Sandra manages to construct the *Morse* audience, and particularly that part of the audience for whom the programmes represent a 'way in' to high culture as 'other'. This is particularly interesting since it suggests an identification with the researcher, rather than the researched, and shows the difficulty of regarding oneself as 'object' rather than 'subject'. This may be particularly marked in relation to media texts, where an identity as an intelligent person makes it necessary to differentiate oneself from the duped and beguiled masses. I will return to this point in the conclusion of this chapter.

Perhaps one of the most interesting differences between the groups in this area, however, is in the association of 'quality' with Englishness. Although this is referred to in the second group, it is less developed, and frequently framed by the predominantly ironic and self-aware mode of reading. In group 1, however, the discussion of the pleasures afforded by the representations of Englishness in the programmes really takes flight:

Matthew: I think another thing about it, I think it was the second series I first started watching it, they obviously filmed it in a lovely summer, if we had one a few years ago and that I found very appealing was the English countryside in summer and it was kind of slightly idyllic.

Sandra: Like *Lovejoy* or something, really nice.

Matthew: When it comes across in the film, it's always better than it really is and I think that was quite appealing.

Sandra: With the music, the sun and

Matthew: Yeah, and the country lanes and the jag.

Lyn: And Oxford as well.

Malcolm: And the country pubs they go to, don't they, they're always sitting outside and it's all

Matthew: Well, that's it, and it's that sort of *Darling Buds of May* sort of beauty about it, you know.

Malcolm: But not as sweet though as

(766–81)

...

LIVERPOOL JOHN MOORES UNIVERSITY
Aldham Roberts L.R.C.
TEL. 0151 231 3701/3634

Matthew: I always did like them going at the end of the programme, the episodes, went to the pub. I thought that was great, you know, just so human and real, British.

Sandra: Yeah, it's like you can go to the opera and you can still enjoy a pint, you know, you don't have to be, you know, champagne.

Matthew: If you compare it to all the American series, I mean, it's so

Malcolm: And compare it to the Australian.

Sandra: Well, I mean, they don't have to explain it at the end, do they?

Matthew: Well, no, but it's just so much more real than all that ruddy cop stuff.

(793–804)

This reading is entirely consistent with the versions of Englishness so prevalent in the reviews of *Morse*. In this context Englishness is marked by at least three significant elements: the past as national heritage, English culture seen as predominantly rural, and the belief in English cultural superiority. If the first of these elements is slightly less noticeable here than in group 2, the second and third are strikingly present, in the discussion of a topic which was introduced by one of the members of the group, rather than by a question from me. As in the review quoted earlier, cultural superiority is expressed mainly in relation to American popular culture, or more specifically crime series, suggesting that what is at stake here is not only the belief in the superiority of all things English, but also the definition of a boundary between popular and high culture. This may have been absorbed from the reviews of the programmes which express similar sentiments but is also part of the dynamic of this event, where the members of the group are particularly exercised by the need to claim *Morse* as 'high culture', and thence to achieve a place in the latter themselves.

However, the notion of claim to high cultural status needs to be nuanced, since the participants in this group remain rooted in the middle-brow culture which Bourdieu has described as 'the illegitimate extra-curricular culture of the autodidact' (1984: 24). Sandra's comment is revelatory in this respect: it is clearly of crucial importance to her that Morse enjoys a pint as much as he enjoys opera. She is rejecting an upper-class or, in Bourdieu's terms, aristocratic notion of legitimate culture in her 'beer rather than champagne' image. This may be one of the keys to the popularity of *Morse*. The programmes contain the whole hierarchy of taste analysed by Bourdieu: put simply, there is perhaps something for everyone, from the most ascetic intellectual to the radical feminist, taking in the Radio 2 listener en route. In terms of this broad appeal, the construction of Morse's character as a combination of highly educated middle-class taste (surely a legitimate autodidact), and working-class origins, and the presence of Lewis as a representative of the 'ordinary', respectable but less well-educated lower middle class play a significant role. It would seem that audience study confirms at least one of my hypotheses about the popularity of *Morse*.

This group's espousal of the 'quality' discourse is marked by a careful negotiation of the boundary between 'high' and popular culture. While the claim for cultural status discussed earlier is certainly a significant aspect of the group's strong interest in the 'quality' of the programmes, there is also a desire to remain in contact with the popular. The ice-cold aestheticism of Bourdieu's 'pure gaze' would alienate this group, who are interested in such homely and earthly pleasures as country lanes and sun-filled pub gardens. I am reminded of the second group's pleasure in the 'sameness' of the programmes set in Oxford. Again, containment of anxiety, in this case through reassuring visuals and cosy Englishness, seems to be a significant aspect of the pleasures sought at particular times by certain kinds of audience. The provision of this reassurance may constitute one of the significant appeals of the *Morse* series, differentiating it from other television genres, or versions of the same genre. Some substantiation of the general thesis that this element of reassurance in part resides in recognition of a familiar, unthreatening and 'middle-brow' culture can be found in the group's discussion of the visual style of the programmes:

Malcolm: Well, the photography's brilliant in every episode, isn't it?

Matthew: Just knits, doesn't it? Everything just]

Sandra: [*Interrupting*] There was one episode where I didn't think the photography was particularly good and that was the one about the brewery].

Lyn: Oh yeah.

Sandra: And that was all angle shots, do you remember that one?

Matthew: Oh yes.

Sandra: You know and instead of just having a head it had to be upwards at an angle.

Malcolm: Oh yes it was.

Matthew: Obviously the director changed.

Sandra: That didn't work at all. It jarred totally. That's the only one I've ever felt]

Matthew: Well, then, it distracts from the characters, you know, the visuals in it are very much].

(161–71)

It is possible to see from this extract that the particular episode of *Morse* being discussed here has strayed into dangerously avant-garde territory, to the interest in form over content which Bourdieu has characterised as typical of legitimate auto-didacticism, the 'purest' and most prestigious form of taste:

Rejecting the 'human' clearly means rejecting what is generic, i.e. *common*, 'easy' and immediately accessible, starting with everything that reduces the aesthetic animal to pure and simple animality, to palpable pleasure or sensual desire. The interest in the content of the representation which leads people to call 'beautiful' the representation of beautiful things, especially those which speak immediately to the senses and the sensibility, is rejected in favour of the indifference and distance which refuse to subordinate judgement of the representation to the nature of the object represented.

(Bourdieu, 1984: 32)

This quotation in some ways summarises the differences between the two groups: in group 1 the discussion is very much concerned with 'palpable pleasure' and with the content of the programmes, and the tone of the discussion is expressive of a close and affectionate relationship to them. In group 2, although enthusiasm for the series is clearly a significant motivation, it is often masked by a more distanced and critical approach which precisely focuses on questions of representation.

The Personal

Group 1 shares with the second group a dominant interest in the representation of the personal in *Morse*. This is the most frequently recurring topic in the discussion, and it takes a number of forms. *Morse* is typical, and to some extent a precursor, of recent developments in British television crime fiction, where the 'one-off' murder mystery is replaced by a long-running series, whose detective hero or heroine is presented in relation to their private as well as professional life dramas. It is therefore not surprising that these regular viewers discuss the programmes not only in terms of their effectiveness as crime fiction but also as soap opera. Much of the pleasure in this discussion lies in the kind of analysis which has been seen as characteristic of soap opera fans, where reality and fiction seem to merge (see Buckingham, 1987: 169). In the short extract below, these *Morse* fans begin to discuss Morse and Lewis as if they were mutual friends rather than fictional characters:

Sandra: It struck me that Lewis knew

Malcolm: Something about her.

Sandra: Straightaway, yet the loyalty he's shown all the way through in every episode, he's always been loyal to Morse even though Morse doesn't always appreciate it.

Malcolm: Yeah, and he didn't want to upset his evening.

(561–5)

At the same time, at other points in the discussion there was a clear awareness of the constructed nature of the texts, as in the example below, where the pace of the programmes is discussed. The potential 'dangers' to the narrative of prolonging the pleasures of spectacle, identified by Laura Mulvey in the 1970s in relation to cinema, do not seem significant to these TV viewers, who, on the contrary, value the opportunity to reflect, and recover from the relentless pace of many fictional narratives (Mulvey, 1975):

Matthew: Yes. Different for a TV series to allow you all that time you know without plot points being made.

Lyn: Yes absolutely.

Matthew: Right up near the end.

Lyn: Yeah.

Matthew: It does give you, I mean, things like that for me give you time to digest the story and you don't have to always keep cutting back and to, you know.

Sandra: It's not intrusive, is it?

Matthew: If you've got all those plot points told, then you can relax a bit which is really good.

(150–7)

Although rare, there are some points in the discussion when this kind of awareness of the fact that the programmes are constructed leads to critique. As suggested previously, the most critical member of the group was Sandra, the only woman present, whose criticisms often centred on the representation of the personal in the programmes:

Sandra: I found in the last series that was just getting every week practically he was meeting a woman and it was just the wrong woman and it just got a little too much. I think you know they're sort of pushing the point. I just felt every week there was a woman. There was the woman who was running the police, no, the gaol, and then there was the opera singer and then there was somebody else and all of it was ending with him just sort of looking forlornly.

(177–81)

Sandra's criticism is not as overtly feminist as those made by the women in the second group, though one can imagine that she would have joined in vociferously if she had been part of that group. She does nonetheless seem to be objecting to the predominance of the heterosexual romance plot, and at a later stage in the discussion expresses a preference for the episode set in Australia because of the focus on the Morse–Lewis relationship and the absence of any love interest.

Although Sandra is mainly objecting to the repetitiveness of the Morse romances or non-romances, there does also seem to be an undercurrent of feminist critique, both of the representation of women as mere adjuncts to Morse, and of the predictability of narratives based on the notion that the most interesting relationships belong to one limited category. Her critique may well be less developed than that of the other group because it is not reinforced by other group members, and it does not gather momentum in the same way. The generally co-operative ethos and friendly atmosphere may also have meant that Sandra did not have to defend her views, or mount an argument in the same way as the women in group 2, faced with Jim's cultural opposition. Nonetheless, it is interesting that Sandra, like the texts themselves, while operating in a fairly 'mainstream' context, is to some extent influenced by feminisms. This point is reinforced by the fact that she raised the same issue right at the beginning of the telephone interview, and reiterated it at several points: 'And this week's (.) I thought it was good to get away. He seems to have a woman in every episode now, that would be the only, um, thing about it, you know, there's always got to be a little sense of female interest' (telephone interview with Sandra, lines 6–8). Later in the interview she explained that she was not objecting to romance *per se* but to the fact that since the women characters only appear in one episode their characters are not developed: 'you lose the impetus of those characters' (161–2). This implied critique of gender representation in *Morse* is particularly significant in a context where praise and enthusiasm are the order of the day.

In group 1, however, a very different kind of reading, made noticeably, though not exclusively, by the two men in the group, emerged. While the only, and culturally isolated, man in group 2 conformed to the analytical and critical tone of the group as a whole, the closer relationships and less competitive atmosphere here allowed the development of a different kind of talk about the programmes, or of relating through the programmes:

Malcolm: I thought it was really good the way (.) and I thought she was perfect. She was really good.

Lyn: How is she perfect?

Malcolm: I always liked her as an actress anyway, and I just thought, that's how I imagined she'd be.

Sandra: She looks the sort of person he would go for, you know, blonde, thin but intellectual.

Matthew: I thought the close-ups and the sort of empathy between them in both their eyes was exactly the same (.), you know, you could see the feeling there, that's what I could see (.) which was quite cleverly done. They obviously had shared something but it was

Malcolm: Long ago.

Matthew: But it could still be there.

(596–604)

Just before this section, Sandra intervened to comment on the closeness between Morse and Lewis, and the concern for Morse which prevents Lewis from giving him the rather disturbing information he has just unearthed about his dinner guest and former fiancée. General praise of the programme as 'fantastic', 'brilliant' and 'so well done' then leads to this exchange. Typed quotations cannot convey the reverent tones in which this discussion, particularly between Malcolm and Matthew, takes place. The emotional nature of the scene, in which Morse is confronted with the woman he loved and lost, is fully appreciated here, in sharp contrast to group 2, where it was wholeheartedly mocked. The sincere expression of emotion in response to the scene is permitted, in this very different social and cultural context. It is nonetheless significant that it is mainly the two men who respond to the romantic content, while Sandra expresses emotion in relation to the Morse–Lewis friendship. This perhaps suggests that the high romance of the scene creates the same feelings of uneasiness for her that are expressed by the women in group 2. In the latter group the anxiety is unleashed in the form of sharp wit, irony and gales of laughter, while in Sandra's case it is less marked, and simply produces a silence.

Just before the extract above, Malcolm had remarked on a visual expression of the empathy between the two characters:

Malcolm: Very good that scene, he was wearing a black sweater, and she was wearing a black dress.

Lyn: Oh yeah.

Malcolm: The husband's just died. It just struck me that he was wearing a black sweater, and she was in mourning.

(556–9)

The small visual detail which Malcolm uses to support the comments on the empathy between the two characters indicates not only that he is a sophisticated reader of visual texts, but also the extent of his concentration, and involvement in the scene. He is also deploying the skills traditionally associated with femininity: sensitivity to others and awareness of the emotional nuances of a social interaction. The women in group 2 are equally aware of such nuances, but their reading is inflected by feminist gender politics: the romance of the scene, and the version of femininity presented by the heroine, are too conventional for them. They object both to the heroine's passive behaviour and coy expression and to Morse's incarnation of lonely masculinity.

Conclusion

Chapter 2 illustrated the complex balancing of conservative and more radical elements in a 'quality' television series of the late 1980s and early 1990s. The programmes oscillate between critique of the status quo and visual affirmation of the securities of English middle-class life, between castigation of heterosexual behaviour and pure romance, and in the case of the hero himself, between the ability to nurture others and his own neediness. The existence of these tensions in the text creates the possibility for a range of readings and identifications, and may be one of the aspects of the series which has ensured its success in winning large audiences. The analysis of the focus groups in this chapter indicates how the image of a uniform, mass audience perpetuated by statistical research masks the range and subtlety of readings and specific fan cultures which a programme such as this may generate.

Two aspects of this research, at least, have also been identified in other audience studies. First, the readings produced here are specific to these particular social contexts, and in this sense, the social dynamics are at least as significant a factor as the text itself in defining the discourses within which the programme may be discussed (see Buckingham, 1993d). The very divergent readings of the text extracts produced by these groups and the contrast between them and some of the comments made in the telephone interviews are ample illustrations of this point. Second, participants in this kind of research are understandably anxious to demonstrate that they are not duped by the media. Although this tendency may be heightened in the research situation, it seems likely, given the low status attributed to television as a medium, and to 'fan' behaviour, that presenting oneself as not 'taken in' by the media may be a general feature of talk of this kind.

In focus group 1, nonetheless, the *Morse* fan identity constructed is predominantly based on unmitigated enthusiasm for the series, and adherence to the view that this is 'quality' television. The critical elements in this discussion are mainly associated with moments when the texts become dangerously avant-garde, with narratives which fail to tie up all the loose ends, or with the representation of the personal. The critique of the latter is not sustained, or shared by the whole group. While the men in the group were strikingly enthusiastic about this aspect of the programmes, the only woman in the group, Sandra, expressed some unease in relation to the romance plots, and found it difficult to reconcile 'quality' with romance. In focus group 2, on the other hand, a feminist identity, based on an ironic and critical reading of the texts, is constructed by the female majority in the group. The only man in the group, whose reading is more conventional, struggles to find a place by resisting these – in this context – dominant readings.

In both cases gender identities play a crucial role in the talk about this mainstream media text, or perhaps more accurately, the text becomes a vehicle for the expression, or construction, of such identities. Clearly, there is a limit to the generalisability of conclusions drawn from the analysis of two focus groups, but it nonetheless seems likely that in many middle-class social contexts in Britain in the early 1990s, feminisms have an impact on the gender identities claimed and constructed. Even in the less politicised of the two groups, feminist critiques of romance haunt the discussion at some points. The analysis would suggest that the programme-makers' decision to alter substantially the gender politics of the original novels was necessary, and that a certain kind of feminism, at least, has a significant, if at times uneasy, place in mainstream popular culture in 1990s' Britain.

   The precise role played by feminist discourses in these discussions is particularly interesting. In both cases, though particularly in the second, feminism is associated with an analytical stance, which is as far removed from Laura Mulvey's notion of the mesmerised cinema spectator as it is possible to imagine. The feminist academic critique of mainstream media texts in which Mulvey played so formative a role is seen here in social contexts which, if not 'real life', are a lot closer to it than the pages of *Screen*. In one sense, feminist critique enables the women in the groups to adopt a powerful position, both within the social context, and in relation to media texts. In another, feminism operates as a constraint, making it possible to talk about the programmes in certain ways, though not in others.

   In the latter sense, the two male participants in the first group, while apparently not insensitive or hostile to feminisms, are free of the constraint which feminist consciousness seems to impose on the women in both groups. The study of these specific instances of social interaction indicates the limitations of generalisations about masculinity and femininity. In this case, two men, who, according to what Deborah Cameron has described as 'feminist folklinguistics', should be confined to competitive non-communication on factual topics, express more emotion than any of the women in the groups (1985: 34). Given that all the group members were sufficiently enthusiastic about these television programmes to participate in my research over a period of months, one could argue that the possibility of giving voice to this evident enthusiasm without constraint is indicative of a more profound freedom of expression. It is ironic that the more critical, feminist readings of the text do not permit this more intimate mode of self-expression. However, it is perhaps not surprising that even in these 'post-feminist' times, women's speech remains censored, and that the power gained through feminist critique at times has an emotional price.

   Clearly, the use of the term 'mainstream' is a crude shorthand to describe the group which did not share the feminist critique found in group 2. The latter could be summarised as a heightened awareness of gender representation and a generally critical (in both senses) and questioning mode of talk. In combination, this political content and critical form seemed to construct a feminist social identity which was politically aware and intellectual. It does not seem surprising that a sustained critique of the representation of women in a media text would emerge in this group, and one might view this as a kind of baseline for the characterisation of such an event as 'feminist'. However, the group also developed an ironic mode of talk, which seemed to be a determining feature of the cultural identity it constructed. These characteristics are not unique to a feminist identity, or applicable to all feminists or feminisms. However, they clearly have explanatory power in the analysis of *Morse* group 2, and it seems valid to investigate whether similar combinations may manifest themselves in other contexts, such as fan talk about *The Archers*.

   In some ways the description of *Morse* group 1 as 'mainstream' is more problematic. The connotations of the term are very broad and general, so that it may in fact be quite unsuitable for the description of the subtle nuances of readings revealed by qualitative audience research. In the words of Sarah Thornton:

'Ethnography is a qualitative method that is best suited to emphasizing the diverse and the particular. The mainstream, by contrast, is an abstraction that assumes a look of generality and a quantitative sweep' (1995: 107). There is also a problem with the kind of binary opposition which the characterisation of the two *Morse* groups as 'feminist' and 'mainstream' might suggest. Readings are complex and varied within one discussion or even speech act, and as David Morley (1992) found at an early stage of his empirical work, general labels (in his case, 'oppositional', 'negotiated' and 'preferred') can mask these complexities. Thornton has also provided a detailed analysis of the limitations of the mainstream/subculture dichotomy, commenting that 'inconsistent fantasies of the mainstream are rampant in subcultural studies' (1995: 93). She concludes that the 'chimera of a negative mainstream' has led academics in cultural studies and sociology to an ill-founded and under-researched celebration of the subversive potential of subcultures. My own difficulties seem to stem not from the excessively celebratory tendency (in fact, my analysis is well aware of the limitations imposed by feminist discourses on *Morse* group 2) but on the inadequacy of the term 'mainstream' and its binaries, such as 'subculture'. This effect was reinforced by the comparison of only two groups. In the *Archers* research, the deconstruction of the term 'mainstream' is facilitated by the fact of studying a range of research events, thus aiming to avoid dualism.

In an article on feminist audience research, Cathy Schwichtenberg (1994) has commented: 'in order to understand the formation of gender in dominant culture, we must look to the margins where gender has always been a problematic negotiation'. My research implies that while the opposition of centre and margins, of mainstream and alternative cultures initially provided a useful framework for the analysis of these events, the analysis in the end transcends it. In this case, both in terms of the texts, and of the instances of fan culture I have analysed, gender is just as problematic and contradictory a negotiation in 'dominant' culture as outside it, and the study of that culture is as enlightening as the contemplation of the manifold forms of radical chic.

Chapter Five

'Archers Addicts'

Introduction

The official *Archers* fan club – '*Archers* Addicts' – seemed a logical place to look for fans of the soap opera. It is perhaps necessary here, however, to distinguish between 'fandom' and 'audiences'. I have used the term 'fans' to describe the participants in the *Morse* focus groups at various points, but as the analysis of the groups demonstrated, this may mean very different things. It may also be dangerous to assume that participation in research is an indicator of 'fandom'.[1] Although a fan culture around *Morse* clearly has developed (manifested, outside this research, by the existence of *Morse* tours of Oxford, and the successful merchandising of music and books), it is less established than that around *The Archers*, where there is a fan club regularly organising weekend and day events and even two-week *Archers* cruises. There are also a number of *Archers* websites, 'official' and 'unofficial', and the programme is often the topic of letters to the Editor in the press.

In general, it could be argued that the continuity and 'everydayness' of the soap opera genre is more likely to promote the more intense level of investment indicated by the word 'fan' than a crime fiction drama which was televised in blocks of four or five programmes at irregular and increasingly unpredictable intervals. In researching *The Archers*, therefore, the question of what it means to define oneself as a fan, or to be a member of a fan club, is likely to be significant – particularly in the first phase of the research, carried out at an *Archers* fan club weekend. By definition all I would know in advance about the participants in this weekend would be their possession of the enthusiasm for the programmes which membership of the club and/or participation in its activities implies, and the social disposition, time and material means to participate in a residential weekend costing £200.

Joli Jenson has argued that the term 'fan' is associated in both academic and journalistic writing 'with two fan types – the obsessed individual and the hysterical crowd' (1992: 9). She also describes how fandom is associated with the alienation of modern mass society by cultural commentators: the socially isolated individual is seen as easy prey for the psychic compensations of fandom (ibid.: 17). This characterisation, according to Jenson, allows academic writers, for instance, to project any fears of irrationality onto 'fans' who then become the social 'other' or 'they' while 'we' can rejoice in our rational, educated stability (ibid.: 24). Jenson's view has been critiqued by Barker (1993), who claims that it is based on insufficient evidence and an inaccurately homogeneous view of discourses describing fan cultures. Barker is undoubtedly right to suggest that Jenson's picture is not the whole one, and that positive representations of fans do exist. Nonetheless, the negative stereotypes do seem to be a significant cultural presence; the name of the official fan club of *The Archers*, the '*Archers* Addicts', immediately invokes the negative image of the obsessed fan, though it may also imply an ironic, or gently self-mocking 'take' on this image. In either case, the name of the fan club represents a response to the kind of negative discourses identified by Jenson.

The presence of these discourses in representations of an event such as this is indicated by two newspaper articles on the *Archers* weekend I attended, entitled 'Addicted to Ambridge' and '*Archers* Fans All A-quiver'. These two pieces, published in the *Radio Times* (Graham) and the *Birmingham Post* (Ameghino), respectively, both used terms which associate fandom with excessive, irrational behaviour, and which maintain the vocabulary of drug addiction, for example: 'odyssey of obsession', 'blanket of enthusiasm' (Graham, 1997: 26–7), 'they are all obsessed', 'each addict has forked out £199 for this particular "fix" ' (Ameghino, 1997: 37–8). Both pieces begin with a pen portrait of a participant in the weekend which reinforces this impression: 'V.'s life would not be the same without *The Archers*. "I wouldn't have done any of these things if I hadn't been a member of the fan club." Membership of *Archers* Addicts has taken V. on an odyssey of obsession: conventions, gatherings and special weekends like this' (Graham, 1997: 26);

> S. can barely contain his emotion. 'When you dash home from work to turn on the radio, … when you think about it all day and tell your friends not to phone you while it's on because you won't answer them. Then,' he announces to the surrounding faces who are enthusiastically nodding their agreement. 'Then you are an addict.'

Irrational and childish emotional involvement is conveyed through images such as the audience 'squeaking' with excitement in the *Birmingham Post* piece and an excessive and obsessively detailed level of knowledge about the programmes through phrases such as: 'her trivia is frighteningly thorough' in the *Radio Times*.

Although, clearly, these articles were written and published after the weekend, it seems reasonable to assume that the discourses they mobilise did not appear from nowhere. In their recent research on the Judge Dredd films Barker and Brooks found that some of their respondents systematically linked the terms 'fan' and 'sad', suggesting that the negative connotations of fandom are not confined to commentators in the media or academe (see Barker and Brooks, 1998: 175). It is very likely that the participants in the weekend would have been aware of them, and that this awareness would have coloured their presentation of themselves as fans. As I have already indicated, being a fan of a 'quality' media text is particularly contradictory. Sue Brower found that the middle-class, well-educated members of the Viewers for Quality Television organisation which she researched negotiated this contradiction by appropriating the 'quality' discourse 'in order to permit themselves the pleasures of fandom' (1992: 182). The negotiation of the negative connotations of fandom is also likely to be a question posed here.

The '*Archers* Weekend' Experience

My own membership of the '*Archers* Addicts' allowed me to discover the possibility of attending an *Archers* weekend at Wood Norton Hall (a BBC-owned country hotel/short course centre) in Worcestershire in January 1997. Although I had joined the fan club before I even dreamt of doing research on the programmes, my motivation to attend this weekend was definitely research-based. Before I began research, my 'fan behaviour' was restricted to listening to the programmes regularly, reading the fan club newspapers (*The Village Voice* and *The Borsetshire Echo*), buying the occasional bit of merchandise, and of course discussing the soap with women friends. In 1989 I had stumbled on an *Archers* stand at Euston station – this was my first discovery of the fan club. On this occasion I bought an *Archers* sweatshirt for myself, one for a close friend and a postcard of 'The Bull', which various members of the cast autographed. In subsequent years purchases included Christmas cards to be sent to carefully selected friends and colleagues, a calendar, mug and tea towels. Most of these artefacts were given away as presents to people I would talk to about *The Archers*. They are a clear indication of participation in some kind of fan culture. Despite all this, I did not attend any fan club events; arguably this position allowed me to maintain an ironic distance and to see myself as part of an alternative, sophisticated and even subversive *Archers* fan culture – the kind of culture which emerged, partly under my influence, in *Morse* group 2.

This then was the cultural 'baggage' which I took to Wood Norton. I was apprehensive about participating in something which I would not normally have chosen to do, and fairly convinced that I would remain an outsider during the weekend. An interesting split is recognisable in my attitude to the weekend – despite my own clear membership of a fan culture, I viewed the participants in the weekend as 'other'. They were to be 'mainstream' fans, from whom I expected to be culturally and politically different. They would be more conventional and more conservative than me. Writing this is not entirely comfortable, but it seems important to reveal my own prejudices and preconceptions. Sarah Thornton's comment on the role of the term mainstream in youth dance cultures may be equally applicable to my own, middle-aged claim to subcultural identity: 'For many youthful imaginations, the mainstream is a powerful way to put themselves in the picture, imagine their social world, assert their cultural worth, claim their subcultural capital' (Thornton, 1995: 115). This kind of process also seems to be at work in the hostile relationship to Jim which dominated *Morse* group 2 – his views were systematically rejected and mocked in the same way that Thornton's 'Techno Tracys' and 'raving Sharons' could be laughed at by hardcore clubbers (ibid.: 100). It seems likely that the negative connotations of the word fan, the associations with 'anoraks' and 'being sad', were also in the back of my mind, though if anyone had questioned me on this, I would have vigorously denied such stereotyping. This denial would, however, have revealed the sense of being 'above' or 'outside' ideology which may be one of the pitfalls of academic work on popular culture, though, as I have already suggested, there is probably nothing very unusual in these attitudes generally. Later in the weekend a member of the cast also expressed his dread of the weekend and his expectation of being 'surrounded by anoraks'. For him, as for me, the weekend turned out to be quite surprising.

As a result of the hand-out I had distributed, all the participants in the weekend knew I was a researcher as soon as they were introduced to me. The question which almost always followed was whether I was only interested in *The Archers* for my research, or whether I actually listened to the programmes. I usually responded by saying I was a fan too. Whether this dispelled the slight suspiciousness and distance encapsulated in the question is a matter for speculation. 'Othering' was clearly a two-way process and my status as researcher did separate me from the group to some extent, at least initially. The weekend's main organiser, Hedli Niklaus, managed to pick me out in a group of twenty-one people (the total number attending) with the words, 'You must be Lyn'. I was clearly in some way conspicuous, perhaps because of the external accoutrements of the North London radical culture I aspired to – black garments rather than floral prints, earrings the sanctioned form of jewellery. All of this raised issues for me on a personal level. Throughout my adolescence, when I studied for and gained a place at Oxford, I was the academic 'black sheep' of my working-class Wolverhampton family. My parents constantly made excuses for my strangely studious behaviour, and my social awkwardness at family occasions. During the Wood Norton Hall weekend I was torn between feeling confident in my ability to relate to a wide variety of people (which I have always seen as a positive result of the experience of belonging to two social classes) and feeling that as an academic I really did not fit in. I was not, however, the only outsider: Alison Graham, the journalist who wrote the *Radio Times* piece on the weekend, was also present throughout. My impression was that the fact that some of the participants had read and appreciated articles she had already published on *The Archers* (and perhaps her prowess in the quiz!) meant that she was less 'suspicious' than I was as an unknown researcher.[2]

The Friday evening began with drinks in the bar with some cast members. I entered the bar feeling apprehensive – my first glance round the room seemed to confirm all my suspicions about the differences between me and the participants in the weekend. In fact I had already made contact with one of the participants on arriving at the station – a Scottish woman of about my age (early forties) who had been given the weekend as a present by her husband (she told me that her husband approved of her interest in *The Archers*, as 'although it's soap opera, it has some "snob value", being on Radio 4'). I almost immediately got into conversation with her, with two women in their mid to late thirties and with Sara Coward, the actress who plays Caroline Pemberton in *The Archers*. This conversation was mainly about France: the actress had just bought a place there and was planning to commute to Pebble Mill, and I teach French. I began to feel considerable empathy with her and the two women, one of whom was American, the other from the North of Ireland. I was disappointed not to be sitting next to them at dinner. For the meal I sat opposite another young woman, also a fan of *The X Files*, who talked about saving up to attend this event, and collecting memorabilia for both series. She was particularly keen on Eddie Grundy, and described having pictures of him in her bedroom. She was living in '*Archers* country', not very far from Wood Norton Hall, and knew the places we were to visit the next day quite well. I was aware of having a more middle-class occupation than the people I was sitting near to, who made jokes about French teachers. In this context I was very much the outsider. This was reinforced after dinner, when the main organisers of the weekend 'Kathy Perks' (Hedli Niklaus) and 'Eddie Grundy' (Trevor Harrison) ran an *Archers* quiz. I was completely out of my depth as many of the questions related to decades when I had not being listening (the 1950s, 1960s, early 1970s, early 1980s). Unfortunately my team, despite being keen fans, did not fare much better, and our score was the lowest! The winning team and runners-up displayed a phenomenal knowledge of the programmes. After the quiz I 'escaped' to my room as soon as possible.

The next day began with a coach trip round the Cotswolds, taking in the church where *Archers* weddings often 'take place' and lunch at 'The Bull'. Another journalist, writing for the *Birmingham Post*, joined us for the trip. As we sat on the coach she moved around, interviewing people. At lunch a group photograph was taken by photographers from the *Radio Times* and the *Post*. In some ways it was amazing that participants in the weekend remained good-humoured despite being interrogated by journalists *and* an academic researcher. In fact they seemed to enjoy the opportunity to talk about *The Archers*, and the sense of being 'celebrities by association'. The media interest clearly placed the issue of fandom on the cultural and social agenda of the weekend, as much of the questioning focused on 'what it means to be an *Archers* fan' (see above for an analysis of the resulting articles). While the journalists interviewed and took notes, I was in slightly 'off-duty' mode. During the coach trip, and particularly the pub lunch, I spent time with the three women I had talked to in the bar the previous evening. I was enjoying their company, and began to feel part of a friendship group. I began to hope I would be sitting next to them at dinner. The afternoon was taken up with the 'From Roots to Radio' performance in the studio at Wood Norton. This involved talks by a writer, producer, actress and sound technician, as well as a specially written 'scene' and questions and answers. After this I did the first focus group, which was attended by five people, sitting round a table in a luxurious meeting room, where I had arranged for tea and biscuits to be served.

I was pleased that I had been placed next to my two new friends at dinner that evening. We were also sitting near a cast member who expressed his surprise that we did not fit into the 'anoraks' category (see p. 106). As the evening progressed and the wine flowed, I felt slightly disappointed that he seemed to monopolise my new friends' attention, and that the women-centred evening I had envisaged did not really materialise. This disappointment indicates the extent to which I had become involved in the proceedings, and exactly like all the other participants, had begun to make friends. I retired early, leaving my companions in the bar till the early hours. The next day, after chatting to a number of other participants at breakfast, I did the second focus group which was attended by three people. Then, in the words of Alison Graham, 'we say our goodbyes and scatter to our different homes and our different lives' (1997: 27).

The '*Archers* Addicts'

Eight participants in the weekend (40 per cent of the whole group; see Appendix 2) attended the focus groups; which were composed as follows:

Group 1

Elspeth*: sixties, white, allergist/speech therapist/lecturer

Norman: fifties, white, retired technician

Joan: seventies, white, retired

Pam: fifties, white, finance officer, Joan's daughter-in-law

Viv*: forties, white, housewife, former legal secretary

Group 2

Janet*: seventies, white, retired senior home economist

Tim*: seventies, white, retired senior executive officer, Janet's husband

Alice*: fifties, white, history teacher

An asterisk indicates that a telephone interview was also conducted with this respondent in 1999.

Focus Group 1

Social Dynamics and Class

In focus group 1 the line count and topic map both indicate that Viv (157 lines) and Joan (199 lines) were the most dominant members of this group, followed by Pam (102 lines). The only man in the group (Norman), Elspeth, and I spoke least (75 to 80 lines), although Norman and I introduced a relatively high number of new topics (eight and seven respectively), and when she spoke, Elspeth often introduced a new and more analytical theme. My participation in both the Wood Norton focus groups was significantly less in terms of lines spoken than it was in both the *Morse* groups (193 and 198 as opposed to 77 and 59 lines), although I introduced a relatively high number of new topics in each case. A possible explanation for this is the more highly developed fan culture around *The Archers* which the weekend was symptomatic of; these groups may have been more used to talking about *The Archers* in a sustained way, because of their participation in the fan culture and the 'everydayness' of soap opera already noted. In any case it is clear that I played a different and less influential role in these discussions. In the *Morse* discussions the fact that I was inevitably more acquainted with the programme extracts I showed established me as an expert and meant that some of my more lengthy interventions were responses to requests for information, rather than facilitation of the group. Thus the difference in method – no extracts were played at Wood Norton – may also have reduced my agenda-setting role in the *Archers* groups. Further factors may have been age and knowledge of the programmes: as several of the Wood Norton group members had been listening to *The Archers* since the 1950s, and had already displayed their expertise in the previous evening's quiz, I did not play the role of 'expert' in the same way. The difference in location – my own place of employment, an H.E. institution in the case of *Morse* – and the more neutral territory of a country hotel/BBC training centre for *The Archers* may also have played a part, as the former might have been more intimidating, and certainly more likely to reinforce my centrality to the event.[3] In general there were few pauses in the talk, and the Wood Norton groups responded to my questions and to each other fluently and in depth.

Joan and Pam were perhaps slightly advantaged by the fact of coming to the group together, and Viv's confidence may have been drawn in part from her status as a fan of *The Archers* who had attended many similar events before, was known to cast members (particularly the fan club organiser Hedli Niklaus) and was the organiser of an *Archers* fans penfriends' circle. It is interesting that in this context two women who are not in employment play the most active role in the discussion. Sarah Thornton has argued that status in a youth subculture may be a way of resisting economic and social exclusion: 'Subcultural capital is the linchpin of an alternative hierarchy in which the axes of age, gender, sexuality and race are all employed in order to keep the determinations of class, income and occupation at bay' (1997: 207). It may be possible to argue on similar lines that the expertise both these women demonstrate in relation to *The Archers* provides them with a level of social reinforcement which they may not derive from their roles as a housewife and a retired woman. However, as the analysis below suggests, Viv and Joan may be positioned in very different ways in class terms, and it may well be misleading to group them together in this way. It may also be dangerous to link enthusiasm for a media text with a form of vulnerability (see Barker and Brooks, 1998: 237). Nonetheless, it is significant that 40 per cent of the weekend participants were not in employment. Could knowledge of *The Archers* perform a similar function for older, but nonetheless in some senses marginalised, people, as a particular haircut and style of music might for young people? Can Thornton's term, following Bourdieu, 'subcultural capital', be used here? If so, where does this leave my initial characterisation of these groups as 'mainstream'?

The general ethos of this group was co-operative and polite. Disagreement was contained by this ethos, though it did occur. Social class differences, rather than a gender-based divide, as in *Morse* group 2, seem to underlie most of the disagreement, suggesting that the apparent homogeneity which I found in my application of standard categories to the weekend group as a whole conceals a range of nuances. The issue of class was raised by Joan early in the discussion:

> *Joan*: Going back, quite a few years now something which jarred on me at the time, I've just remembered it, was when George married Christine. I felt that was to me wasn't right, it didn't gel. They were so completely different, from such completely different worlds, that I couldn't understand what brought them together – what she saw in him. Or perhaps it's just me that I couldn't see anything in him. But you know she seemed such a different <u>type</u>. And somehow I never could understand that.
>
> (170–5)

Joan is very clearly identifying with Christine, the upper middle-class woman, in these remarks. In typically analytical mode, Elspeth commented:

> *Elspeth*: Yes, they brought out in the storyline, if I remember, they have brought out the fact that George comes from a different class from Christine.
>
> *Joan*: Oh yes, they did.
>
> *Elspeth*: Yes, so they have covered it.
>
> (182–5)

Elspeth seems to be countering Joan's criticism by suggesting that the issue was adequately dealt with by the scriptwriters; she thus deflects the discussion away from the more loaded issue of psychological and social realism and introduces the notion of the agency of its scriptwriters and producers, and its construction as a media text. Joan is still unconvinced, returning to the theme of realism: 'Yes, they did cover it, but it just, to me, didn't ring true.'

Interestingly, at this point Viv goes off at an apparent tangent:

> *Viv*: What do you think about John and Hayley – do you think they'll make a go of it – do you like them?
>
> *Joan*: There again, no, I don't I really don't.
>
> *Viv*: Because they're very (*inaudible*)]
>
> *Joan*: I mean, I like her] although she would irritate me terribly. A woman I couldn't stand too long – she's alright but that voice gets on my nerves. I really can't stand that voice [*Laughter*]. No, I don't think so.
>
> *Norman*: Don't you think though that surely (.) any people – I mean, Christine and George – surely it's the attraction that, I mean, you read in the paper]
>
> *Joan*: The attraction of opposites]

Norman: about millionairess marrying someone like a tramp or something.
   It's the love, it's the attraction]

(188–99)

The tangent is only apparent: although Viv introduces a completely different pair of characters there are parallels between them and Christine and George (who 'married' in 1979). John is (or more accurately was, since he 'died' in 1998) a member of the Archer family, and as a result quite solidly middle class, both culturally and economically. Hayley comes from Birmingham (the part is played by Jasper Carrott's daughter, Lucy Davis, who provides the requisite accent with some panache). It is clear that Hayley's family is working class: when her father (a non-speaking character so far) visits Ambridge he spends most of his time doing odd jobs for villagers such as the very upper middle-class Mrs Antrobus. The introduction of John and Hayley into the discussion is therefore a development of the class issue, and it is significant that Viv, who speaks with a Midlands accent, should introduce them. In the telephone interview which I conducted with her two years later (March 1999), Viv cited Hayley as one of her favourite characters: 'Well, I like Hayley. I've liked her from the start. I think they've given her a lovely personality, I think she's quite true to life' (111–14). She did not voice this opinion in the discussion, perhaps because of the negative attitude towards Hayley expressed by Joan. This temporarily silences Viv, and the laughter which accompanies Joan's comment about the awfulness of Hayley's voice may be due to the unease which its basis in class difference evokes. It would be fair to comment that the Midlands accent is one of the least favoured of regional accents, and that representations of Midlanders in the media tend to associate it with stupidity.[4] Viv's interest in Hayley, a rare positive representation of a working-class Birmingham woman, is perhaps therefore not surprising. Norman, who speaks with a working-class London accent, takes up the theme and offers another form of resistance to Joan's interpretation of George and Christine's marriage. Joan concedes that such an attraction 'of opposites' is possible, but wonders whether Christine was on the rebound from a previous relationship and making a big mistake. Norman points out that the couple are still together twenty years later: 'It seems to have lasted though.' Joan agrees and everyone laughs, perhaps with relief that this rather tricky issue has been dealt with and agreement and humour maintained. In fact, during the course of this exchange all the participants may have been saying something about their own class identification: Joan began by affirming a middle-class identity and Viv and Norman by resisting a negative view of working-class culture and characters. Elspeth tried to introduce a more neutral and intellectual approach, perhaps reflecting her own version of middle-class culture.

The class issue does not return in the form of disagreement in the discussion, but in a sense it is omnipresent. Although caution should be exercised in assuming a class basis for identification with fictional characters (similarly in the case of ethnicity or 'race' – see Chapter 3, note 4), the favourite characters enumerated in this group do seem to relate to social class identifications, perhaps in part as a result of the early disagreement on this issue. In this analysis of the role of class in the discussion, I am putting into practice one of the tenets of the theory of discourse analysis developed by Potter and Wetherell: 'The basic theoretical thrust of discourse analysis is the argument that people's talk fulfils many functions and has varying effects' (1987: 167). Thus the positions adopted (through opinions expressed on *The Archers*) by participants in this group are *functional* in the context of the group, a way of marking out an identity and of asserting difference. They in turn generate effects in the discussion as a whole, which may set the parameters for, or trigger off, other identifications. There is no automatic correlation with class in socio-economic terms, and these positions may not be adopted in a different context. It is for this reason that I use the term 'class identifications' and that I would emphasise their shifting nature.

Later in the discussion Joan selects two middle-class women as her 'favourites':

Joan: I like Mrs Snell and I like Mrs Antrobus – they are women, yeah, I feel a sort of sympathy with actually, you know. I feel they are women I could rather like. If I met them.

Lyn: Have a gin and tonic with.

Joan: Yes [*Laughter*]. And I'm desperately sorry for Clarrie – it's so awful she has a dreadful life and I think 'oh that poor, down-trodden little girl'.

(328–33)

The fantasy of crossing the boundaries into the fictional world and the strong identification with women of a social milieu perceived as similar to her own (or one she aspires to) seem to motivate Joan's remarks here. My 'gin and tonic' quip suggests that I was both making exactly this reading of Joan at the time, and entering the fantasy of her meeting Mrs Antrobus (who is known to have acquired the gin and tonic habit in an earlier, colonial existence in India). This is clearly a more positive possibility for fantasy than its correlate: the 'poor, down-trodden little girl' of the next lines, which seems to be an expression of distance from working-class characters. Significantly, Clarrie is a 'girl', despite the fact that the character is a middle-aged mother of two, while the more middle-class Mrs Antrobus and Mrs Snell are 'women'. The notion of working-class people precisely as 'characters' revealed itself more fully later:

Joan: Yes. She was the sort of woman that one met during the war. I mean, I met during the war – Cockneys – but they don't seem to breed them like that now.

Pam: No, they're a breed of their own.

Joan: They were strong, they were, they were strong women, and they had this lovely quirky sense of humour. You could never get them down. They were incredible women.

Elspeth: So really there's only Prue.

(463–9)

They may be 'incredible', 'strong' and 'quirky', but working-class women are here identified as very clearly other. Elspeth deflects this 'salt of the earth' line of argument by pursuing her earlier theme – a discussion of the women characters in the early *Archers* programmes of the 1950s and 1960s – and this is then taken up by other members of the group.

Shortly after this, Viv makes several attempts to comment on two of her favourite characters – Sid and Kathy Perks – and eventually manages to speak:

Viv: You asked earlier on – I'd forgotten then – but I don't always agree – you know, I don't – I didn't like them making Sid into this homophobe, you know, with Sean. He's very easy-going normally, isn't he, and I think that's a bit – I didn't agree with that. And the way they made Kathy put her foot in it with Sean. Because she's such a sweet and intelligent person, I don't think she would have handled it like that at all. I thought that was very contrived somehow – do you remember the scene?

(548–53)

Here Viv is defending two characters she feels particularly close to: 'and when Sid and Kathy were reconciled – I really loved that. Um, I think I lost weight that week I was so happy, I was on a high because they'd got back together' (61–3). Perhaps, significantly, she has again chosen one of the Ambridge 'Brummies' (Sid) as her favourite, and she is arguing strongly against his depiction as a political *Sun* reader. Sid is more working class than Kathy, who is a teacher; in combination they could be said to represent lower middle-class or respectable working-class culture in Ambridge. They are portrayed as capable of relating to the posher Ambridge residents, who occasionally patronise their premises as well as the farm workers who often end the day in their bar (until their final split in 2000 Sid and Kathy kept the village pub, 'The Bull'). Viv reiterated her concerns that Sid should not become one of Ambridge's working-class 'characters' in the telephone interview (and in a subsequent letter): 'But I hope they don't make Sid a sort of, I don't know a semi-caricature character. I'd rather him be (.). They're making him a bit too comical almost [*inaudible*] I hope they don't go too far down that road' (97–9). I would argue that some of this defence of these characters is based on recognition of region and class-based cultural and social similarities, and that in this focus group the allegiance to particular characters expressed is perhaps unusually consistent in these terms. Again it is likely that the reasons for this are in part at least connected to the specific dynamics of the group, where class became the pivotal, if almost unspoken, issue. In the telephone interview Viv expressed her dislike of perhaps the most upper-class woman in Ambridge – Julia Pargetter of Lower Loxley Hall:

Lyn: Are there any characters that you really don't like?

Viv: Julia, I'll say that straightaway. The sooner she goes back to Spain the better. I don't like her. She's in the programme but to me she doesn't ring true anyway. But that's me again, I mean, there are probably people who like her that are actresses and Lady of the Manor, but I find everything at Lower Loxley surreal.

(122–5)

Further enquiries lead Viv to cite Peggy Woolley (a *nouveau riche* 'Lady of the Manor') and her daughter Jennifer as disliked characters, thus completing a map of the class hierarchies of *The Archers* and clarifying her own investment in the characters who are closest to urban working-class and lower middle-class culture.[5]

The criterion used both by Viv and Joan in their rejection of situations or characters who seem remote from their own social milieu is modality, expressed in phrases such as 'something which jarred', '[it] doesn't ring true', 'I find everything ... surreal'. The dominance of modality demonstrated in the topic map for both the Wood Norton Hall groups and for many of the telephone interviews is also noted in other research on media audiences (see Buckingham, 1993d). This is indicative of its potential for the expression of significant discourses and subject positions: to say that something is not 'realistic' is to imply an alternative view of the world. The expression of that alternative view may be based on politics or social allegiances, and it is likely to be inextricably connected to the dynamics and power relationships of the social interaction. In the words of Barker and Brooks: '"Reality", then, is not a descriptive criterion at all; it is a moral version of or selection from the world' (1998: 296). Here it is in the end Viv's version of reality which generated some level of consensus in the group: there was general agreement with her concerns about the representation of Sid as a homophobe, perhaps because of the shared belief in the benign nature of Ambridge society. The inclusion of this issue in the programme has created anxiety among these listeners perhaps because it questions the notion of the ideal community which *The Archers*, like other soap operas, negotiates. Joan's critique of Christine's marriage to George is still more controversial, perhaps again because it reveals the possibility of social hierarchies which are inadmissible in the rural utopia of Ambridge (and perhaps uncomfortably present within the group).

If Viv and Joan expressed class identifications most clearly, with Pam in general supporting Joan, Elspeth chose the linchpins of the programme, Phil and Jill Archer, as her favourite characters: 'They're dependable aren't they? They are *The Archers*. Everything in some way radiates from them' (291–2). Norman agreed with her, expressing a particular preference for Jill: 'Well, I have to say, I agree about Phil and Jill. Jill seems to be a sort of matriarch of the whole – as you say the whole Archer clan' (297–8). Elspeth has chosen characters who are in some sense represented as 'above' class, as the benchmark of normality, rather than a particular upper or lower middle-class milieu. She seems to have chosen these characters more on the basis of their role in the narrative, than identification, and her choice is entirely consistent with the reflective and slightly distanced role she plays in the discussion. Norman here does not engage with the class theme of the discussion, but shifts it onto gender, a topic which then is sustained for ten pages of a 25-page transcription.

Romance and Gender

As the topic map shows, this theme and the question of modality were the two issues which promoted the most sustained discussion. Questions of external and internal modality were an important aspect of the whole discussion, and they are often intertwined with the issue of gender representation.[6] Gender is an issue in the discussion almost from the beginning, as some of the extracts already quoted indicate. Inevitably it underlies the talk about characters and relationships even if the issue is not always raised overtly. The discussion of the relationship between George and Christine is in some ways the moment when the gender issue (along with class) does become overt, but it is Norman's description of Jill as a matriarch which reminded me to ask one of the questions on my list – 'about the women in Ambridge'. The response to this question was the expression of a consensus that the Ambridge population is characterised by strong women and weak men and a sustained and co-operative exploration of the reasons why women and men are represented in this way in the programmes. A consensus was much more easily reached in relation to gender than in terms of the class issue, perhaps because it was a less contentious topic in a mainly female group where the only man present spoke relatively little and did not take a controversial line on gender.

Joan introduced what became the group's most sustained rationale, linking the two dominant themes of the discussion – gender and modality: 'Is it a modern trend though? Do you think it is something which is coming in our society that women are becoming the dominant sex?' (400–1). Joan's comment is immediately met with agreement from all members of the group, and the consensus seems to be based on a general belief in the progress made by women since the war. Joan and Pam then provide a narrative of their own lives which is clearly marked by feminism. Joan comments that her daughters-in-law are all stronger than her sons:

> And looking back at me and their father it was the other way round. He was the strong one. And, in fact, to be honest since he died I have changed a good deal and I know that I have become my own person, and looking back I was not.
>
> (412–14)

Pam concurs with a similar version of her own life, though the change in her case is brought about by paid employment, rather than widowhood: 'I was at home for fifteen years and until the children were older you know at secondary schools, and then I went out to work. You sort of become a different person' (422–4). These narratives, with their emphasis on 'becoming your own person' after a period of subservience to the needs of others, bear some resemblance to the narrative structure of much feminist confessional writing of the 1970s (see Felski, 1989). They could also be described as a version of liberal feminism in that they emphasise the individual's role in escaping from oppression; indeed they give the impression that personal will combined with a change in circumstances will suffice to combat social inequalities. On this basis *The Archers* can be read as confirming progressive social development in the area of gender. Thus Pam concludes: 'Probably, going back, *The Archers* are the same really. Because I think most of the women work' (435–6).

However, at this point a few cracks appear in the consensus. Viv (who describes herself as a housewife) opens a discussion of Ambridge women who like Jill Archer 'don't work', and thus questions the implied inactivity: 'Jill at one time was doing a lot, looking after the children and doing her B&Bs. I think she's wonder woman she is' (430–1). Although the discussion becomes excited at this point, with several people talking at the same time, suggesting that a contentious issue has been touched on, the critique of traditional gender roles is not developed. The costs of being the person 'who's there when anyone's in trouble' (Norman, 298) and the low status attached to such work are not questioned by this group. The discussion focuses on further examples of strong women and weak, wimpy men, until Viv introduces her critical point about Sid's homophobia. Here again the analysis is predominantly liberal – there is a reaction against a sympathetic character being portrayed as homophobic, and against his wife Kathy's politically correct but tactless response: 'I was cringing you know, I thought "she wouldn't do that" ' (Viv, 555–6). These characters, perhaps like *The Archers* generally, are seen as too nice to embody such attitudes. Although there is a general approval of the presence of 'modern issues' in the programmes – 'otherwise it gets too bland' (Joan, 577) – there is also an attachment to the basic goodness of the main characters, and to the benign nature of the community as a whole. Interestingly, the issue of 'race' and racism, although one of the most dramatic examples of the recent and contested inclusion of 'issues' in *The Archers*, was not referred to at all in this group.

The main discussion of the gender issue then turned to speculation about romantic developments in relation to various characters. What was most striking was the repeated recurrence of a motif originally introduced by Joan and Pam:

Joan: They're very short of

Pam: Bit short of people.

Lyn: Short of men.

   [*Laughter*]

                                                            (663–5)

Here I am participating in the traditionally feminine occupation – talking about relationships, and particularly, the lack of decent men – which then becomes a major theme of this discussion:

Joan: There are youngsters growing up of course, aren't there?

Pam: Yes, they're no good for the old ones – Caroline's on her own.

Joan: Yes, she's on her own.

Pam: And there's Shula.

Viv: Debbie.

Pam: No one for Debbie, you see.

Joan: But they'll be coming up – she's young, you see, a lot could happen there.

Pam: They did have that tractor driver, didn't they, but he's gone out of it now.

Elspeth: Yes he has.

Norman: The thing is

Pam: I mean, there's no one to, for romance, is there?

(673–83)

As this extract demonstrates, the theme of romance, or, more accurately, its absence brings all of the women into the discussion, and generates a general agreement among them. Norman attempts to interject, but fails, in the face of this overwhelming interest. Pam reiterates her point four times in the next fifteen lines, concluding that the romance narrative is the key to involvement in the programmes:

Pam: There's no romance going and it is romance that gets us all, you know.

Viv: That's right, yeah.

(678–9)

It is Norman who ends this phase of the discussion of romance: 'Can we turn back to the original question about the difference between John Archer and Simon Pemberton?' (689–90). This seems to confirm that his earlier attempt to intervene was expressive of slight unease; he perhaps feels that the topic of romance is somehow not appropriate for this kind of serious discussion, and is anxious to return to the 'real' agenda. However, despite this intervention, and a follow-up question from me on the representation of business, after a few lines, the theme of lack of romantic interest is returned to. The two levels of engagement which the discussion of gender has revealed seem typical of the kind of contradictions which are fundamental to talk about media texts. On the one hand, Ambridge is full of strong women 'becoming their own person', while on the other, what really keeps us listening is their potential for romantic involvements with men. Joan and Pam express the view that independence of men has been a positive force in their lives, and yet the single women in Ambridge are clearly a problem. Lack of, and the drive towards romantic fulfilment, as was the case for *Morse*, are clearly significant sources of pleasure in this group's engagement with *The Archers*. This does not, however, mean that their narratives of their own lives are similarly structured.

Fandom, Critical Reading and 'Quality'

The discourse of fandom was inevitably foregrounded in a weekend organised by the fan club and entitled '*Archers* Addicts' Weekend'. It was very clear that participation in the weekend implied membership of a particular culture, and that the weekend offered numerous opportunities for the display of appropriate forms of subcultural capital, such as knowledge about the programmes' history. In focus group 1 this kind of display is particularly marked and there is a relatively high number of references to the production of the programmes (7 as opposed to 1 in group 2). This may in part be the result of the timing of the group: it immediately followed the studio session where we had been addressed by members of the production team. However, it also seemed to result from Viv's position as a kind of 'honorary' *Archers* fan, who was particularly active in the fan club, and knew the weekend organiser, Hedli Niklaus, quite well. A further factor was Elspeth's analytical approach, combined with her involvement in the fan culture (which emerged more in the telephone interview in April 1999); she made several remarks which indicated reflection on the production process and on the audience: 'Maybe they're not skilled enough at tuning in the audience to get the idea and they do it too obviously. Perhaps they underestimate our intelligence sometimes' (110–11).

The display of knowledge of *The Archers*' past was also a significant feature of this group. The effect of all of this accumulated 'capital' in the discussion was at times, as Elspeth's contribution indicates, to introduce a critical mode of talk. However, at other times, it operated as a way of reinforcing a sense of closeness between the group members and the programmes. For instance, members of the production team and the actors are discussed in much the same way as the characters themselves, so that feelings of ownership of the programmes are reinforced (see Hobson, 1982, Chapter 7). In this way, as Buckingham has already noted, the ideal community is extended beyond the text, to include the production team and actors (1987: 184). This was particularly the case in relation to the Editor, Vanessa Whitburn, who was repeatedly referred to as 'Vanessa':

> *Pam*: As you say, there isn't any – but then I wouldn't think Vanessa was – is a romantic sort of
>
> *Viv*: She doesn't come across
>
> *All* : No.
>
> *Pam*: Her heart – she comes across to me as quite a hard sort of
>
> *Viv*: But we have had some nice storylines though while she's been Editor.
>
> (746–51)

Ambivalence about Vanessa's 'hardness' and her role in suppressing the romance narratives is contained by Viv's reassertion of loyalty. This was very much the dominant mode of this discussion. As well as displaying considerable knowledge of the programmes, its participants were conversant with 'secondary texts' such as the media debate about Vanessa Whitburn's introduction of contemporary issues. Although there is quite a lot of criticism of the programmes (about 119 lines, as opposed to 82 lines of overt praise) – about the absence of romance, the unrealistic nature of some storylines or the behaviour of some characters – fundamental loyalty is always reasserted, particularly in the face of criticism from the press. On the topic of gender, interestingly it is Norman who defends the programmes, though he clearly has some doubts about 'Vanessa':

> *Norman*: Er, well, actually, I was just thinking of something that was in the
> paper – it's a few weeks ago or was it months, time goes by about *The Archers*
> being taken over by the women. The article there – and I don't agree. I
> don't agree at all. I mean, there are – I haven't done a headcount recently
> mentally but I've got the photograph so I can have a headcount and see if
> there's more women than men, but it seems, you know, a fairly balanced
> programme – I mean there's the – Vanessa Whitburn's a raging feminist
> you know – as you say, I agree with you about the strong men though.
>
> (370–6)

Comments such as this, which discuss the programme as text, and demonstrate awareness of the agents of its production were often combined with talk about the characters or narrative from 'inside' the diegesis. The line count reveals that the more critical, 'outside' the diegesis, mode is dominant here (approximately 480 lines in this category, and 170 'inside' the diegesis). Furthermore, as I have already indicated, when defining 'critical' more conventionally as criticism or negative comment, the count revealed more criticism than direct praise of the programmes. In some ways this is surprising, given the strong fan culture and commitment to the programmes of the members of this group. However, the tensions between the critical and enthusiastic modes, and the dominance of the former (in both senses), can be seen as reflections of the context itself. On the one hand, the BBC-organised weekend, and the presence of actors, a producer and a scriptwriter, were likely to encourage positive identification. On the other, the discussion took place in a fairly formal setting, and my introduction of myself as an academic researcher was likely to encourage critique. I possibly reinforced this by asking questions which encouraged this mode of engagement with the text.[7] However, these tensions are also indicative of the difficulties of negotiating the negative discourse surrounding fandom; the dominance of the critical mode is expressive of the need to present oneself as a critical reader in the research context.

Nonetheless, it was possible in this group to express a high level of involvement. Joan described herself as 'hooked', Pam commented: 'I can't sort of give it up and not knowing what's going to happen to them' and Viv was worried that she might be too emotionally involved:

> *Viv*: I don't think it's always relaxation though, I think, I don't (.) because I get emotionally involved but (.) I can get quite worked up if I think, you know, or very sad]
>
> *Joan*: Oh, so do I, the tears will flow]
>
> *Viv*: I wish I wasn't (.) I didn't believe in it so much. It wouldn't make me feel like that.
>
> (46–9)

At the start of the discussion several of the participants attributed their involvement with the programmes to the fact that they had been listening for several decades: 'I think the reason I like it is the way you can follow the characters through, from when Lizzie was born, hole in her heart, right the way through from, you know, now she's married to Nigel' (Norman, 39–41). This sense of continuity, which is clearly offered by all soap opera, but particularly by a programme which is as long running as *The Archers*, was also commented on by Viv, who linked it with the 'everydayness' of the series: 'It started like reading a book really, but it never ends – it's every day, you know it's going to carry on and it's very personal on the radio' (4–5).

The importance of the medium, because of the possibilities for visualisation and imagination which it offers, was also commented on by other members of the group, often in connection with the short duration of the programme: 'I think I like it because it's only fifteen minutes out of my life, not too long and I like the feeling that, yes, to me it's visual, I can imagine the characters as I want them to be, not as they are at all' (Joan, 14–16). These expressions of involvement in some ways resemble talk about soap opera generally, but there is also a sense in which special qualities are being claimed for *The Archers* in this talk. Listening to a soap opera on the radio is perhaps now an almost eccentric activity, given the dominance of television, and this in itself may lend it a certain *cachet*. Here it seems that the low status of soap opera is being combated by differentiating between radio (particularly Radio 4) and television soap: radio is depicted as requiring creative work, rather than passive reception, and the fact that the programme lasts only fifteen minutes perhaps also 'protects' its listeners against sustained inactivity: the idea of 'fifteen minutes of relaxation totally to myself' (Elspeth, 31–2) in an otherwise very busy life is a way of containing and combating the negative associations of fandom with complete immersion and passive addiction.[8] Elspeth's remark, quoted above, on the intelligence of the audience is a further instance of this kind of defence. In all of this, and in the references to the high standards of acting, or realism and 'relevance', claims for the 'quality' of *The Archers* are being made. Whereas in the case of *Morse* these claims rested in part on the visual qualities of the programmes which were similar to those of the heritage film, here it is precisely the lack of visuals which connotes 'quality'. In requiring attentive and imaginative listeners this lack guarantees that this is no ordinary soap and that to be an *Archers* fan is not equivalent to declaring a passionate interest in *Coronation Street* or *EastEnders*.

Unease about the level of involvement, or at least about some of the terminology of fandom, was also expressed on at least one occasion by denial: 'I wouldn't call myself an addict. I listen, I like *The Archers*, I wouldn't say I was an addict' (Joan, 789–90). More frequently, accounts of the reactions of others indicated a self-aware version of fandom; the ability to see the absurdity of such a degree of involvement in a fictional text could perhaps also become a guarantor against this extreme, while simultaneously allowing its expression:

> *Elspeth*: Here we are talking about these characters, it's surely getting across to you how much they mean to us. That we think about them.
>
> *Viv*: Well, they're like another family really, aren't they? To me they are. They're another family.
>
> *Joan*: I know. Sometimes if I've got a group of friends and we all happen to be together and one or two of us who are, you know, we listen to *The Archers* all the time, suddenly we will be talking about somebody, about something that has happened in *The Archers* and the others are looking at us cos they don't sort of listen to it – well, who's that? You see. Because they thought we were talking about someone we know and then we say to the other 'Oh, them you know'. But good gracious! They get up and say 'Well, what are you worried about, I mean, it's only a programme, you know'.
>
> [*Laughs*]
>
> (211–22)

Here, Joan carefully avoids the word 'fan' in her account of herself and her friends ('one or two of us who are, you know, we listen'), and Elspeth introduces the exchange in analytical mode. Elspeth's role as mediator between the group and the researcher is consistent with the position she has adopted throughout. The telephone interview conducted in April 1999 confirmed that she would be likely to identify with an academic approach, and that this might in part be her strategy for dealing with the negative connotations of fandom:

> When it's actually going on, I can feel part of it and tears will come into my eyes (.) and then I start to then put on my (.) academic side and think, now then, how did they achieve that, and was it effective, and why did they do it. But when I'm actually listening to it I'm part of it.
>
> (372–6)

This comment encapsulates both Elspeth's individual mode of engagement with the text, and the tensions in focus group 1 between involvement and distance generally. Her comments are frequently operating on two levels: enthusiasm and involvement (for example, throughout the telephone interview she spoke of the characters as 'real people', using their fictional names rather than the actors' names) and academic commentary. This is more noticeable in the telephone interview, since in the discussion group, probably for reasons associated with the context, the reflective mode was dominant.

While Elspeth was perhaps the most striking example of this split in group 1, as I have already noted, the discussion as a whole combined the expression of enthusiasm and involvement with self-aware deconstructions of their own fan behaviour; in a letter which she wrote to me after the telephone interview, Viv confirmed her awareness of the negative stereotypes associated with fans of media texts: 'It was good to be able to talk at length on one of my favourite subjects, though I'm not completely sad – I do have other interests!' Viv's use of the word 'sad' implies a sophisticated, self-reflexive and 'cool' version of *Archers* fandom.[9] A development of this mode of *Archers* fandom occurred when Viv told the story of how a letter she had written was read out during an interview with Hedli Niklaus on local radio. Initially she was reluctant to tell the story – 'well, I don't want to go on too much' (242–3) – but when encouraged by me to continue, she gave quite a lengthy and excited account:

> I was there just polishing the furniture, and the presenter, Gordon Atterley, said 'Now I've got a letter that's come into my possession' and he started reading this letter. And it was my letter. [*Laughter*] I couldn't, that's my letter that I wrote and she'd kept it you see, and she'd given it to him, and read it out. So I had to ring up then – you've just given me the shock of my life.
>
> (259–63)

The jumps from telling the group the story to re-enactment of the radio presenter's words or of her telephone call, the repetition, and the short, rushed explanations are all indicative of Viv's excitement (which is confirmed by the rising intonation heard on the tape). In this very exciting narrative she is able to take one step further in the appropriation of the media text which I noted in the discussion of 'Vanessa'. She is no longer a housewife in Wolverhampton, but has crossed the boundary between audience and performer. The performance of fandom may in part be yet another defence, along with denial, critical reading and self-awareness, against the negative connotations of fandom. It is also without doubt a significant source of pleasure. When I rang Viv in March 1999 she began the conversation by telling me that 'so much had happened' since the Wood Norton weekend. She then described writing articles on *The Archers* and on 'My Life as an *Archers* Addict' for a magazine. In a subsequent letter she told me that she and a 'handful of Addicts' and four cast members had taken part in a BBC documentary the previous week. Some of this activity bears some resemblance to the active and creative fandom described by Henry Jenkins (1992) in his discussion of science fiction fans. Barker (1993) has pointed out the dangers of Jenkins's tendency to feminise and idealise fan cultures, on the grounds of their subversive potential. I would not make such claims in this instance, but the performance of fandom has certainly empowered Viv, and added to her pleasure in the programmes: 'The events I have experienced, the friends I have made, learning to use a wordprocessor for the penfriend scheme and the articles, have all enriched my life' ('My Life as an *Archers* Addict', January 1999).

Focus Group 2

Group Dynamics In and Out of the Diegesis

The first point to make about this group is that it is more positive than critical of *The Archers* – there are approximately 123 lines devoted to overt praise and only 41 to criticism (out of a total of 786 lines), and that this is a more marked feature than it was in group 1, where the balance was 119 praise to 82 criticism. The generally positive and enthusiastic tenor of the group seems related to the dynamics generally, which were relaxed and co-operative. As in *Morse* group 1, this is a small group (of three – a couple and a single person) who are not competing for space in the same way as the larger, less-well-acquainted groups (*Morse* group 2 and Wood Norton group 1).[10] Although the three participants in this group are not long-standing friends like the members of *Morse* group 1, they had become friendly during the course of the weekend, having played together as a team in the quiz on the first night (and won!).

In group 2, consensus was the order of the day, as the group members co-operated in the construction of a positive view of *The Archers*. This may in part be attributable to the stage of relationship which they had reached: Alice, Tim and Janet were in the early stages of an acquaintance which they were to maintain for some time after the weekend. Perhaps some of the early work in this process, in terms of expressing an identity, had already been done, whereas in group 1 five people who have scarcely met each other before (and were not destined to become friends) are confronted with a situation in which they need to assert their own identity. There are some instances where this developing intimacy is expressed through humour which seems connected to the various imbalances in the group: couple/single woman; two women (or three including myself)/one man (see discussion of gender, below). Making jokes and laughing at each other's jokes were quite a significant feature of the dynamics between Alice and Janet and Tim, with humour functioning to include Alice in the intimacy of the couple. There were times when Alice was required to observe and be amused by the banter between the couple, but there was also a high level of reciprocation, and reinforcement of Alice's contributions:

Alice: Well, when I first came in my favourite character was Lilian … I've gone off her since she became a gin-soaked harpy on Guernsey.

[*Laughter*]

Tim: I like that, a gin-soaked harpy

[*Laughter*]

(363–8)

123

Alice spoke noticeably more than anyone else (337 lines, as opposed to Tim's 183 and Janet's 178), and she introduced more than twice as many new topics (28) as either Tim or myself (12). This can perhaps in part be attributed to the couple/single person dynamic referred to above (as a couple, Tim and Janet perhaps have to work less hard to express an identity), but it may also result from the fact that Alice is a teacher, and therefore used to the social context of a discussion group. For Tim and Janet, who had left school at 14 and 16 respectively, this may have been a slightly less familiar activity than it was for Alice, although clearly they were quite at ease (perhaps also as a result of their professional backgrounds). My role seems to have been relatively limited; again this discussion was extremely lively, and my interventions were brief and interrogatory, rather than explanatory as they had been in the *Morse* groups. I spoke considerably less than any of the participants in group 2 (whereas in group 1 I spoke roughly as much as two of the five participants). This was probably because of the growing friendship in this group and its small size. I also seem to have picked up on the generally good-humoured tone of the interaction, and I made a few jokes, which seem aimed to demonstrate my knowledge of and participation in the programmes. Thus, as in the *Morse* groups, and indeed most of this research, my role was split between that of 'objective' researcher with a list of questions, and fan, participating in the display of specialised knowledge.

The good-humoured and relaxed tone of this discussion does not, however, mean that this group were less analytical than group 1; if anything, the reverse is probably the case. Both groups had a similar level of talk 'inside the diegesis' – about 168 lines in this group and 178 in group 1, and commentary 'outside the diegesis' (410 and 480 lines respectively), and a similar tendency to slip from the critical commentary mode, often expressing awareness of the text as a construction and of the agents of its production, to talk about the characters, or stories, as if they were real:

> *Janet*: ... So that makes it real in a sense that you begin to feel worried about the things that you aren't told about and aren't, aren't happening. But you get involved to that extent, but like recently with Nigel and Elizabeth running [*inaudible*] in all these conferences and things (.) they must have help to run conferences like that. There's never mention of staff=
>
> (26–30)

Here Janet has moved from critical observation of the programmes and of her own involvement to anxiety about how two of the characters 'manage' their business. The comment is particularly interesting in that it focuses on a practical issue rather than on lack of psychological realism which is a more common version of this kind of move 'into' the diegesis in both of these groups. On one level it demonstrates the flexibility of the modality discourse, which can be used both in speaking 'outside the diegesis' – 'this character or situation would not be like this in real life' – or 'inside', as here, and which almost forms a bridge between the two

speaking positions. Janet's initial remark could have led to a discussion of the limitations of the codes of realism in the programmes, but instead it becomes a
stepping-stone to the expression of the anxiety which they generate.

The comment also seems to demonstrate the fundamental frustration inherent
in this kind of involvement in a media text; entering the diegesis in this way carries
with it both the pleasure of the fantasy and a strong sense of loss or lack, inevitably
generated by the limitations of the narrative, the fact that the programme must
end somewhere (in the case of a fifteen-minute episode this seems particularly
acute). The tension between the desire for closure and pleasure in process is a
structural feature of fictional narratives (see Neale, 1980). In the case of soap
opera, where closure is clearly less of an issue, realism and attention to detail seem
to create their own anxieties. As the programme-makers carefully research each
detail of the narrative, and fans follow every episode over years, there seems to be
a desire for the diegesis to expand exponentially, for more characters, more detail,
as here, or more romance as in focus group 1. The desire for more narrative and
more information seems to involve an inevitable disappointment since expansion
must of necessity be finite and limited. In some senses the activities of the fan club
are designed to meet these desires for more, and in both groups the negotiation of
the fan club's inevitably only partial fulfilment of this desire was an issue. In the
case of focus group 1, Norman introduced the notion of a self-protective resistance to the fan club's activities: 'I've got friends of mine who listen to *The Archers*
and are *Archers* fans, but they don't want to know what the characters look like, ...
they would never come to a thing like this' (769–70). In focus group 2, I introduced
the idea, which was then taken up by all three participants, first of all affirming
that while others of their acquaintance would not attend an event like this for fear
of disappointment, it had not curtailed their own pleasure, and then allowing a
slight note of disappointment to creep in: 'The one who disappointed me most
was Tony, because he's much older than his character and he's almost completely
bald' (Alice, 694–5). Clearly the provision of a visual dimension constitutes a very
specific 'threat' in relation to a radio series. This 'stretching' of the diegesis into
another mode of perception renders particularly acute the dilemma involved in
meeting the actors, a process which constitutes both a satisfying extension of the
fantasy and its complete annihilation. Resistance to the latter can be seen in the
tendency to use the fictional character names, and to slip from the fictional narrative to the reality of the weekend, and vice versa:

Alice: That's why she was sympathetic of course to Kathy, wasn't she, when
Kathy got thrown out of The Bull?

Tim: I thought Kathy was very hard-working this weekend.

Alice: Oh yes, wasn't she just!

Janet: Lovely lady.

(352–6)

Here, 'Kathy' remains a character, rather than becoming Hedli Niklaus, the actress. This kind of collusion in resistance to the sense of lack described above may be a typical feature of *Archers* fan cultures or of fan activities generally. It was certainly a strong feature of these groups, who were totally united in their praise of the weekend, even if criticism of the programmes themselves was permitted in both groups.

Tradition, Modernity and Gender

Early on in this discussion Tim expressed the view that one of the pleasures of *The Archers* was 'a degree of escapism about it coming from an urban environment as we do' (43–4). Although she did not comment' on this in the discussion (unlike Janet, who agreed), Alice probably shared this view, since in the telephone interview in 1999 she described herself as a 'townie' learning things about the rhythms of country life from *The Archers*. I returned to this theme towards the end of the group discussion:

> *Lyn*: You said that living in an urban area, it was a kind of escape into a country life. To what extent is this idea about being a country village important to you?
>
> *Janet*: Community spirit, I'd say, I like the community spirit that comes over.
>
> *Tim*: Yes. It's all part of our country, I think. One as much as the other, and it's a part now which I think is disappearing, this farming thing, because apparently a lot of big firms are buying up farms rather than small farms.
>
> (702–7)

Janet's comment seems to support the notion of an ideal community as one of the pleasures of the programme. My question prompted a lengthy discussion of the loss of the countryside and of a traditional way of life which was linked to the rejection of the enterprise culture also found in the programmes: 'There's so much of it disappearing at an ever increasing rate. Everything now devolves on money. If it isn't making money it's not worth anything in the minds of many people' (Tim, 741). The topoi surrounding the 'tradition' discourse identified in Chapter 2 – nostalgia for essentially rural traditions and communities, rejection of enterprise, and an enthusiastic espousal of Englishness – were all present in this part of the discussion which culminated in celebration of the delights of home: 'I mean, I very rarely go abroad (.). I love England so much there's so many different areas and they're so beautiful' (Alice, 750–1). Much of this was reiterated in the telephone interviews two years later, suggesting that *The Archers* has struck a deep chord with these listeners. The celebration of Englishness which emerged here is reminiscent of the expression of similar themes in *Morse* group 1, and, as there, is linked to the 'quality' discourse.

However, despite the pleasures of tradition which were described here, and despite the fact that Alice had been listening for thirty years, and Janet and Tim for forty-five, as in group 1, the modernity of the contemporary programmes was still more consistently praised. Interestingly, and again following similar lines to the group 1 discussion, it was immediately linked to the representation of women (I had introduced this topic by asking about the 'Ambridge women'). Positive comments on the contemporaneity of these representations were substantiated by the ubiquitous discourse of modality: 'But that is quite realistic, isn't it, where a husband and wife are both working and yet they've got a child and they've got lots of things to think about and that's very much a sort of modern problem' (Alice, 148–50). Alice's comment generated a fairly sustained discussion of changing representations of women in *The Archers*, during the course of which both Janet and Tim agreed with her view. Janet described Jill Archer as 'a wife of that genera-tion', but emphasised how the programme had moved on:

> Yes. I think her way of life shouldn't be demeaned at all because she is to be admired really in lots of ways and she does that, but I think Pat and Ruth are more the modern attitudes, the attitudes of the last twenty years (.) so I think *The Archers* reflects that very well actually.
>
> (163–6)

Tim participates fully in this discussion, agreeing with the two women:

> I can remember my mother, my father couldn't get a shirt out of the cupboard you know she used to get them out and put them on the bed. Well, that doesn't happen nowadays. But you know it is a commentary of the time, I think, *The Archers*.
>
> (185–8)

There seems to be a general approval of these changes, though Alice is the only one who expresses it overtly: 'I'm very happy with them being their strong charac-ters so (.) you know I think it's very important that women don't just sit at home and (.) these days very few women can afford to' (179–81). As in group 1, the version of feminism expressed by this group could be characterised as liberal: the group members observe and approve of the progress made by women in the past forty years, and this progress seems to provide sufficient evidence of a basically benign social status quo: there is no critique of contemporary gender inequalities, either in society, or as represented in *The Archers*.

Interestingly, social class is discussed immediately after this exchange relating to gender, and in similar terms. Alice describes the Vintage *Archers* tapes: 'It's quite fascinating to listen to the way in which people talk and the attitudes they adopt and you think they could never get away with that now' (196–7). While Alice's comment is more general, Tim focuses on the issue of class, describing Grace Fairbrother, Phil Archer's first wife, as 'a complete non-starter' in the modern context:

Well, her manner of speaking, her accents, attitudes, she was a squire's daughter and it shone out of every word she ever uttered. It did to me anyway and for her to marry a farmer, a farmer's son as Phil was, then didn't ring true.

(203–5)

This appeal, as ever, to modality expresses an understanding of the more rigid social hierarchies which pertained in the 1950s, and an implied critique. The description of Grace as a 'non-starter' now also implies a sense of progress, similar to that expressed in relation to gender.

The telephone interviews permit some further nuancing of this consensus, as Alice referred to the topic of gender representation about seven times, whereas Tim and Janet referred to it only once. She also made comments which imply a more critical perspective on gender relations: 'I think that's realistic, in fact. I think there's an awful lot of men who pay lip service to women's rights, but like to have it all ways themselves' (telephone interview with Alice, 299–300). The fact that Alice did not develop this more critical line of thought in the focus group may be attributable to the context of the discussion, and the push towards liberal consensus which dominated it, with minor dissent in the area of gender fairly systematically diffused by humour. It may also reflect the couple/single woman imbalance in the group. As a single woman, Alice seems to have developed a more critical view of gender relations; however, for a couple in their seventies the more conventional view, expressed here in jokes, that women are powerful despite appearances to the contrary, and that real progress has been made, holds sway, and it is this more sanguine vision which dominated the discussion.

Discerning Fans, 'Quality' and Education

The topic map reveals that the 'quality' discourse was quite dominant in this group; only modality, narrative and character are referred to more frequently and there are more references to 'quality' than in group 1 (seven as opposed to two) . This seems consistent with the greater predominance of praise of the programmes here. Most of these references are concentrated in the early part of the discussion, which then pays more attention to character, narrative and, predictably, modality. The 'quality' discourse is first introduced by Tim:

But we do enjoy *The Archers* and it has that something which may be hard to define (.) but it's got something that grips one and you can't always put your finger on it altogether. You can put forward ideas but there's still a bit of mystique about it somehow.

(60–3)

This notion of the special qualities of *The Archers* is one which Tim returned to both later, in this discussion and in the telephone interview. This could be said to represent the apogee of the 'quality' discourse: the fact that the programme's success is a mystery which cannot be explained merely adds to its status. In some ways this is also reminiscent of Bourdieu's notion of the legitimate autodidact, whose wider cultural knowledge is acquired through experience rather than study and often relies on mystique rather than analysis: 'Knowledge by experience ... feels and deplores the essential inadequacy of words and concepts to express the reality "tasted" in mystical union' (Bourdieu, 1984: 68). However, the attempt to introduce the notion of mystique into discussion of soap opera would, in Bourdieu's terms, be doomed to failure, because of the low status of the genre. The display of detailed knowledge of such a text would probably condemn both of these groups to the category 'illegitimate autodidacticism' (ibid.: 24; see also discussion of Jim's role in *Morse* group 2). Thus Alice, who as a teacher could be precisely one of those pedagogues abhorred by Bourdieu's aesthetes, immediately provided detailed reasons for the programmes' success, which she attributed to the writing, acting, directing and strong storylines. However, Tim's notion of 'mystique' is of interest since, as Bourdieu has noted, it is a discourse more readily associated with the appreciation of high culture. The possible claim for the superior cultural status of the *Archers* fan which it may imply is consistent with the analysis which follows.

This association of agency with 'quality' reoccurs on a further two occasions on the topic map: first, Tim praises the writing, using the programme's longevity as proof of its unusually high quality: 'It's in its 46th year now so they must have done something extraordinary to keep it going for all that time' (168–9). Alice develops the theme of 'modern issues' discussed above, associating it both with the quality of the programmes and realism. She begins by making a general comment:

> I think (.) I think since Vanessa Whitburn came as the editor, I think a lot of the stories developed in much greater depth than they used to be. Sometimes in the past when things have happened and then it all suddenly came to an end and you were left a little bit in the air thinking I wonder what they did actually do about that. Nowadays the major issues, she really, I mean, they are really very thoroughly researched.
>
> (216–20)

She then goes on to cite the treatment of racist attacks as an example, and concludes: 'It's that kind of thing that I feel really makes it real these days. (.) I do think she explores her stories very well' (233–4). The first thing to be noted here is the loyalty to 'Vanessa', and to the controversial storylines she has introduced, which was shared by both groups, even if in the case of discussion group 1, a more critical attitude was expressed by one participant, Elspeth, in the telephone interview. Second, it is evident from this, and from the general dominance of the modality discourse in the discussions, that realism is one of the main criteria for 'quality' in relation to *The Archers*. For the soap opera genre, based as it is on the notion of 'everyday life', the codes of realism are clearly crucial, whereas in the discussion of *Morse*, while realism was certainly an issue, other, more aesthetic concerns made up a large part of the 'quality' discourse (see Chapter 4). Finally, we can see fragments of academic discourse in Alice's comments: 'developed in much greater depth', 'thoroughly researched', 'she explores her stories very well'. This is not surprising, given her profession, but it may also indicate a particular, more academic version of the display of knowledge about the programmes identified as a feature of the fan culture in the discussion of focus group 1. Like Tim, Alice may be attempting to shift her appreciation of *The Archers* into the realms of legitimate auto-didacticism. The autodidact became a theme of the discussion at one point:

> *Alice*: I always find know-alls terribly boring in a way in that they won't listen to other people's point of view, do you know what I mean? And then Lynda's the sort who reads an article or something and goes on a one-day course and then she's an expert.
>
> *Janet*: That's right.
>
> *Tim*: But you do find there are people like this.
>
> (486–90)

These comments seem to support the notion that the participants in group 2 were attempting to differentiate themselves from an unprestigious form of knowledge – that of the 'know-all'. At the same time they were concerned to define how the programmes might play an educational role, and transmit more useful, or valid, information; in the discussion of modernity and gender Janet commented: 'and you see this business of contemporary issues and in a way they might help people listening to solve their problems' (172–3). Shortly after this, unlike Janet who here sees other people as the target of the programmes' possible educational function, Alice describes them as beneficial to her: 'I mean, I think you can learn a tremendous amount from the programme really, the way in which things happen' (242–3). The idea that *The Archers* might have educational value clearly gives the soap opera an added status, thus reinforcing the 'quality' discourse. It may in part at least emanate from the original role of *The Archers* which was to educate post-war farmers, and the continuing socially responsible airing of issues which characterises the programmes (see Chapter 1). The notion also seems consistent with the group's positive view of the ideological role played by the programmes: they reflect positive social change, and may even contribute to it by helping people acquire greater understanding of some issues, or solve contemporary problems such as drug addiction.

Like the participants in group 1, these listeners saw the medium of radio as one of the distinguishing features of *The Archers*; Tim pursued his idea about the programme's special qualities, demonstrated by its success, in this context: 'But I think for a programme of this kind to maintain four million people (.) it's really something. I mean TV has overtaken so many radio programmes but it hasn't overtaken *The Archers*' (213–15). The comparison with television was more developed in the telephone interviews with the participants in this group than in the focus group itself. Tim and Janet commented that watching television soap would not fit into their lifestyle, and Tim described himself as hating programmes such as

Coronation Street. Alice also commented that she did not watch television soaps. In this preference for radio, and association of the medium with the claim for 'quality', the two Wood Norton groups were broadly similar. If the superiority of radio over television can be claimed, the status of the fans of the radio soap is increased, here, as in group 1. Janet describes herself as 'believing in' *The Archers*: 'but not to the extent that I believe they are a real family, if you know what I mean, like some people do' (40–1). This statement seems to demonstrate aware-ness of the negative discourses surrounding fandom which I discussed in the introduction to this chapter, and by conjuring the image of the fans who believe in the programme blindly, to claim a more discerning version of fandom. Commenting on her involvement in the fan club, Alice developed the idea much later in the discussion: 'I think that I've been to almost everything, and it's always enjoyable. You know, the people who listen to *The Archers* always seem to be pleasant and there's always people to talk to, and all the actors and so on that have ever been involved have been absolutely delightful' (645–8). This comment encap-sulates the version of fandom constructed in this group, and it is significant that in a move similar to that already described in relation to 'Vanessa', the actors are somehow appropriated into the fan culture.

In this group there was no problem about expressing praise and enthusiasm for the programmes, or in emphasising their involvement, though terms such as 'addicted' and 'hooked' which had been used in group 1 were avoided here. The emphasis was on the construction of a rationale for the enthusiasm, and this move was spearheaded by Alice, and based on the description of *The Archers* as high quality, socially relevant and realistic drama, with an educational function. The discussion of the shared excesses of fandom, or indeed the performance of self-aware fandom found in group 1, were not present here. The higher proportion of overt praise in fact masks a more distanced and calmer discussion: belief in the benign nature of the programmes and the English village world they represent, and the identity of a genteel and discerning *Archers* fan, were the basis for this harmonious accord.

Conclusion

In this chapter I have been at pains to emphasise the uniqueness of each of these discussions; nonetheless some common features emerge, and in conclusion I will draw attention to them. The first of these was the belief in the realism of *The Archers*; this appears to be almost a condition of the serious interest these listeners express in the programmes, and although criticisms were made, the fundamental conviction that the series is realistic was not questioned to anything like the extent, or level of critique, which occurred in *Morse* group 2, for instance. The realism of the programmes was associated with a general emphasis on their 'quality', particu-larly in group 2, and in this sense these discussions were reminiscent of *Morse* group 1. This was accompanied by a sense of the benign nature of the world depicted; while it was seen as important to include social problems, their contain-ment within a basically utopian vision of village life was crucial. The educational function of these inclusions was emphasised by both groups, suggesting a positive vision of society as capable of change and progress (and an equally positive, almost Reithian view of the relationship between society and media texts). In this way the discourses of tradition and modernity which are omnipresent in the text itself emerged significantly in these instances of talk about *The Archers*. The programme seemed to encapsulate a harmonious balance between the two elements: on the one hand, the inclusion of contemporary social issues was seen to make the programmes realistic and relevant, and on the other, the presence of more traditional heritage features such as the village setting and activities was associated with the preservation of an endangered culture, particularly in group 2.

It was in this context that the only socio-political critique emerged: in group 2 Tim commented negatively on the materialism of contemporary society – 'everything now devolves on money'. Whereas in group 1 the text was seen to reflect social progress, in group 2 this idea was accompanied by a more socially critical view of the programmes as a counterpoint to negative developments in contemporary society, such as the threat to the environment and over-emphasis on profitability. In this sense group 2 could be said to have produced a more politically critical reading than group 1, although in Morley's terms, the alignment between the textual representation of enterprise and tradition and the views expressed does not indicate an oppositional reading. The nostalgic Englishness expressed in group 2 could also be seen as a conservative element. In group 1 the discussion of gender encompassed not only an emphasis on romance, but also a critique of homophobia, and the erroneous – at least in relation to the contemporary programme – but interesting inclusion of lesbianism as a positive example of the social breadth of the programmes: 'some of the things they bring out are quite good – little things like abortion and or there's been lesbian, hasn't there – and then there's been a bit of homosexual – it's all things that – OK, they happen, they're part of life' (Joan, 67–8).[11] It is interesting that Joan, who expressed more conservative views on the topic of social class, took such a liberal stance in relation to sexuality. Her response is consistent with (though not substantiation of) the view that awareness of gender, sexuality and arguably 'race' has to some extent replaced class consciousness and struggle in contemporary Britain. These differences of interpretation and politics between the groups are significant, and along with the specificities of social context and relations which I have described in this chapter, they indicate the difficulty of attaching a common label to these groups, particularly one as vague and broad as the word 'mainstream'. Nonetheless, attachment to the idea of social progress, and to the potential of *The Archers* to contribute positively to society by raising social issues, were recurring features of both discussions. Joan's phrase 'OK, they happen, they're part of life' epitomises the liberal ethos of both groups, which could be described as tolerance of social and sexual divergence, rather than its positive affirmation.

This liberal ambience was nowhere more evident than in relation to the question of gender. As the examples from group 1 cited above suggest, feminism was a tangible influence on the talk in both of these groups. Both groups described *The Archers* as a reflection of the changes in the position of women, and in gender relations in the post-war period, and welcomed these changes, both in the text, and in society and the participants' own lives. There was no suggestion that these changes might go further, or might still be perceived as highly inadequate in either group. Unlike *Morse* group 2, these groups did not develop a critique of the representation of gender in the text, even though, as I have demonstrated, critical and analytical elements were strongly present in both discussions. The fact that a feminist decon-struction of heterosexual relations as represented in *The Archers* did emerge in the telephone interview with Alice indicates that individual participants might have reacted differently to this issue in a different social context. Irony was not a strong feature of either discussion in this area; in group 1, for instance, romance was a dominant topic, and it was referred to only as a highly desirable narrative develop-ment, and never critically or ironically. All of this suggests that a liberal version of feminism formed part of the generally liberal politics I have described, and that this is very different to the feminist identity constructed in *Morse* group 2.

It is striking that the men in both of these groups did not play an oppositional role in relation to this liberal feminist identity, and in group 2, Tim positively espoused feminist views. Like the men in *Morse* group 1, neither of the male partic-ipants in these groups seemed unwilling to express emotion or more anxious to downplay their involvement in the programme than the female participants. In these respects, the strong gender differences discovered by Jo Tacchi (2000) in her research on radio consumption are not replicated here.[12] As aficionados of a soap opera who are keen enough to join a fan club weekend, these men are unlikely to be typical male radio listeners. Nonetheless, Norman's unease with the romance discourse seems illustrative of the kind of gender difference identified by Tacchi.

A further determining feature of these groups was the negotiation of the nega-tive connotations of the term 'fan' by groups of mainly middle-aged and middle-class *Archers* listeners. This apparent contradiction in terms was managed by emphasising the 'quality' of the programmes, by occasional denial, and more frequently, by self-aware and self-reflexive presentation, and even performance, of fandom. It is equally important to see these activities as positive pleasures. The process Sarah Thornton describes, where the mainstream is a negative pole against which more positive subcultural identities can be constructed, may well be in play here. Both discussions emphasised the special qualities of *The Archers* and of the fan culture surrounding them. Identity and difference, rather than being in the nondescript middle or mainstream of everything, may be even more important for those who do not have the cultural status of extreme youth. Allowing oneself the excesses of participation in a fan culture, even to the extent of becoming 'sad', may be a useful antidote to maturity:

> Actually I had never considered myself a fan club type of person, they were for worshippers of pop singers, film stars or football teams. Not for listeners to a radio drama and definitely not for a mature woman who had never been a groupie of any kind.
>
> (Viv, 'My Life as an *Archers* Addict', January 1999)

Chapter Six

Feminisms, Fans and Country Folk

This chapter is concerned with the second phase of my research on the *Archers* audience: the questionnaire survey, which aimed to gather responses from a broader group of listeners to the programme than the fan club weekend could provide, and the follow-up interviews, where the principal respondent (Mary) was chosen because of her feminist views. The first part of the chapter discusses the responses to *The Archers* presented in the 110 questionnaires returned. The rest of the chapter analyses the face-to-face interview with Mary and her partner Ben, and the telephone interviews with her friend Jan, and her student, friend and colleague, Louise.

The Questionnaire Survey

Although this sample was demographically broader than the Wood Norton group (see Appendix 1), it is almost 100 per cent white, predominantly female (78 per cent) and lower middle class (62 per cent of men and 49 per cent of women belonged to social class 11). The age range is much broader than at Wood Norton with 41 per cent of this sample under 45. Nonetheless, the dominant age group is 46–55 (38 per cent of men and 34 per cent of women), and about one quarter of the sample were over 55. The high proportion of respondents in the 46–55 age range may be particularly significant in relation to *The Archers* since the programme itself is 50 years old, and many of its listeners have been following it since child-hood. The responses to the questionnaire seemed to bear out this notion; 20 per cent of women and 25 per cent of men in the sample had been listening to *The Archers* since the 1950s, and 68 per cent and 50 per cent, respectively, had listened for more than twenty years.

The retention of an audience over such a long period of time makes *The Archers* a very unusual media text, and in response to question 3 – 'What do you like about *The Archers*? (what makes you listen?)' – many respondents referred to the sense of security and continuity which this long-term listening generated:

> I recall listening as a child, going to early mass, then having breakfast while the *Archers* Omnibus episode was on, on a Sunday. It is my bit of

continuity ... My earliest memories are Sunday mornings and Walter Gabriel's voice, whilst eating bacon!!

(m., 36–45, Anglo-Irish, senior healthcare worker)

The association of the programme with pleasurable rituals of everyday life was often cited in this way, and seems to be a particular strength of radio as a medium, since it can provide a background for other activities. Thus many associated the programme with domestic tasks such as preparing meals, washing-up or ironing, while others saw it more as a moment of indulgence and relaxation, and would listen while eating or 'when I get home from work. Put my feet up for 15 minutes to listen' (f., 26–35, white, British, administrator). The nostalgic dimension of the pleasures of *The Archers* thus seems to be the result of the interweaving of the experience of listening with other sensations and experiences, over a long period, perhaps a lifetime. This 'Proustian' connection of *The Archers* with emotionally charged early memories seems to be intensified by the nature of the medium. Like the participants in the Wood Norton Hall groups, these respondents referred to the particular pleasures of a sound-based medium, and the stimulation to the imagination which it provides: 'I close my eyes while listening and I am in a country pub, a farmhouse kitchen or feeding ducks on the village green' (f., 46–55, English, retired registrar).

The images of country life described by the listener quoted above form a significant part of the pleasures of listening. Almost all respondents found the rural setting an important aspect of the programme and 79 per cent of men and 84 per cent of women responded positively to a question on the portrayal of English traditions (question 9). Like the experience of listening over a long period of time, the content of the programmes, particularly the traditional English village aspect, reinforces feelings of security: 'The intro music, security in listening every Sunday a.m. to such a "solid" institution, very English' (f., 36–45, white European, manager of drug rehabilitation project). At the same time, only very small numbers of respondents commented negatively on the recent introduction of contemporary social issues into the programmes, while 41 per cent of women, and 21 per cent of men, commented positively on this aspect.[1] The relationship of tradition and modernity in the programmes was identified as significant by some respondents: 'The whole essence of Ambridge is its retention of traditional values and a sense that time has passed it by, so that it struggles to encompass the modern ways – but knows it must do if it is to survive' (m., 56+, 'wasp', market research consultant). This tension, present at many levels in the content of the programmes (see Chapter 2), the production policy and the audience response, was often expressed here more indirectly. The majority of respondents found the traditional elements crucial to their enjoyment, yet at the same time, the more dramatic, issue-based storylines seemed most popular. In response to a question about recent stories they had disliked or found boring (question 12), a number of respondents cited those based on village activities, suggesting that it is the *idea* of the village, rather than the minutiae, which is attractive, and that this is a more complex issue than the overwhelmingly positive response to question 9 would at first suggest. The relationship of tradition and modernity in contemporary British culture clearly emerges as a theme in these responses, which seem to be balancing the pleasures of nostalgia and an imaginary rural English past with a need for engagement with contemporary social issues and interpersonal relations.

If a significant feminist fan culture did not emerge from the questionnaire survey, for a very small number of respondents, gender and sexuality, and their representation in *The Archers*, did seem to be burning issues. These responses could crudely be divided into two groups: the first consisted of those who expressed an anxiety that the programmes might become dominated by 'political correctness'. Thus in response to the question on the role of women one respondent wrote: 'Pat and Ruth are a bit too militant re feminist issues. I prefer to see them succeeding by their own efforts, in a quieter way', and at the end of the questionnaire: 'don't let them become too politically correct' (f., 46–55, English, lawyer). The 'p.c. discourse' almost inevitably saw political correctness as a strong, if entirely nebulous and ill-defined, threat, whether to the positive representation of women, as above, or to the equally ill-defined 'tradition': '... like so many things "English" or "British", or "traditional" they are not P.C. *The Archers* could be the only radio programme concerned with "tradition" – and even it will lose that soon I suspect' (m., 56+, British/English, retired). The linking of a threatening modernity with changing representations of gender was more directly stated by a female respondent: 'Bring back the good old days when Ambridge was a real place not a women's commune' (f., 46–55, English white, property manager). However, these responses and the two negative comments from male respondents on the inclusion of gay characters in *The Archers* were very much the exception to the rule, and in general the kind of liberal consensus in relation to gender which emerged in the Wood Norton Hall groups was dominant. In this consensus the women were seen to be stronger than the male characters and this was found to be justified, often because this is 'just like life' (m., 46–55, white British, charity administrator).

Among the female respondents a small minority (about 8 per cent) gave answers which seemed to be informed by feminism. Perhaps the most overt was the following: 'I enjoyed the change of emphasis when there was a change of scriptwriters and the female characters were more feminist in their outlook' (f., 26–35, African-Caribbean, educational psychologist). Only two or three women respondents took issue with the representation of gender in the programmes. There was one request for 'more active roles for women' (f., 26–35, white British, student/social worker) and one critique of the conventional nature of women's lives and relationships in *The Archers*: 'Not many single women in *The Archers* – predominance of conventional heterosexual relationships which is a bit tiresome' (f., 26–35, white British, administrator). This respondent also took up the issue of the representation of gay characters: 'Encouraged by recent revelation that Sean is most likely homosexual (recent references to Gay Pride)', and three other women and two men also voiced these concerns: 'at last a gay character who is openly gay rather than hinted at (as in Shane makes delicious quiches)' (f., 36–45, British, civil servant). Interestingly it was a male respondent who specifically raised the question of a lesbian character: 'Good cross-section of characters: a lesbian is all there is to come?' (m., 46–55, white British, market research). Another male respondent criticised the programmes' failure to introduce 'more than a token "gay" character' and more unusually, the general representation of masculinity: 'On the whole, terribly stereotypical in being emotionally insensitive and unspiritual. They could do with a "men's group" to allow "sharing of vulnerabilities" – just as the women get a dose of assertiveness' (m., 46–55, white British, computer systems manager). It is clear from these responses, and those at the other extreme, analysed above, that *The Archers* attracts a broad spectrum of listeners, at least in the area of gender politics. The kind of feminism which approves and even takes for granted the positive representation of women, rather than making the kind of critique found in this small group of responses, was more generally characteristic of the respondents to the questionnaire survey.

The questionnaire method of enquiry itself was clearly less conducive to the emergence and sustained maintenance of a playful and ironic stance than a focus group such as *Morse* group 2, but gentle irony was an element of many of these responses, particularly while describing their own fan behaviour. A number of respondents answered the question on when and how they listened in this vein, for example: 'Quietly, dedicatedly. Nobody is allowed to interrupt or disturb me on pain of death (or worse)' (m., 56+, 'wasp', market research consultant). Question 20, which asked respondents whether they talked about *The Archers* with friends, also elicited descriptions of a self-aware and playful entry into the diegesis:

> Frequently, usually about the storylines – often very seriously when non-Archers' fans are present. We enjoy pretending that it is real life and see how long it is before they catch on. … We all take it very seriously but with our tongues firmly in our cheeks.
>
> (m., 36–45, white Caucasian, teacher)

A slightly ironic presentation of a serious interest in the programme was also a feature of a response from a woman listener who said she talked to women and homosexual men about *The Archers*: 'My male friends listen on a Sunday morning – if anything exciting happens during the week, I phone them at 7.20 p.m. to warn them (they don't like surprises)' (f., 36–45, British, civil servant). This tongue-in-cheek mode was also adopted in the general approach to the questionnaire by some respondents, who answered in humorous style; a female listener answered the question on the role of women, for instance, as follows: 'They do bake well, but seem to be emotionally unstable. Poor Caroline can pick up a dud virtually as he puts his foot in the Shire' (f., 46–55, 'wasp', teacher). Some expressions of loyalty to the series were couched in this mode: 'If the BBC ever decide to axe it I'll personally lead a demo to Downing Street or Buckingham Palace or wherever I have to go' (f., 36–45, white, teacher).

The persona of the mock-serious, middle-class *Archers* fan that emerges here seems to be a further instance of the delicate negotiation of the fandom discourse in the context of 'quality' radio, suggesting that the tensions identified in the focus groups might be quite generalised in a predominantly middle-class audience.

Although 43 per cent of female respondents and 25 per cent of the men said they followed television soaps, several were at pains to differentiate between the latter and *The Archers*, and the quality of the programme was widely emphasised and praised. The need to differentiate oneself from fans of other series, or even other *Archers* fans, was also expressed here; one respondent described how she had attended an *Archers* weekend with friends: 'Had a really good time though we were probably a bit frivolous compared with the other somewhat ageing aficionados' (f., 46–55, white British, teacher) and another commented: 'Although *The Archers* is a soap, it seems to be a soap through which one meets a nice type of person! (God! that's just the sort of snobby thing Jennifer would say!)' (f., 45–55, white, housewife).

The desire to express emotional involvement was combined, in one instance particularly, with a more ironic stance: 'I find it very comforting – it seems like an oasis in a very frightening world (I'm not being sarcastic here!). Ideally I would like to live in Ambridge … it's my dream' (f., 26–35, white British, administrator). The denial in parenthesis in fact distances the writer from the more 'involved' statement, and this is reinforced by the hint of self-parody in the dream of living in Ambridge. This careful balancing act, combining the critique of gender representation (see above) and ironic humour with expression of emotional involvement, is very reminiscent of *Morse* group 2, and interestingly this respondent is in the same, young age-group as the most dominant member of that group, Sarah, and her friend Lisa. The isolated nature of the response indicated that for the reasons discussed above the questionnaire survey had not led me to the feminist subculture I had hoped to find in the sample. I also began to realise that even if such a shared subculture had emerged, inviting individuals who did not know each other to a focus group would merely replicate the *Morse* research, both in terms of strengths and limitations. I decided that the investigation of the role of talk about *The Archers* in a friendship group with some of the feminist subcultural characteristics I had identified in the *Morse* research and in my own social relation to *The Archers* would enable me to take the research into a new sphere (see Chapter 3). Fortunately, one questionnaire offered particularly full and interesting responses, as well as the possibility of finding such a group.

Introducing Mary, and Friends

Mary's initial questionnaire, completed in 1997, led me eventually to interview her, in December 1998. By this stage I was looking for a small network of *Archers* listeners who would talk about the programmes with each other naturally (i.e. outside the research context). The emphasis on the social aspect of listening in Mary's questionnaire suggested that she would be able to introduce me to exactly this kind of network:

> Several of my closest friends, male and female, listen to *The Archers*. We make jokes about them all the time especially in our e-mail communications. … Also at work several professional colleagues put up newspaper articles about *The Archers* on the staff noticeboard and you can have a good old

chat with colleagues when otherwise you might not have much in common. Ben also finds this at work, at least with women in his work-place – there's a sort of *Archers* 'in-crowd'.

This description of a network of social relations enriched by, or even based on, *The Archers*, which also implied a jokey, playful relationship to the programmes, seemed an ideal subject for further investigation. Mary's response to the questionnaire also stood out immediately as she had typed her answers, and as a result they were much fuller than the hand-written replies. The wealth of information which she provided made it irresistible to enquire further, even though initially I had some qualms because Mary and I had once met socially, many years previously, through a mutual friend. As the acquaintance was very slight, and distanced by a lapse of time, I eventually decided that it would not impede the research, and might even enhance it, particularly if its possible impact was openly declared, and the subject of careful reflection.

Several aspects of Mary's questionnaire and the telephone interview with her suggested an 'oppositional' relationship to *The Archers*. Unlike the members of the Wood Norton Hall groups who praised the programmes for being true to life, Mary found little that she recognised in *The Archers*. In response to the question 'Which (if any) characters do you identify with?', she wrote:

> No … I can't say there is anyone. They live lives that are so different from mine. I think I enjoy NOT identifying and feeling critical of them, though there have been moments. When Mark died, and Shula was grief-stricken, it brought tears to my eyes.

This sense of belonging to a very different world, or world-view, and yet still engaging emotionally with the fictional text was very much a feature of *Morse* group 2, and of my own relation to *The Archers*. The distance from the 'reality represented' in these comments is reminiscent of Ien Ang's ironic viewers of *Dallas* (1985: 99); however, the crucial difference is that Mary describes an emotional response to the text at the same time. It was precisely this combination of involvement and distance which led me to investigate Mary's readings of *The Archers* in more depth.

A further significant factor in my choice to focus on Mary and her circle in this phase of the research was the (almost) overt feminist views she expressed, particularly in the telephone interview, where a sense of complicity between myself and her emerged fairly early in the discussion:

> *Mary*: I mean, it (.) I have to say I take it on several levels – I'm sure you do as well.
>
> [*Laughter*]
>
> *Lyn*: Yes.

(88–9)

As this quotation suggests, some of the complicity was connected with recognition of each other as critical readers. This sense of complicity in a shared culture encompassed and possibly stemmed from feminisms, as well as a similar social and professional milieu and age-group. I introduced the topic of gender representation quite early in the discussion and asked three further questions on the topic. The length of Mary's replies (in response to my question on feminism, 34 lines) and the fact that she was already engaged in a discussion of the representation of the personal in *The Archers* before I asked my questions suggests, however, that this was far from being alien territory for her. As in the questionnaire, the Wood Norton concern for balance was entirely absent here, and Mary had no qualms in expressing her greater interest in the women characters:

> *Lyn*: Yes, what about the [*cough*] the male characters, recently? Are you finding them any more interesting or more or less the same?
>
> *Mary*: I don't think I do find them very interesting. Um –
>
> *Lyn*: Are you more interested in the women characters?
>
> *Mary*: I suppose I am. The men have got to be there for the women to develop their interesting characters (*laughs*) I suppose.
>
> (138–43)

The fact that Mary could summarily dismiss the male characters as mere adjuncts to the women without any fear of a reaction from me suggests a shared, mischievous sense of humour. The remark would probably not have gone unchallenged, or at least unnoticed, in either of the Wood Norton Hall groups, where in one case the lack of strong male characters was perceived as a problem.

A similar moment of collusion occurred a little later when I asked Mary her view on the idea of the programme being 'taken over by feminists':

> *Lyn*: Um, I don't know whether you've read any of the stuff in the press about *The Archers* and that, but one of the themes in the last few years has been that it's been taken over by feminists. Um, I think that might have been by a feminist producer at least. I think it might have been mentioned at the Theatre thing. What do you think about that?
>
> *Mary*: I suppose – in the sense that they've got some storylines that are about, um, – I mean, I don't think for a minute that it's been taken over by feminists [*laughter*] if they tried I don't think Radio 4 would let them. And also that what being taken over by feminists might mean could be very complicated.
>
> (169–77)

The shared laughter over the absurdity of the notion of *The Archers* being taken over by feminists indicates that both Mary and I are constructing an image of Radio 4 as part of a conservative establishment or mainstream culture which we do not belong to. The feminist social identity we are constructing relies on a sense of opposition to this symbolic cultural centre. Mary's next sentence emphasises the complexity of feminisms, and by implication, of the cultural identity being constructed in this exchange. This becomes more obvious when feminism is explicitly linked to the two levels of her way of talking about *The Archers* which has already been established as something we both share:

> Or maybe they're targeting at different audiences. I mean, they're recognising that – there are feminists. I mean – I know a lot of women that listen to it. It's very kind of tongue in cheek that kind of – and it's a lot to do with, um, what I said before about looking at it at two levels, like quite often when I'm talking to friends about it, we don't talk about the characters, we talk about what the writer is going to do with the characters, and what would be right to do with them.
>
> (201–6)

In this reply Mary comes as close as anyone does in this research to actually saying that she is a feminist; the clear implication is that feminism is a recognised cultural identity: 'I mean, they're recognising that – there are feminists'. The fact that this feminist identity is sophisticated and analytical is equally clear. Later in the interview Mary also suggested a relationship between gender and the jokey 'double-take' on *The Archers* which had already emerged as a significant characteristic of her talk with friends about the programme:

> There's two things, one is the actual experience of listening, and the other is having a jokey discussion with people who listen in much the same way as I do, which is – they don't make a priority but when they hear it, so that we can have kind of jokey conversations, often all female actually.
>
> (299–302)

This contains, in encapsulated form, almost all the elements of *Morse* group 2 – a women's culture of talk about a media text which involves a distanced relationship to it – 'they don't make a priority' and the use of the programme as a source of jokes and camaraderie. Interestingly, although Mary seems to see women, and particularly feminists, as a significant part of the *Archers* audience and as the dominant group of her own *Archers* 'in-crowd', in fact three significant participants in the latter – her partner, ex-husband and a former colleague – are all men. Clearly, biological gender is not the issue in participating in this mode of talk on *The Archers*, and the men concerned may well be strongly influenced by feminisms (see the Ben and Mary interview below).

Mary portrayed herself as an 'oppositional' reader of *The Archers*, not only in the field of gender, but also, quite unusually for this sample, in relation to the representation of Englishness in the programmes:

I lived in the country from 1954 to 1964 and my experience of the village was NOTHING like Ambridge. I hate the kind of Englishness at one level and I have never been part of it, coming from an Irish family. In fact, I would say that I was excluded from it. On the other hand, it amuses me and I feel rather superior listening to it!

Generally, Mary places herself firmly on the 'modernity' side of the tradition/modernity equation in the questionnaire: 'If there has been a change in the direction of more controversial subjects being introduced, then I would say it was for the better.' However, her responses in the telephone interview suggested a complex balancing of negative and positive elements, like that of other respondents. At one point I had asked Mary about the representation of Englishness, phrasing the question ironically, and referring to the 'relentless English village' (line 247). Mary resisted the ironic mode of reply, and spoke positively about the picture of spontaneous, warm social relations depicted in *The Archers*:

Yes, I suppose it can be a bit superior, but there's a bit of me that also likes – I'd like – I think I'd like to live, I think, I sometimes think, uh uh, not always, that it would be nice to have a less regimented, compartmentalised life. That is, I think there are aspects of being able to go to a pub where you might meet people you know, whereas the social life I have is that everything's arranged, um, I meet people because, you know, I meet people – I arrange things like two weeks in advance, and they come to my house, or I go to their house – which is – … that's how I live my life, but the thought of just popping into the local and meeting up with people and having a good chat, is so remote from my experience and yet there's something about that – I sometimes think that it would be nice to go somewhere and just bump into people and you could go or leave as you felt like it.

(249–58)

This suggests that one of the main pleasures of *The Archers* for Mary is the recognition of precisely the kind of utopian ideal community which I discuss in Chapter 2, and which is in sharp contrast to the time-managed existence of the modern intellectual. The fact that the ritual of listening intensifies the structure and security provided by home life was also suggested by Mary's notion of listening to *The Archers* as part of 'being comfortably domestic': 'Yes, it gives a certain sort of structure. I actually do try to get home, if – I try not to stay at work, and I use *The Archers* as my target for being at home cooking supper' (292–3). The comforting nature of the social world of *The Archers* is closely connected to representations of traditional, rural Englishness: Mary's response demonstrates that it is perfectly possible to relate to this at an emotional level, while maintaining a political critique of the programmes on feminist and other grounds.

However, the sense of being 'outside' Englishness was also reiterated at several points. In a follow-up questionnaire, which concluded the research, Mary expressed pleasure that one of the recent new characters in *The Archers* was an Irish woman. Both Mary and her partner Ben were relating to a media text which is generally viewed as the epitome of Englishness from a complex position, both inside and outside Englishness, since Mary is Irish and Ben is Jewish American, and they live in a southern British town. The other respondents discussed in this chapter, Louise, who described herself as having 'northern working-class roots' and who was brought up overseas, and Jan, whose parents are Australian, may also have a complex relationship to Englishness. Inevitably this introduces a different kind of oppositionality to their readings than that focused on gender which I had identified in *Morse* group 2 and sought here. In choosing to place them, and particularly Mary, at the centre of this phase of the research I am engaging with questions of national and ethnic, as well as gender, identity, and with another form of oppositional reading – that of audience members who do not entirely share the dominant forms of Englishness which the text expresses. This represents a development of the research which may also interrogate the cultural Englishness which so far has emerged as a focus of recognition and identification for my respondents.

The rest of this chapter analyses talk about *The Archers* by people linked in some way to Mary. Mary gave me a longer list of friends: one man did not respond to my e-mail, and the remaining two women were missed out simply because I felt that I already had enough material for this phase of the research. The class, age and ethnicity profile of this group of respondents is as follows:

> **Mary**: f., 51, academic, white, born in Ireland of Irish parents but grew up in Britain
>
> **Ben**: m., 47, academic, born and brought up in USA, white, Jewish family background; lived in England since 22
>
> **Jan**: f., 43, freelance consultant, white British, born and brought up in London but with Australian parents
>
> **Louise**: f., 34, postgraduate student and part-time lecturer, white English, brought up overseas (mainly Hong Kong)

Interview with Mary and Ben

Context and Relations

This discussion took place about one month after the telephone interview with Mary, at the house she shares with her partner, Ben. When I arrived Mary immediately took control of the situation, by suggesting where we should sit, where I should set up the tape-recorder, and that we would do some of the interview first and then have tea. My nervousness about the interview was expressed in a joke I made as I arrived about having a tape-recorder with me, 'like a real researcher'. The nervousness stemmed in part from the meeting of my professional and private lives; since Mary, Ben and I share friends in common (and friends could be considered as the people we most want to impress), there was more pressure to do the interview well than there had been with people I didn't know at all, in the Wood Norton Hall groups. In fact I rapidly relaxed, since a sense of complicity developed early on in the discussion. This is demonstrated not only by the content of the discussion but also by its length (one and a half hours), and by the fact that talk about *The Archers* commenced even before I switched on the tape-recorder (almost as soon as I crossed the threshold), and continued after I switched it off. I followed my list of set questions less assiduously than I had at Wood Norton, partly because of the complication that Mary had already answered most of them in the questionnaire and telephone interview, and also because it seemed important to follow up the interesting and unpredictable lines of thought which emerged.

I was very much more split between the role of fan and that of researcher than I had been at Wood Norton: Mary and Ben plunged into two topics (would Shula's new husband Alastair turn out to be a paedophile? and would *The Archers* ever include a lesbian character?) before I asked any questions at all, and my first interventions were responses to these – their – topics as a fellow fan. My first question occurred only at line 131 of the transcript, and while for most of the discussion I mainly asked questions (often follow-up questions, as described above), there were also several instances, particularly in the last half hour of the discussion, where my desire to join in with a mode of talk about *The Archers* which I recognised immediately was irresistible. The fact that, even accounting for the length of this discussion, I spoke much more than I had done in the second group at Wood Norton, which is similar in size (211 lines as opposed to 59), substantiates the notion that I was participating as a fan more in this instance.

As the topic map makes clear, the discussion was divided between talk about the programme, consisting mainly of recounting favourite stories or scenes or discussing characters, and talk about the audience, which was the topic referred to most frequently – no less than twenty-nine times.[2] The third most frequently referenced topic was agency, indicating, again, a strong tendency to analyse the programme as a fictional text, rather than entering the fiction. The very strong emphasis on audience and, to a lesser extent, agency here indicates a very different understanding of the research context than that evidenced in the Wood Norton Hall groups. Although in the latter case agency and audience were significant topics, they were much less so than modality, and references to the audience were on the whole concerned with describing their own fan behaviour, '*Archers* Addicts' activities and so on. Here, Mary and Ben, in a complete role reversal, were so apprised of the aim of the research and the nature of my interests that in some ways they were actually doing the work of analysing talk about *The Archers* for me. Modality was referred to, but on only seven occasions, so that interest in realism is outweighed here by concerns about the composition of the *Archers* audience, modes of talk about the programme in particular social groups, influences on its production and, last but not least, favourite stories from the programme and from their experience as listeners.

Mutual recognition as critical readers was also a strong feature of this discussion, where unashamedly academic language was used from the outset. Thus at line 50, Ben described the scriptwriters 'putting down markers', then at line 94, referred to a 'funny intertextual thing', while later Mary described *The Archers* as Ben's 'acculturation' project, and he talked of 'being positioned' as an *Archers* fan at work (244) and of 'a recognisable *Archers* discourse' (514). The discussion was also more sustained than most of the talk analysed in the rest of this research project, in that topics were developed in some detail, and there were references back to earlier themes or ideas. The analytical mode was accompanied throughout by a version of the playful talk about *The Archers* which Mary and Ben analysed so effectively, and indeed the two opening topics are instances of this. One of the main sources of humour and of play consisted of switching between speaking 'within' the diegesis, and from 'outside' in analytical mode, as unpredictably as possible:

Ben: But there's something odd about Alastair. There's something about the particular way he became unhinged when the whole thing with Richard blew up that was not quite believable. I don't know.

Lyn: Or the way he recovered from being very angry –

Ben: Overnight.

Lyn: Very quickly.

Ben: Yes.

Lyn: And went back to her. It was like=

Ben: =And he's always=

Mary: =You've got to distinguish between an unstable personality and inconsistent writing.

[*Laughter*]

Lyn: No no no.

(69–80)

In this example Mary pricks the bubble of Ben's and my excursion into the diegesis, and her analytical comment, from 'outside', is in effect the punch line, demonstrating the need to be funny and clever at the same time in this context.

The inevitable result of this switching between talking about *The Archers* as if it were real and demonstrating very clear awareness that it is not is that the former mode takes on a slightly self-conscious air, and as Ben's analysis of 'the *Archers* discourse' demonstrates, this self-aware 'suspension of disbelief' is a general feature of Ben and Mary's talk about *The Archers*:

Ben: But there's a recognisable *Archers* discourse which is, um, which I recognise and it is, it is earnest, you suspend disbelief completely, and you talk about it in slightly hushed tones, um, a bit like you would talk about your own friends – um 'yes, well, what will happen indeed?'

Mary: I don't think it's suspending disbelief exactly –

Lyn: It's pretending –

Ben: It is a kind of pretence.

(514–20)

Later in the discussion I commented on my recognition of this phenomenon in my own social circles: 'I immediately knew what you were talking about. I think. That you're sort of playing at seriousness, aren't you?' (1198). I also made the point about switching between modes of talk:

It's part of the game to totally talk about *The Archers* as if they were real, um, and every now and again somebody will say something that admits that they're not real, and you sort of giggle a bit then. But mostly you try to keep it up.

(1205–8)

Clearly, the result of these moments of shared analysis and recognition is a reinforcement of the sense of complicity, of being on home ground.

Another aspect of the dynamics of this event seems to result from the gender imbalance of the group. Mary had already ascribed to Ben the role of performer, and here Ben was very much performing for his audience of two attentive and appreciative women:

Ben: Anyway, um, but Glenda Jackson played Prue Forrest who actually approached the other Christmas celebrity for his autograph, I can't remember who it was – was it Terry Wogan? Terry Wogan, and Glenda Jackson played Prue Forrest saying, 'Excuse me, Mr Wogan' [*assumed country accent*], 'can I have your autograph?' Uh ... er.

[*Laughter*]

Lyn: I can see that if I miss a programme you can act it all out for me.

Mary: And he does – he's got all the voices and I don't need to watch – in fact, I enjoy his version of it more than listening to it.

Ben: I've tried doing Jennifer Aldridge.

Lyn: Have you? Do a bit of Jennifer for us.

Ben: Darling [*in 'Jennifer's' voice*].

(687–96)

I was perhaps responding particularly positively to Ben as this was my first contact with him, and I was anxious to replicate the rapport I felt I had established with Mary on the telephone. My general desire to please and to be accepted also meant that I was happy to play the role of appreciative audience of Mary's and Ben's 'double act' of *Archers* fandom. Ben was the most obvious performer, as the quotation above suggests – telling funny stories involving both humorous moments from the programme and the excesses of his own fandom, and imitating the characters' voices. Mary in some ways acted as the 'straight man', adding supplementary material to the joke, or the punchline, as in the 'inconsistent writing' line quoted above. Some of my appreciation of Ben's mimicry and humour probably also stemmed from recognition of a fellow performer, and there are points in the discussion, particularly towards the end, when I join in. Ben's, anxiety about providing the right kind of material for me is evidenced by his question – 'Is this any good?', which occurs about half-way through the discussion, and suggests that even for academics 'being researched' is quite a demanding process. The fact that all of these efforts were successful, that Mary and Ben 'hit the spot' as far as I was concerned, and that I was accepted into their 'group', are indicated by the length of the discussion, and the fact that the talk is extremely fluent, fast, uninterrupted and punctuated by gales of loud laughter.

The discussion was built on mutual reinforcement, with a high level of listening attentively to each other, finishing each other's sentences, laughing at each other's jokes, and constructing a particular story or line of thought co-operatively. The line-count revealed that Ben spoke most. Since I had already interviewed Mary, inevitably some of my questions were more directed at Ben, and this probably contributed to the relatively high number of lines he spoke. While it could be argued that to some extent quite traditional gender relations are being maintained here – with a male participant performing for his female audience – in fact, as I have suggested, both Mary and I intervene frequently and with some energy. The difference in number of lines between Ben and Mary is only about eighty, and she introduced slightly more new topics, so that it would be excessive to describe Ben's role as dominant. In the next section, where I will focus more on the content of the discussion, the question of gender will be examined in more depth. It is sufficient to say here that more traditional forms of masculinity probably would not encompass Ben's detailed knowledge of a soap opera or his performance – verging on camp – of the voices of female characters from *The Archers*.

Gender, Englishness and Ironic Fandom

A defining feature of Mary and Ben's talk about *The Archers* is their portrayal of the programme as in some way outside their normal cultural and social world, permitting forms of talk which would not normally be possible for them:

> *Mary*: I think that if it – given that you're so much more into it than I am, I
> think. I think it has provided – I don't mean because you're American but

I think it allows you, and this is just my – I'm just thinking out of the top of my head – this is just a theory, you don't have to react, it allows you to talk about some quite difficult things as a man, with women, like feelings and emotions and relationships.

Ben: Possibly.

Mary: At a kind of jokey, slightly ironical way – I mean, for me, I think it allows me to say really horrible things about people – cos I try to be good and kind and counselling to people, most of the time – supportive. But, you know, I'm quite happy to call – it allows me to say really rude things about people, that if they were real I'd be nice about them. But I do think it provides a kind of –

(293–303)

This extract is revealing in relation to the versions of masculinity and femininity being constructed. In talk about *The Archers* Mary is able temporarily to abandon her mature and caring version of femininity. Generally, this seems similar to the escape from middle-class maturity through *Archers* fandom which I noted in Wood Norton group 1. The possibility of expressing aggression which Mary highlights may be a surprising, but heartfelt, pleasure for 'nice' women.

Mary's comment suggests that talk about *The Archers* creates the possibility of a new kind of masculinity for Ben, and this is borne out by the fact that both Mary and Ben emphasised that he was the real *Archers* fan of the two of them, in a reversal of the relationship to soap opera more frequently found in couples in audience research (e.g. Morley, 1986). A discussion of the extent of Ben's commitment to the programme was characterised by a mixture of affirmation and denial:

Lyn: Do you listen more or less every day?

Ben: Yeah, yeah. I mean, there are times when I miss it – um, and there have been – when it gets particularly interesting I do (.) organise my life around it without putting too – I don't want to put it particularly strongly but [*laughter*] I wouldn't –

Mary: More than I do, more than I do.

Ben: More than Mary does, but I wouldn't – I mean, I wouldn't cancel a work commitment or, you know, or leave something early –

Mary: But you might ask someone not to phone you.

Ben: I might ask someone not to phone me, or I might – if I'm sitting in the office I might think, um, you know, if I (.) if I hurry up – you know, if it's about ten to seven – if I hurry up I can get out of the office in time to hear it, um, or I think I'm actually gonna – I get this kind of slight feeling of panic when I hear that I've got – you know, when it's quarter to seven and I've got another hour to do – what can I do? And I have been known

> either to go out to the car and sit there for quarter of an hour to listen to it, or – it's true, I have, –
>
> [*Laughter*]
>
> *Mary*: I didn't realise how bad you were, Ben.
>
> (149–67)

On the one hand, this establishes the ironic and self-aware performance of fandom – 'I don't want to put it particularly strongly', with Mary colluding with Ben's description of himself as an 'addict' and reinforcing the joke. On the other, the hesitations and repetitions which occur suggest that there might be some genuine unease about admitting this. Nonetheless, in emphasising Ben's soap opera fandom, Mary is presenting Ben as a suitable partner for a feminist, a man who is capable of questioning the boundaries of masculinity. The dynamic here seems to illustrate how awareness of gender issues generates performance of newly defined gender roles – a clear, if limited, instance of the impact of feminisms on at least some social milieus. It also perhaps illustrates social constraints within such circles, such as the unspoken but subliminally present need for feminists in hetero-sexual relationships to justify their choice to their women friends. Here, it is the 'feminine' soap opera text which is used to mark out these differences, by both partners. If Mary could be said to take the lead in this, Ben certainly colludes with her construction of his social persona. Ben himself comments that the programmes display 'a kind of modern middle-class female orientation' (498). Mary agrees and asks 'in that case, why does Ben like it?' (501–2). I would argue that this might be exactly the reason for Ben's interest in the programmes and that in his talk about *The Archers* he has constructed a different, 'feminised' masculinity, incorporating elements of camp performance. The fact that Ben's talk about *The Archers* was also intellectual and analytical aligns it even more with the feminist identity which had already formed part of the complicity between myself and Mary in the earlier interview.

The question of national identity was a significant focus of this discussion:

> *Ben*: But the script would always be about the same, so it would always be this – 'So, how are you?' 'Well, you know'. 'Yes, go on' [*a laugh*]. 'Well, I don't like to – '. 'It's OK. Go on'. 'Well, it's just that – '. 'Yes'. 'Well, I – '. 'Yes.' [*laughter*] And then it would finish, and – so there's always been this problem about getting people to talk about themselves. This very British thing they do in *The Archers* which is 'I don't want to pry' [*laughter*] and 'I don't want to say too much about myself cos it would monopolise things'.
>
> (96–102)

The most obvious observation about this is that Ben is positioning himself outside British, or perhaps more accurately English, reserve. However, this kind of ironic self-mockery is a well-known aspect of Englishness, so that at another level, he is demonstrating just how British, or English, he has become.[3] The fact that I immediately recognised and responded to the joke supports the idea of it operating among 'insiders', rather than from outside the culture.

A later comment clarifies Ben's perspective as that of an outsider, far more as a result of the social milieu he inhabits in British culture than his American origins:

> I have never identified at all with anyone in *The Archers*, either as personal-ities or in life style. Um, um, nor do I recognise any of them as personalities or in terms of lifestyle in life. In my working life or social life – there are very, very few points of connection – that kind of, that kind of nostalgic strand of British village life.
>
> (304–8)

In the discussion of favourite characters which then ensued Ben continued to affirm his sense of difference and distance, describing, for instance, how he had been disappointed by one of the actors he had seen at the *Archers* performance:

> Actually, I found Nelson particularly disappointing to see in the flesh. Because I've often thought of him as this vaguely, kind of outré figure. A bit racy, and he's got this amazing past and reputation, and yet he just seemed like a kind of colonel type, with a blue blazer with brass buttons and a little moustache. And it was obvious that all they really wanted was his voice. And as a character he was very different.
>
> (400–4)[4]

Unusually in this research, Ben was unable to think of a favourite character, thus entirely affirming his own point about lack of recognition or identification with the characters. In some ways it could be said that both Mary and Ben had a kind of safety valve for fandom. If Mary's was about emphasising the casual nature of her listening, for Ben this consisted of counterbalancing his description of organising his life so that he could listen, with his performance of the obsessive fan (and being teased about it by Mary), and the expression of distance and cultural difference at crucial points.

The importance of these expressions of distance, and of the ironic and playful mode of talk about *The Archers* they described, and to some extent adopted here, was emphasised towards the end of the discussion, when Mary and Ben raised the topic of how they are viewed as *Archers* fans by people belonging to their own milieu:

Mary: The other thing is that I do – I am aware of the hostility of some people towards the enthusiasm for *The Archers*.

(*Ben agrees*)

Lyn: Really?

Ben: Oh, yes.

LIVERPOOL JOHN MOORES UNIVERSITY
LEARNING SERVICES

Mary: The superiority, or a horror and a shock that people like me or Ben might even listen, might descend, sort of, –

Lyn: What sort of – where's the hostility coming from?

Ben: It's kind of establishment and middle class, and terribly, terribly English, and we're not seen like that.

Lyn: So it's a politically correct hostility, in fact, is it?

Ben: Would you say?

Lyn: That it's – it's incorrect to be listening to *The Archers*?

Mary: Well, all the people on this list,[5] I think, would regard themselves as quite radically left and socialist, or feminist. So it's not those people. Or least, it's not authority, it's not those people –

Ben: I think it's people who have a kind of stereotype of what it means to be, you know, vaguely academic and left-wing. And they're shocked that anyone who they've slotted into that category could also listen to *The Archers*. Which I think in their minds is a completely different category.

(1152–70)

This can be interpreted as suggesting that the ethos of their own political and cultural group (which interestingly is described here as 'radically left', 'feminist' and 'vaguely academic') is a major determinant of the ironic and playful mode of talk about *The Archers* which Ben and Mary adopt. It could also be argued that, like Ien Ang's ironic viewers, Mary and Ben use irony in their talk about *The Archers* at least in part to demonstrate their resistance to 'the ideology of mass culture' in this case, more specifically, the ideology of middle-class Englishness and of the conventional family (Ang, 1985: 99). The irony is clearly crucial – in order for *The Archers* to become cool in the 'radically left', and 'vaguely academic' milieu they describe, the talk about it must demonstrate an ironic take on these elements. However, the kind of criticism which Mary and Ben describe, and which is akin to Ang's 'ideology of mass culture' position, clearly emanates from groups outside their own immediate circles. Mary and Ben effectively turn the tables on their critics, with the result that *Archers* fandom becomes very cool indeed, and non-participants are viewed as rather straight, boring, and excessively wedded to high culture institutions such as Radio 3:

Mary: It comes out of – I think it comes out of a general (.) distaste for soap opera generally. Um, and the assumption that people who –

Ben: Lowbrow –

Mary: People who listen to those soap operas are people who've got boring lives and who live out some kind of excitement through the dramas in the soap opera and that, you know, there're various stereotypes that the people who like soap operas do it because they have a gap in their lives. It's like other people.

(1177–83)

These two extracts, where Mary and Ben analyse how they are perceived by others, constitute a particularly interesting part of this discussion, in that they portray *Archers* fandom as unconventional, or even transgressive in the context of the wider left-wing milieu which they inhabit: they are thus constructing their own identities in opposition to the anti-mass culture position described by Ang, rather than being ironic about *The Archers* out of deference to it. The reclaiming of popular culture which the second extract describes is also probably influenced by some recent academic writing on the media, which Mary and Ben may well have read. Their position is more complex than either Ien Ang's ironic viewers or her 'mass culture' respondents. Although, like the former, Mary and Ben certainly derive pleasure from their ironic comments and jokes, their object is as much their own fandom as the popular text, and irony is certainly not their only form of engagement with, or pleasure from, the programmes (see below). Like cultural studies itself, they have moved on from the 'ideology of mass culture' critique Ang describes, and *Archers* fandom is a way of demonstrating a more contemporary approach to popular culture. These differences illustrate changes which have taken place since the 1980s when Ang researched her book, as well as differences in research methods: Ang tends to attach one all-encompassing label to her groups of respondents, on the basis of entirely written evidence, whereas the focus group and interview methods I have used lead to more complex and contradictory results.

The idea of an escape from mature, middle-class seriousness discussed in relation to the performance of fandom in Wood Norton group 1 seems relevant here, though in this case that maturity takes on a particular intellectual and political form. Like the Wood Norton fans, Mary and Ben were also aware of being disapproved of for their *Archers* fandom by younger people, particularly their own son, who is described as critical of their intellectual talk about *The Archers* on moral grounds:

Mary: A style of language and discourse which is associated with being academic, actually, and that actually you might be excluding people because I think Liam, my son, feels a bit like that. That actually we're being clever, we're being clever. And, um, the ability to move between the different levels of belief and non-belief is what academics do. And –

Ben: Even if the actual –

Mary: And we're playing with real life because that's what academics do, they abstract theory from everything, and, of course, Ambridge isn't real life so – again, it's this thing like 'Do they know real people, there are really people struggling in the countryside, they're real poor people, and you're spending your time playing academic games'.

(1232–42)

Whereas Viv's son teased her for being a 'sad' *Archers* fan, Liam is critical of his parents' talk about *The Archers* precisely because of the escape from an otherwise politically sensitive and responsible stance which it implies. Like Louise (see below), he is also critical of academic disengagement from political realities. This seems to be another version of the political critique of *Archers* fandom described earlier in the discussion by Mary and Ben, and it is interesting that it emerges quite late. Despite the force of their son's critical comments, Ben and Mary do not defend themselves: there is a brief comment, and then the compelling game, and the respite from 'political correctness' which it offers, resumes.

However, playful and transgressive talk about *The Archers* did not preclude the possibility of real emotional engagement, as in the telephone interview with Mary. As then, Mary was prepared to admit both to a favourite character, and to the notion of the programme fulfilling an emotional need:

Mary: I quite like Jill.

Ben: Really!! [*Laughter*] Jill!!

Mary: Yes. I think she's a kind person. I wouldn't like to be her, but I wish she was my mum.

Ben: Oh, I see. She is the, she is the amazing mum.

Lyn: Do you like her voice?

Mary: Mmm. I do. I think – I think it would be wonderful to have an older friend, an older woman friend – that I could go and offer me coffee and – there's nobody like that in my life. Maybe that's significant – I don't know any older women but, you know, or maybe the ones that are around are so – you know, so flawed, like my mother, or my stepmother, or my mother-in-law, or my first mother-in-law [*laughs*]. Oh, my first mother-in-law was a bit more like that.

(364–75)

This was a level of self-revelation which despite the 'new masculinity' described above did not emerge in Ben's comments. It was, as I have suggested, probably easier to combine the description of casual listening patterns with that of a more emotional engagement, and may also result from a higher degree of trust between myself and Mary as a result of the telephone conversation and gender-based complicity. Nonetheless, if Ben did not delve into his past, a little later in the discussion he was quite open about his own emotional response, the fact that the programme had sometimes made him cry, for instance, and that he had found some speeches very moving:

Ben: And I have – I have cried.

Mary: Yes. [*Laughter*] We've both –

Ben: At Shula's – at Shula's famous speech about having, um, you know, paid the video bill – um, having put – you know, the speech she did a couple of months after Mark died, when she talked about having tidied it all up and, and then there was nothing left and it was beautifully written, I think, as a kind of, um – and I think she's actually a very good actor. One of the best and it was actually brilliantly done and we were just (.)

(*laughs*)

Mary: It was very powerful, wasn't it, the way they –

Ben: Utterly believable, and there've been a few times like that, haven't there?

(537–45)

Interestingly, the 'quality' discourse re-emerges at this point, and although it is referred to slightly less frequently in this discussion than in the Wood Norton groups, it is clear that despite all the irony and distancing, the notion that the programme is well put together is in fact crucial to Ben's and Mary's involvement. What evolves is thus a complex and ambiguous relationship to the text. The pleasures are partly about playing with it, satirising it and seeing oneself as very different from the world it depicts, in a slightly superior way (as Mary suggested in the telephone interview); the ironic and playful reading of such an apparently conventional and mainstream text enables the construction of an identity which is both intellectual and capable of making links with popular culture. At the same time it is important to feel that in choosing this particular soap opera they, or, more accurately, we, are relating to a programme which is in fact sufficiently well written and well acted to keep us listening regularly and occasionally have us riveted or traumatised. Here again, there is a crucial difference between this and Ien Ang's *Dallas* research. Although a soap opera, *The Archers* relies more on the codes of realism than melodrama, and some left-wing and feminist discourses are represented in the text. *The Archers* therefore permits a wider range of responses than the total mockery of the excesses of the text by ironic viewers described by Ang. Nonetheless, the difficulty of expressing this level of involvement in this context is evidenced by the hesitations and laughter in the above extract, and the 'quality' discourse could in some ways be seen as rescuing the speakers from their disarray. Despite this a baseline of involvement and admiration, similar to that expressed at Wood Norton and in many of the telephone interviews, is clearly present, indicating that there is some common ground in the responses I am analysing.

Telephone Interview with Jan

Jan is a close friend of Mary's who lives in a city in the North of England. I contacted her by e-mail, and organised the telephone interview which took place about a month after the interview with Mary and Ben. Throughout the interview my aim was to be as affirming as possible, since Jan and I had never met, and I also aimed to confine my interventions to asking questions as much as possible.

These aims proved in practice to be rather conflicting, and in fact I asked thirty-six questions, made twenty-six affirming responses (which ranged from 'yes' to repetition of what Jan had said or commenting that others had said the same thing) and fifty-two comments as a fan or regular listener. The interventions 'as a fan' consisted of joining in with accounts of the narrative, making jokes about characters or stories or displaying knowledge about the production process or names of characters. They also included a discussion of the audience at one point, and references to secondary literature such as articles in the press and books on *The Archers*. The high number of these interventions surprised me, as I had imagined that I had played a neutral but encouraging role. It suggests that I have found common ground and empathised with my respondent, so that the interview becomes an instance of a shared culture, as well as a research event. This is evidenced by the use of the pronoun 'we' in the interview by both speakers, and by the shared jokes which, if less numerous and energetic than in the Mary/Ben interview, are interspersed throughout:

> *Jan*: And I ended up hearing it so often, because it was a repeat and then it was on things like *Pick of the Week* – I felt I really died with John.
>
> *Lyn*: Um, um. Yes, and now we're going through it all again
>
> [*Laughs*]
>
> *Jan*: Oh, I know. I know. There's a very interesting article in *The Guardian* about how he hasn't got much work since.
>
> *Lyn*: Yes.
>
> *Jan*: Did you see that?
>
> *Lyn*: Yes, I did.
>
> *Jan*: I felt a bit sorry for him.
>
> *Lyn*: Yes, because he was supposed to be going off for a glittering career, wasn't he?
>
> *Jan*: Yes, one of his new parts had been – sort of mute. [*Laughs*] But it was a bit like the character of John. I think – I found that quite interesting as well – the sort of real people and the characters. And the confusion – that it can have on this masthead of *The Guardian*, John Archer. I think in a way we can work between those two levels is too interesting.
>
> (136–49)

The jokes at the beginning of this extract combine involvement and just a hint of irony – through overstating the case – 'dying' with John, or 'going through it all again'. Jan's reply 'Oh, I know, I know', with its slightly exaggerated tone of commiseration, confirms the very subtle hint of camp performance we are both engaging in here. The shared culture is also demonstrated by the fact that we had both read the newspaper article; this is one of many instances when recognition of each other's knowledge about the programmes has a cohesive effect on the dynamics of the interview – just as in the Wood Norton groups sharing this kind of knowledge seemed to be one of the pleasures of the event and of fandom generally. The extract ends with Jan taking up the pronoun 'we' which I had introduced at the beginning. Although the exact parameters of this 'we' are inevitably unclear, it implies Jan and the friends she talks to about *The Archers* and quite possibly includes me. The fact that Jan uses exactly the same phrase – 'two levels' – which Mary had used several times in her interview suggests perhaps that they have talked inbetween the two events. The phrase carries with it all the connotations of a sophisticated reading culture around *The Archers* which it had also implied in the earlier interview with Mary. This exchange can be seen as typical of a developing complicity as critical and slightly playful readers of *The Archers* which underpinned this whole interview, and is to some extent similar to that shared with Mary, and with Mary and Ben. The complicity developed at this early stage in the interview was probably crucial to the feminist analysis which Jan subsequently initiated.

The topic map of this interview nonetheless reveals significant differences from the interviews with Mary and with Mary and Ben. Narrative and character are the most frequently recurring topics, with audience third, whereas with Ben and Mary audience occurs significantly more than narrative (twenty-nine as opposed to twenty occurrences), and audience and agency more than character; in the interview with Mary both agency and audience are mentioned more than narrative or character. The topic map for Jan's interview is more like that of Wood Norton group 2, where character and narrative are the most frequently recurring topics after modality. The topic counts indicate that Jan expressed her involvement with the programmes more directly than either Mary or Ben, and was less concerned with establishing critical reader status through the analysis of the audience or production of the programmes. Very early in the interview, she described her long-term involvement with *The Archers*: 'I think I was probably about 12, which makes it 31 years' (83). Like Mary, and many of the respondents to the questionnaire survey, Jan described the programmes as a source of security, a kind of 'anchor' in a busy life. She particularly emphasised their role in helping her re-settle at home after work trips abroad – 'it probably is an anchor-point for returning and feeling the world's the same'. Jan is also more similar to the respondents to the questionnaire survey than either Mary or Ben, in that she has been listening since childhood, and she emphasised the importance of this: 'I mean, I can tell that people who've only listened recently enjoy it a great deal, but I think it – things resonate more deeply if you've had that length of contact' (437–9). Nonetheless, the interview with Jan was similar in tone to the telephone interview with Mary, that is, quite serious, strongly empathetic and co-operative. It was generally more relaxed than the interview with Ben and Mary, where the specific dynamics of a group of two women (who were both clearly feminists) and one man led to pronounced elements of performance and ironic humour.

Almost immediately after the start of the interview, Jan described her dissatisfaction with the programmes: 'Cos I can't say that I'm sort of ecstatic after my fifteen minutes hit. But I hate missing it. So it's an ambivalent pleasure really' (111–12). When asked about her likes and dislikes, Jan mentioned storylines based on difficulties in relationships – 'sort of heightened emotional things' (127–8) – and also described herself finding the 'stuff around Usha and racism very compelling' (126–7). Like Mary, she described her interest as very largely based on the increasing number of 'personal relationships' storylines, and on the inclusion of modern social issues. Jan's interest in the women characters emerged early on, and her alternative view of them was suggested by her description of Shula as 'smugly complacent' and Shula's wedding as 'repugnant'. The fact that her oppositional reading was a feminist one emerged soon after these comments, and it was Jan who introduced the topic:

> *Lyn*: … they've had quite a lot of press coverage, some of it quite negative, about the programme being too modern.
>
> *Jan*: Yes, and too feminist as well
>
> *Lyn*: And too feminist, yes.
>
> *Jan*: It's a laugh.
>
> *Lyn*: What do you think about that?
>
> *Jan*: God, I wish it was feminist. I mean, I think that the women characters probably do come across quite strongly, but that to me isn't feminism. And –
>
> *Lyn*: What would you like them to do with the women characters?
>
> *Jan*: Um, a bit more sort of – I suppose more connection between the women, and more solidarity between the women, which does come in fits and bursts but they are mostly portrayed sort as based in their family settings, and not doing activities together. That's why I've always liked the Shula–Caroline thing. And I suppose to some extent Usha and, um –
>
> *Lyn*: Ruth –
>
> *Jan*: Ruth. Have a friendship.
>
> *Lyn*: Yes.
>
> *Jan*: But it's very much round the edges of the commitments to family life. And I'd like more of the single women, I suppose. Debbie's not been really developed much. I think – I think she's quite interesting, but she's quite in the wings.
>
> (264–82)

Jan 'comes out' as a feminist even more directly than Mary, though her line on feminism in the programmes is similar to Mary's, and very different to the Wood

Norton groups. For Jan, feminism is perhaps an influence on the programmes, but this does not make them feminist; *The Archers* is depicted as being part of a conservative, or more accurately liberal, culture, where the representation of strong women characters is permissible, but where the heterosexual and familial status quo remains unquestioned. It is clear that in Jan's view a feminist text would involve a more radical and questioning approach, particularly in the area of sexuality:

Jan: … I mean, one of my other interests is sexuality, because I'm a lesbian, so I'm always listening out for any hope. [*Laughs*] Any woman in Ambridge coming out. Friends of mine went to an Ambridge – some sort of an *Archers* occasion in Leeds – and spoke to Vanessa Whitburn afterwards about the lack of any lesbians in it. Or gay characters. I mean, the great disappointment has been what's his name, Shula's twin? Kenton.

Lyn: Kenton, yes.

Jan: That's been a great disappointment, because we all thought that he was gay. And he had to go to Australia to express it and so that's –

Lyn: Yes, yes, and now he's been –

Jan: Oh, awful! Awful! That's been a great disappointment.

(286–95)

The high level of shared understanding here is demonstrated by the fact that I did not even need to finish my sentence about the fate of the unfortunate Kenton (a secret marriage in Australia) for Jan to respond, and that she had no qualms at all in describing another marriage in very negative terms. Her cry of 'awful' is also another instance of the use of exaggerated language in a humorous, slightly camp manner.

This shared understanding develops even more in the discussion of the possibility of a lesbian character which follows. This discussion begins outside the diegesis, with Jan recounting the meeting with Vanessa Whitburn, and commenting: 'I know it's become very modern in TV soap operas, but I find it almost impossible to imagine in the context of *The Archers*.'[6] I then developed a theory about Jan's 'unrealisable hope':

Lyn: It would be – it would be interesting, I mean, in some things – I can't – I imagine that they entertain the idea, the scriptwriters and Vanessa Whitburn, you know, but it wouldn't be in any way, er – it would be something that they might be quite interested in including or developing, given their sort of general approach, but [*coughing*] I sort of imagine them being a bit frightened of the reaction of the more traditional bits of the audience.

Jan: Yes.

Lyn: Who are probably a very large part of the audience, um.

Jan: Yes. And probably have less of a problem dealing with

Lyn: With men.

Jan: Yes. And Sean and Peter in their nicely settled sort of way.

Lyn: And also in a sense although they're obviously now they're in the 'Cat and Fiddle' in the village in a big way, whereas it used to be less – it used to be referred to, um, but they're still not main characters in a way, are they?

(315–27)

The level of mutual understanding here is expressed by the fact that I complete Jan's sentence about the greater tolerance of gay men in mainstream media correctly, and that this is taken as a given, rather than a point to be argued. My analysis at the start of this extract firmly places me on Jan's side, and in the 'bit of the audience' which would welcome, rather than be threatened by, a lesbian character, thus confirming and reinforcing the shared culture of the discussion. The fact that I am also including Vanessa Whitburn and the production team in this follows on from Jan's references to the meeting with the producer. Both of these references are instances of the inclusion of production staff as characters in the ideal community of soap opera. Interestingly, here, this ideal community is an alternative feminist one, where a lesbian character might play a central role, whereas in the Wood Norton groups, it is characterised by a 'balanced' approach to the question of gender. The ideal community is thus clearly an extremely flexible notion, which is adapted to different reading cultures and contexts. It is also clear that like Mary in her response to my question on feminism we are differentiating between ourselves and a more conventional, less feminist 'mainstream' – the 'traditional bits of the audience', and that the notion of this 'Other' is a crucial part of the feminist identity being constructed.

Just as Mary and Ben could find almost no-one they liked, and certainly no-one they identified with in Ambridge, Jan comments: 'When I sort of boil it down, it's worrying how few [characters] I really like in a completely wholesome way.' Jan does not share Mary's fantasy of living in a place like Ambridge:

Jan: There can be a sort of slightly cloying feeling that makes me 'Oh, thank God, I don't live there', but I'm quite happy to listen in cos that – that's the way the whole village works. I mean, I wouldn't want to make my home there. But I like the eavesdropping feeling about it. And I have really liked Usha moving in. And I don't know what they're going to do with her now. She's gone very quiet.

Lyn: Again – yes.

Jan: Um, but I – but I suppose I was interested to see the whole thing through her eyes. And I wouldn't mind more sort of marginalised people living in – but I think it's unlikely. (.)

Lyn: Yes, yes. So in a way one of the pleasures is – I was just thinking as you were talking, why do we listen to this, you know, when it is quite conventional in many ways, and it's not really reflecting the kind of lives we lead – I mean, I shouldn't speak for other people but, you know, I don't think – I mean, I certainly don't live in a completely different world, you know, which doesn't – I mean, there are lots of ways in which I think, 'Uh, they should have done that', or, you know, they could have been experimental, um, but I still find I'm very compelled by it. Um, and it's almost like it's more interesting to listen to something where there's the sort of tantalising hope that something different might happen – you know, in this very conventional context.

Jan: Yes, and they do have threats to it, don't they, of developments and – it is, you know, the community is in – I mean, a bit like all this unemployment, low employment thing at the moment, but it's not static. And it does reflect some of the social changes that are going on. So I think that raises the hope that – um, it could – people could be challenged, I suppose. Or whether that's rather shocking – to think of, I mean, to think of Jill being challenged.

Lyn: Yes, you wouldn't want them to be too challenged, would you?

[*Laughter*]

(399–420)

The theme of Englishness returns here in an indirect way, since Jan mentions Usha, the only Asian character in *The Archers*, as one of the few examples of a person from a 'marginalised' group in the soap. There is a general identification with such groups, but the question of national or ethnic identity is not developed. The dominant issue here is the representation of gender and sexuality, perhaps as a result of Jan's own marginalisation by a programme where there are no lesbian characters, and where, as she says, female homosexuality, like cancer (until recently), is an unmentionable subject. It is not surprising that the fantasy of the spontaneous and warm connection with others which Mary (and others) associated with *The Archers* is not entirely shared by Jan; even if, like Mary, she says she would like to tell Jill all her troubles, she is also 'ambivalent' about Jill, finding her too complacent and moralising – the fantasy of a supportive, even utopian, community clearly has its limits. This extract also reflects the very high level of complicity between researcher and 'researched' which has developed, and it is interesting that I find myself speaking on Jan's behalf, again using the pronoun 'we'. Even though I correct myself, and am momentarily reduced to incoherence by this possible gaffe, the sense that we are speaking from a similar (though clearly not the same) place almost becomes a given in the relationship between myself and Jan from this point. She does not deny the similarity of our viewpoint, and in fact continues as if she is also identifying with my analysis. The joke at the end contains the essence of this version of fandom which consists of 'chafing' (Jan, line 490) against the programmes and expressing distance from the conventional gender relationships and wider society they depict, while at the same time needing this very stable status quo to persist. The conventional nature of the text makes it an effective spring-board for a distanced and critical reading.

Jan's choice of language to describe the lack of inhibition she feels in talking about being a fan of *The Archers* is revealing:

> *Jan*: Yes. I'm very open about it, cos I think some people are a bit closet, [*laughs*] about listening. Or they say things very irritating, like, 'I some-times catch it in the car', and then you find out that they know absolutely everything, so they must make much more of an effort than that suggests – to listen to it. But they're not going to own up to it. I do own up. I think it can be a very bonding thing.
>
> (476–80)

Here the language of gay and lesbian culture overlaps with that of *Archers* fandom in the use of the term 'closet', suggesting the embeddedness of the latter at least in some lesbian subcultures. Here Jan is talking about encounters outside her circles of friends (in fact while working abroad), and she demonstrates her awareness of the constraints involved in being a middle-class soap opera fan which have emerged in the rest of this research. As she says, she is not particularly affected by them, and is quite willing to talk about the extent of her involvement (though, like Mary and Ben, she expresses this later in the interview, and after the political critique):

> *Lyn*: But it's sort of one of the reasons that you listen, perhaps? That it's fairly predictable and the same characters –?
>
> *Jan*: Well, the thought of not listening is impossible.
>
> *Lyn*: Um, is it?
>
> *Jan*: I rarely miss (.) it would be like (.) I think I mean, I know they call us the *Archers* Addicts. I think there is something in that. I would feel very bereft if I, you know, resolved not to listen. But it's hard to quite pinpoint what the pleasures are.
>
> (506–12)

Jan uses the term 'addict' here, without any of the accompanying denials, qualifi-cations or irony which the term evoked even in the Wood Norton Hall groups, just as earlier she had referred to her '15 minutes hit'. The fact that 'the thought of not listening is impossible' is confirmed by the incomplete sentences in her final utterance – 'I rarely miss (.) it would be like (.)': the thought is so impossible it's actually unsayable. The term 'bereft' clearly implies a very strong level of emotional involvement, and can in some ways be equated with comments made by the Wood Norton Hall listeners about *The Archers* having become a second or surrogate family. In Jan's case, her position as a lesbian reader of *The Archers* means that she is automatically distanced from a text which focuses on heterosexual relationships and family life; once this, and her feminist analysis, have been declared in the interview she does not have to work quite as hard at establishing her identity as a critical and oppositional reader as a heterosexual couple, and is freer to express her involvement than Mary and Ben. Her ability to immerse herself in the narrative, and to declare her allegiance to the programmes also suggest that being an *Archers* fan is not particularly shocking in her circle of friends. Jan clearly participates in a feminist fan culture which derives both pleasure and frustration from the programmes' mainly conservative depiction of family life, sexuality and the utopian English village. Through the story about meeting Vanessa Whitburn she also refers to a specifically lesbian subculture, where the kind of romantic speculation which flourished in Wood Norton group 1 is replaced by another kind of 'unrealisable hope', for a lesbian character or couple in the village. This could clearly be the topic of further research; my conclusions here are based only on the interview with Jan, and on conversations with my own lesbian friends, for whom speculation about 'Vanessa's' sexuality is equally fascinating. The contrast between this interview and the previous two indicates the possibility of specific lesbian fan cultures, while the activity of narrative, and particularly romantic, speculation is common to almost all fan cultures around both *The Archers* and other soaps.

Telephone Interview with Louise

Louise was interviewed in early March 1999, about two weeks after Jan. Mary had explained to me that Louise was one of her postgraduate students, and I had exchanged e-mails with her to arrange the interview. Like Jan, Louise asked about the research, and I sent her the same reply. It emerged at the start of the interview that Mary and Louise had had a conversation about *The Archers*, and that this had led Mary to ask Louise if she could give me her number. Although Louise and Mary were friends outside work, Louise told me later that they did not often talk about *The Archers*. As a postgraduate student, Louise is similar in terms of education to the other participants in this phase of the research (who are educated at least to MA level). At the beginning of the interview Louise expressed some anxiety about whether she was 'an appropriate person' to answer my questions – I wondered if this concern may have stemmed from the student–teacher dynamic. In her response to the draft of this chapter, Louise questioned this view:

> I think perhaps you put too much emphasis on my student status (which I am not any longer!). I do in fact also teach at the University. ... Feeling

you are not a suitable person to be interviewed, from my experience is quite a common occurrence.

At thirty-four Louise is ten years or more younger than the others in this chapter, and this may also be a determining factor. Prior to becoming a student, Louise was working in community publishing and she also mentioned 'northern, working-class roots' in e-mail correspondence after the interview. Like the others, Louise was in a middle-class profession but she is the only person who specifically mentioned a working-class background. Mary and Ben focused on their Irish and American Jewish backgrounds, and Jan did not raise the issue. While she is not necessarily the only person of working-class origins in this sample, Louise was the only person who mentioned it, and this in itself may have some significance in terms of the identity she constructed in the interview. However, Louise's comments are a useful reminder that such interpretations must remain speculative.

The interview was shorter than Jan's, but about five minutes longer than the half-hour interview with Mary. Louise spoke more, compared to me, than Jan had done (though clearly much less overall) and much less, again compared to me, than Mary. Although Louise spoke a similar number of lines to Mary, her responses were shorter, with the result that I intervened more to ask questions and follow up on answers than I had done with Mary. It is also striking that while almost half of my interventions in the interview with Jan were as a fellow fan or audience member, and this was also a feature of the interview with Mary and Ben, here I made no such interventions at all. My utterances consisted of forty-five questions, fourteen affirmative comments (repetition or 'yes') and just two rather weak jokes – both aiming to be affirmative. This difference indicates that the recognition of a common culture of talk about *The Archers* did not take place here, and as a result this is a more classic research interview, where the researcher's interventions are almost entirely confined to questions and facilitation of the interviewee. The topic map also reveals differences from the other interviews discussed in this chapter, as well as some similarities with the Wood Norton Hall groups. The *Archers* audience was discussed quite substantially, mainly at the end of the interview, when I asked Louise if she had any further comments. In this sense Louise demonstrated similar preoccupations to the other participants, and an awareness of my research interests, which is not surprising, given her location in Higher Education. After this, however, the picture looks rather different, with modality, 'quality', intertextuality and character emerging as equally important topics. The importance of modality, 'quality' and character makes this interview more similar to the Wood Norton groups and telephone interviews than to the other interviews in this chapter. Although Louise said quite a lot about gender representation, this was in response to sustained questions from me, rather than spontaneous. There are few references to narrative developments, and Louise rarely spoke within the diegesis: this perhaps also indicates that Louise does not speak as a very involved fan in the same way as the other respondents in this research – the Wood Norton groups, Jan, and to some extent Mary and Ben.

Despite these differences, Louise described her positive feelings about the programme early in the interview:

> Um, well I mean – I guess I enjoy it – it's kind of become a ritual because I'm the Sunday morning Omnibus listener. ... And I actually really like having that big chunk on the Sunday – so I really enjoy like Sunday morning and put that on for an hour – and I sit in bed and have a cup of tea, so it's kind of become my Sunday morning ritual now.
>
> (43–5)

This meshing of the pleasure of listening with other rituals of domestic life is similar to the accounts provided in many of the questionnaires. Louise also described herself as a 'social' listener who enjoyed talking about the programme with her partner: 'but I listen much more intently on a Sunday, cos it'll usually be the first time I've heard those ones, whereas he might have heard some, so he dips in and out and then – we do end up talking about it afterwards' (60–2). However, the sustained talk, jokes and e-mails about *The Archers* which were a feature of Mary's, Ben's and Jan's relation to the programme were not part of Louise's description of talking about it with friends:

> *Lyn*: But do you talk about *The Archers* to other friends as well?
>
> *Louise*: I do, yes, if – I mean, (.) not – not that often. I guess it's kind of – I find like with any sort of soap, if there's something that, like, kind of happens, you know, John's death or something like that, and everybody's been listening to it, you know, because they didn't play the music at the end of it – this big thing, and you get caught into it. So, if it comes up in conversation sort of in passing, I will do.
>
> (67–71)

In this account of an altogether more casual kind of talk, the comment that it's like 'any sort of soap' is significant – suggesting that rather than specifically focusing on *The Archers* Louise and her friends would talk about particularly dramatic episodes in soaps generally. In this, Louise was very different from Mary, Ben and Jan, who hardly mentioned any other soaps.[7]

It is even more significant that in response to my first question about how long she had been listening, Louise described herself as a 'TV soap person', clearly placing *The Archers* among other programmes, rather than defining it as a special interest as the others had done:

> *Lyn*: Yes, Yes. Has it made you switch, or do you watch the TV soaps as well?
>
> *Louise*: I watch [*laughter*] soaps on telly. Yeah. I mean, I quite like soaps.
>
> *Lyn*: So this has just added another one?

> *Louise*: Yes. It's just another one to my sort of collection of listening and watching. Yes.
>
> (31–6)

The laughter in the middle of her sentence about watching TV soaps perhaps indicates a slight nervousness, or at least self-consciousness about saying this in an interview on *The Archers*. The self-definition as a TV soap person, and here the use of the familiar term 'telly', seem to contribute to the identification with popular culture which is a feature of the whole interview. This could be described as a kind of resistance to the 'highbrow' connotations of *The Archers* and Radio 4, which Louise clarified right at the end of the interview:

> *Louise*: … you talk to people about listening to *The Archers*, they're often people who don't watch any soaps on TV at all. Um, that's like a lot of my friends, you know, they – you can talk about *The Archers*, but then if I say, 'oh, you know, *Emmerdale*' they'll go, 'I don't watch TV'. And it'll be, like, '*Emmerdale*'s so similar to *The Archers*' and it'll – there's this sort of gulf there as well, that it's sort of – that *The Archers* is seen as being a kind of higher soap, because it's on Radio 4. Um, –
>
> *Lyn*: Um, um.That's interesting.You think that some people would listen to *The Archers* who would not take TV soaps at all seriously. Or think they were worth bothering with?
>
> *Louise*: Mm.Yes. I mean, my friend who lives above me, she is really anti-TV, and – but she listens to *The Archers* every evening. And you can have a conversation about *The Archers*, about oh, you know, 'blah, blah, blah, and Susan ran off', or something like that, but you couldn't talk about, you know, I don't know – you know, someone running off with someone in *Emmerdale* or something. It would be considered – you know, 'Oh, I don't watch TV' or, 'That's rubbish, that is'. And she has this connection that, you know, Radio 4 has got some kind of rubber stamp that means it's OK to have a soap on the radio and listen to it, but it's –
>
> (350–65)

Interestingly, the 'other' audience which Louise constructs might include the other people interviewed here who expressed a strong attachment to Radio 4 and even an investment in the 'quality' reputation of the programme and the medium. Like most accounts of the 'other audience', Louise's description of this 'high culture' appropriation of *The Archers* also serves to make her own position and identity clear: her references to TV soaps seem subversive of the notion of 'quality' popular culture which was strongly represented in the questionnaires, the Wood Norton groups, and even, in nuanced form, in the interviews discussed here. She is presenting herself as more culturally inclusive than her own view of the typical *Archers* listener.

Louise's resistance to the intellectualisation of popular programmes and pleasures was clearly a key to the lower profile which I took in this interview. Whereas
with Mary and Ben I had been able to join in the game of jokes and camp performance around *The Archers* and with Jan I had become involved in a feminist
discussion of the programmes, here Louise was resistant to these kinds of talk, and
even to some of the questions I asked. Like Mary, Ben and Jan she expressed
distance from the rural lifestyles depicted in *The Archers*; for example, she did not
have a favourite character 'cos they're – they're so far removed from my life,
farming, I mean, I have no concept of farming at all' (151–2). When I questioned
her further about whether this difference from her own life was one of the attractions of *The Archers*, she seemed unwilling to enter into this kind of analysis: 'Um, I
don't know really.(.) I don't know. I don't know whether there is something there or
just that I quite like the escapism that soaps offer me' (159–60). This notion of
watching soaps for the escapist pleasures they provide was reiterated later in the
interview when I asked Louise about the women characters in *The Archers*. Her
response on this issue was a mixture of feminist analysis and unwillingness to
engage in such a discussion. Her first thought was that the Ambridge women were
'a bit mumsy' and when I asked her what she would like the women characters to
be like, her reply was quite ambivalent:

> *Louise*: I don't know, really. I mean, I don't listen to *The Archers* or watch TV
> to get, like, a positive, like, role models of women – you know what I
> mean? Obviously I don't want to see sort of – some of ways they're
> portrayed, where it doesn't – I don't feel any sort of need to identify with
> any characters or – I mean, they all seem – not all of them – again, I
> guess cos there's quite a lot of sort of middle-ageish, kind of women.
> With families, and stuff. But I have that sense of them being mumsy,
> whatever. But that doesn't – it doesn't really bother me. I don't sort of –
> because I don't think, 'I wish they were all career women' cos it would be
> a bit odd in a farming community. And all work. Although, I mean, there
> are actually some – sort of strong – there's Ruth isn't there and Debbie.
> So they've actually got more, haven't they? Like with Shula going into
> business. So, yes, I suppose there are quite a few – and Hayley's quite a
> strong character.
>
> (246–56)

On the one hand, Louise is quite determined to keep the pleasures of watching
TV and listening to radio separate from the kind of analysis of representations
which the question implied. Her resistance to intellectualising these pleasures is
expressed strongly: 'I don't listen to *The Archers* or watch TV to get, like, a positive,
like, role models of women.' At the same time, the rest of the answer shows that
she *is* concerned about how the women characters are represented. Later in the
discussion Louise's contention that the positive representation of women is a baseline for her interest in the programme also suggests that she holds feminist views:
'There are a lot of strong characters, strong women characters in it. But, I mean,

I – maybe I just expect that that there would be?' (268–9). Like Jan and Mary, the fact that there are strong women characters does not lead her to agree that the programme is being taken over by feminists, or that it is feminist, again suggesting that like them she sees the gender politics of the programme as conservative or liberal. She provides a feminist analysis of why *The Archers* might have been written about in these terms: 'maybe, it's this thing that in the past men have always dominated and now women are more up in there that people think, you know, it's becoming a feminist programme, which I don't think it is at all, is it?' (274–6). My interpretation of these comments – that Louise was torn between her feminist ideas and resistance to analysis of a programme she enjoys – seems to be supported by the fact that she returned to this issue near the end of the discussion:

Lyn: Yes, yes. OK then. Is there anything else you want to say, or things that particularly you like or don't like about it? Um, cos otherwise I think that's about it, actually.

Louise: No, I can't really. Um, I guess, cos I – you know, it's not what I'm engaged on perhaps – that I feel that I engage on perhaps a superficial level, when I listen to it. And part of the pleasure of listening to it I think is not having to –

Lyn: Think about it!

[*Laughter*]

Louise: Think about it! You know what I mean?

Lyn: Absolutely. Yes.

Louise: Think about the portrayal of women, and stuff like that. Um –

Lyn: That would make it into work.

Louise: It would make it into work. Kind of, like, oh no – and it's actually. I mean, obviously, I think cos they do have strong women in there, if they were all completely pathetic, then I probably wouldn't listen to it at all. So, on a subconscious level I probably pick out those certain things that I, you know what I mean, I do like? Or want out of something I'm going to listen to. Cos I don't want to be listening to some, um, male programme with the odd woman.

(329–45)

This extract demonstrates that although the shared culture around *The Archers* which manifested itself in the interviews with Jan and Mary and Ben did not emerge here, there were moments of collusion between researcher and researched. The fact that I finish some of Louise's sentences, and that she does not object, and my rather heartfelt empathy with the view that analysing *The Archers* makes it into work, are indicative of this.

Louise's position on class in *The Archers* was very similar to the views she expressed on gender – she was critical about the representations, but ambivalent about going down the critical road:

> Yeah, well, it is, I think it is a bit of a caricature, but I – I find it quite entertaining though. I mean, um, – but if I was a family like, you know, what that was based on I might not be too happy about the way it was kind of portrayed overall.

Modality provided her with a means of making value judgements about *The Archers* which she seemed to feel more at ease with, presumably since unlike questions of representation it is a central discourse in non-academic talk about media texts; it also allowed her to make comparisons with other soaps, and thus maintain the identity of a TV soap person which she had constructed right at the beginning of the interview. She complained that in soap operas such as *EastEnders* or *Brookside*, there were too many 'violent deaths and murders' whereas *The Archers*, like *Coronation Street*, 'kind of plods along at a sort of normal pace' (201). She later associated this slower pace with greater realism:

> Yeah, I mean, I think that I do like – I guess I like that about *The Archers*, the way that they do carry on the things like that. But they don't blow it up into a huge thing. It's just sort of, very – show it as you know, normal life.

> (230–3)

In some ways this could appear to be a reversal of her espousal of the TV soaps in the face of criticism from people who see *The Archers* as a 'higher soap'. She certainly does make the association of realism with quality which was a feature of the Wood Norton Hall discussions. However, the pleasures of stability and of the domestic ritual she described at the beginning also seem to be at stake here. What she likes about *The Archers* is 'the safe pace it tends to go at'; Louise's 'safe pace' is similar to Jan's 'anchor' or Mary's 'structure' – the fixed point in daily life provided by a programme which has been running for over fifty years, and which even at its most dramatic moments does not omit the village fête, the cricket club dinner or the harvest festival. The difference in Louise's case is that she does not combine the pleasures to be found in this stability with critique of the liberal politics underpinning the representations. She expresses neither intense involvement nor a corresponding need to distance herself, and if she describes herself as enjoying the programmes slightly less recently, this is because she's 'overkilled on soaps'.

Conclusion

The Wood Norton Hall groups emphasised that they saw *The Archers* as a reflection of real life, and on the whole could identify with, and relate to, the characters; indeed, one of their main ways of being critical of the programmes was to cite instances when realism was not achieved. In contrast Mary, Ben and Jan (and Louise to some extent) described *The Archers* as a representation of a reality which was completely alien to them and to their lives and showed much less concern about how realistic the programmes were. This was also unlike *Morse* group 2, whose feminist critique often deployed the discourse of modality: the representation of women was found to be unrealistic. Here, distance was expressed in overtly political terms, particularly by Mary and Jan, both in relation to general political issues and specifically to gender and sexuality: representations of gender were more often found inadequate or limited than unrealistic. This is in part a reflection of the very different context: a high degree of trust and complicity was established between researcher and researched, and the meeting of several complete strangers in *Morse* group 2 was not replicated in these one-to-one or small group interviews. As a result, identity and political views could be expressed more directly, particularly in the telephone interviews and questionnaires. However, like some of the participants in *Morse* group 2, Mary, Ben and Jan did not share the Wood Norton Hall groups' belief in the socially positive and progressive nature of these representations and in their educational potential. In political terms, the programmes were a source of dissatisfaction and even frustration.

Even though, as we have seen, various forms of critical reading took place in the Wood Norton groups, here there was far more emphasis on the distance between the participants' own identities and the text. This stemmed in part from the political positions described above, but also from actual social differences – Mary and Ben are Irish and American, respectively, and Jan is lesbian, whereas the Wood Norton participants almost all identified as English, and at the very least, there was a heterosexual majority in each group.[8] As well as being more overtly political than the Wood Norton groups, and even than *Morse* group 2, the mode of critical reading here was noticeably academic, particularly in the Mary and Ben interview, in terms of language used, understanding of the research event and efforts to provide me with answers to my imagined research questions rather than just talk about *The Archers*. Unlike Liebes and Katz my concern here is not to define and quantify the various dimensions of a critical reading, or the likely 'protection' it offers against the ideology of the text, but rather to determine the social role played by making critical (i.e. negative) comments or by being critical (i.e. analysing the text) in the various research events I have described. The analysis of this social role has led to a consideration of the kinds of identities and cultural allegiances which are constructed in these events. One of my main aims in this phase of the research was to locate feminist readings of *The Archers* – in the case of Mary, Ben and Jan, it does not seem controversial to comment that a strong feminist identity emerges in this talk, and that it is closely allied with the academic and analytical distance I have described. It is important to note, however, that while feminisms certainly informed their responses, and in some cases a feminist identity was quite overtly claimed, this was combined with a number of other discourses or identity claims in a complex and shifting manner. A second important proviso is that the kind of feminisms expressed here are clearly specific to this particular social milieu – which can be described as professional middle class (and predominantly academic), middle aged and white. Louise's interview is a useful reminder that the expression of feminist politics or attitudes does not necessarily take this form: while clearly expecting a certain level of feminist awareness in the gender representations in the text, Louise does not here describe or participate in the kind of intellectual games around *The Archers* which are a particular feature of the interview with Mary and Ben.

These games seem to be a fundamental part of a very specific form of *Archers* fan culture which combines feminist and left-wing politics, academic analysis (resulting in part from education to postgraduate level) and varying combinations of irony, camp humour and performance of fandom. The programme's conservative and conventional elements could become the 'mainstream other' against which the members of this culture defined themselves. One of the most significant aspects of this process was about differentiating oneself from the overwhelmingly English and middle-class 'niceness' of *The Archers* – by being less than polite about the inhabitants of Ambridge, or discussing the possibility of something as shocking as paedophilia in Glebe Cottage. To this extent, there is some similarity with Ien Ang's analysis of her ironic viewers who are claiming not only distance from, but also superiority to, the text through this mode of reading (Ang, 1985). Mary, particularly, did describe the pleasures of feeling different and superior to the text, and especially to its Englishness. However, unlike Ien Ang's ironic viewers, Ben, Mary and Jan all emphasised their capacity to be moved by the programmes. Arguably Louise, the person who was least analytical in relation to the programmes (although she did provide a cogent analysis of the audience), also expressed the least emotional involvement. The play around the text – pretending the Archers are real people or speculating about a lesbian romance in Ambridge – is accompanied, particularly in the case of Jan and Ben, by high levels of commitment and involvement – feeling bereft at the thought of no longer listening or organising one's life to be available to listen. It would be inappropriate to comment, like Ien Ang, that these listeners enjoy not the programme 'but the irony they bring to bear on it' (1985: 96).

Perhaps unlike the uniformly melodramatic *Dallas*, *The Archers* permits both distance and involvement for ironic viewers, since it contains a greater range of characters and registers. As I have argued, it also combines tradition and modernity, and adds a hint of subversiveness to a fundamentally conservative structure, whether in the form of attacks on genetically modified crops by a member of the Archer family, or the albeit marginal presence of gay characters in Ambridge. There is enough material there to appeal to the kind of culture I have described in this chapter and to generate a more engaged relationship with the text than that which Ang describes. These elements also feed a form of narrative speculation which is particular to this culture and focuses on how far the scriptwriters and producers will dare to go in this direction. Crucially the producers of the programme are seen as having to curtail their radical tendencies for the sake of the broader audience, so that the identification between audience and textual producers, and the fantasy of becoming the latter, are maintained, even in this group. At Wood Norton, the identification and fantasy were similar, but in that case they depended on a view of the producers as committed to the maintenance of a typically BBC, liberal balance in the programmes, and the very 'niceness' which is critiqued here. As I have also suggested, the script-writing of *The Archers* contains its own version of self-reflexive, and at times ironic, humour, and readers such as Mary and Ben are able to recognise and collude with the jokes about characters who never speak, for instance.[9] This also leads to a further crucial difference from Ien Ang's analysis of ironic viewers where ironic commentary leads only to 'a superior relation to' the programme (1985: 97). In general the kind of commentary which Mary and Ben make does not seem to have the sole aim of 'dominating' the textual object which Ang ascribes to her ironic viewers. The fact that the text constantly provides its own commentary and contains moments of irony, excess and camp humour, such as Julia's discovery of Nelson's stilettos, means that ironic readers are not merely laughing at, but also with, the programmes. The kind of subversive juxtapositions made in the talk are to a limited extent present in the programmes' own humour: Lynda Snell's aromatherapy massage being mistaken for prostitution, or Nelson's amateur dramatics as transvestism. These readers' appreciation of these elements leads to a different definition of 'quality' than that found in the Wood Norton groups or in *Morse* group 1. Here 'quality' incorporates exactly the kind of satirical cleverness and postmodern self-awareness that these readers demonstrate in their talk about the text. A further dimension of pleasure, and perhaps of subcultural belonging, is provided by the opportunity to differentiate oneself from the 'ideology of mass culture' position described by Ien Ang. *The Archers* is 'mainstream' enough to be reclaimed by left-wing intellectuals anxious to affirm their enjoyment of popular culture, while at the same time enjoying its high culture or 'quality' components such as clever script-writing and acting.

A common characteristic of all the talk about *The Archers* I have analysed (and arguably the *Morse* research) is the tendency to construct an identity in opposition to some other grouping. Part of the pleasure of *The Archers* consisted of being in a cultural group with other listeners *from which others are excluded*. In both the Wood Norton Hall groups and here, being in on a secret which non-listeners don't understand is part of the fun. In the Wood Norton Hall groups these excluded others could be younger people who would see *Archers* fans as 'sad' or perhaps even people who are not as 'nice' as *Archers* fans! For Mary and Ben they were left-wing intellectuals who would disapprove of soap opera, for Jan perhaps 'closet' *Archers* listeners. For Louise, they might be people who would integrate *The Archers* into 'high culture'. All of these constructions of 'the other' are associated with an image of the 'mainstream', which the speaker is at pains to differentiate themselves from. The parallel with Thornton's research on the use of the term 'mainstream' in youth dance cultures suggests a similar process of claiming identity in these more middle-aged and middle-class contexts.

Chapter Seven

Conclusion

One of my aims in this research was to assess the influence of feminisms on 'mainstream' media texts produced by dominant players in the media industry and attracting large audiences. The fact that representations of women in the original novels on which *Inspector Morse* is based were substantially changed for television, or that masculinity takes on new forms in the television text, indicates that gender is no longer the unified and monolithic category it once was. In 1997 I wrote that if representations of femininity in *The Archers* had evolved dramatically since the series began in 1951, the male characters seemed largely stuck in a cricket bat- and pint mug-wielding rut. In the early years of the new century, the 'new women' of Ambridge seem a media commonplace, whereas in terms of masculinity the series is arguably breaking new ground.[1] On 22 June 2000, Phil Archer's qualms about talking to his son about his daughter-in-law Ruth's cancer – 'David and I don't … I'm no good at that kind of thing' – proved ill-founded: the programme ended with an emotional scene between the two men, and with David in tears, accepting his father's emotional support. My original aim of 'looking for feminism where one might not expect to find it' seems to have been fulfilled; gender representations in these apparently 'traditional' British media texts are no longer easy to categorise, and modern masculinities, particularly, are represented in ways unimaginable even a few years ago. In this sense, feminisms can no longer be seen as a marginal cultural presence, confined, in media terms, to late night slots on TV channels catering for minority interests (such as Channel 4 in the UK).

Feminisms were a notable influence in the talk about these texts which I analysed. My original characterisation of the two *Morse* groups as 'mainstream' and 'feminist subculture' (see Thomas, 1995) constructed a crude binary, which was complicated and questioned by the *Archers* research, where it was clear that a range of fan cultures were emerging. Furthermore, the term 'subculture' seemed inappropriate for the description of the research events analysed here, and on the whole I have avoided it, since it implies a more permanent and clearly defined mode of cultural belonging than it is possible to study in this kind of research, which does not claim to be ethnographic. While participants in these interviews and focus groups clearly are drawing on particular kinds of cultural and subcultural capital, it is also evident that the views expressed and the mode of talk are unique to, and determined by, the specific dynamics of the events themselves, and in that sense are very far from permanent fixtures. Similarly the identities constructed in this talk – including feminist identities – are far from permanent. Feminism is one of many determining factors (both material and discursive) in the construction of identity. Here I have attempted to analyse how it intersects with determinants such as gender, ethnicity, class, age and sexuality, in a small number of precise contexts. I have also attempted to analyse these contexts in as much detail as space permits.

In the Wood Norton Hall groups, the belief in positive social change encompassed the view that the position of women had significantly improved in the second half of the twentieth century, and that this was a good thing. This was substantially different from the feminist politics expressed by the small group of friends discussed in Chapter 6, and in *Morse* group 2, where dissatisfaction with the status quo both in and out of the texts was the order of the day. In the latter two contexts, my research touched on the issue of what it means to construct a feminist identity in talk about media texts. These discussions took place outside academia, but were clearly influenced by it. Given the dominance of academic feminism it is hardly surprising that the most academic respondents also 'came out' as feminists to varying degrees. As well as the perhaps unsurprising emphasis on deconstructing gender representations in this talk, a form of feminist subcultural capital which was heavily dependent on irony and tinged with camp humour emerged. In these contexts, conventional femininity could be espoused (being 'in love' with Inspector Morse or worrying about soap opera characters) without loss of feminist credentials, thanks to the distancing powers of ironic humour and camp exaggeration. *Morse* and *The Archers* proved to be the ideal textual objects for this combination of intimacy and distance: their popularity and popular genres protecting feminist fans from charges of élitism, their 'quality' acting and scripts nonetheless confirming the links between feminist subcultural and cultural capital *tout court*. The textual inscription of camp elements in *The Archers* made this text highly suitable for feminist appropriations. In Bourdieuian terms, the appropriation of popular texts by feminist intellectuals permitted a simultaneous display and denial of cultural capital: the mode of talk providing the necessary distancing and intellectual display, with the choice of text suggesting a capacity for cultural breadth, encompassing the popular.[2]

It seems important, however, to recognise the role of pleasure in these relationships to media texts; they are not chosen purely in order to construct a certain feminist self-image, but because of the pleasures that they can offer to 'a modern middle-class female orientation', to quote Ben. One of these pleasures, as the interviews with Jan and with Mary and Ben suggested, is indeed the playful juxtaposition of subversive readings and conventional narrative, such as lesbian romance in a village setting dominated by families. However, emotional involvement is at least equally important: crying when a character is 'killed off' by the scriptwriters, leaving work early to catch *The Archers* or learning how to programme the video to avoid missing *Morse*. The pleasures of irony clearly have their limits, and it is the combination of ironic and playful talk with the more conventional pleasures of following a narrative and becoming fond of fictional characters which constituted the fascination of these 'quality' texts for these critical readers. Clearly, the 'quality' element, as well as permitting the construction of the 'discerning fan identity', is crucial to these more conventional pleasures for the predominantly middle-class viewers and listeners I have studied here.

All of this complicates the hierarchy of taste constructed by Bourdieu, in terms of which the 'quality' claimed for these texts raises them slightly from their other-wise middle-brow status. In analysing the 'pure gaze' of intellectuals, who focused on form rather than content, and played games with the texts, as well as the rejec-tion of avant-garde forms by more 'middle-brow' taste, I have produced some empirical illustrations of Bourdieu's theory. And yet, it is also clear that the picture is more complicated than his structures would suggest, and that the purest of gazes is interested in content and narrative, as well as the niceties of form. While the desire to present oneself as a critical reader of the texts placed constraints on the expression of this involvement, none of my respondents were able to disguise or deny their emotional investment completely, and this engagement traversed all of the very varied reading cultures analysed here, suggesting that the strong contrast between distance and involvement in Bourdieu's 'legitimate' and 'illegitimate' cultures presents an excessively unidimensional view of middle-class intellectual taste. The differences between class-based taste cultures identified by Bourdieu exist, but they are fissured rather than monolithic structures, interrogated, and even undermined by similarities which cross these groupings. The pleasure derived from enthusiastic engagement with a low status text in these varying cultural contexts also suggests that individuals do not necessarily define themselves or allow themselves to be defined according to Bourdieuian cultural hierarchies. The '*Archers* Addicts' in Chapter 5 were aware that they might be considered mad or sad by others: if anything this merely added to the pleasure of pretending the Archers were real people. Mary and Ben told a long story about receiving a message on Ben's brother's answerphone while on holiday in Israel. A friend rang to update them on the soap storyline when Shula's husband Mark was killed in a car crash. When Ben's brother heard the message and thought it was about friends who had been in a serious car accident, they were convulsed with laughter in the face of his serious sympathy. The delight of being frivolous, even to the point of rudeness, momentarily overwhelmed the persona of the serious and socially conscious intellectual.

It has also become clear that gender is a major complicating factor, which is not encompassed by Bourdieu's theory of taste. It would be possible to add gender to the Bourdieuian hierarchy simply by placing specifically 'feminine' cultural tastes alongside other most culturally disparaged forms. However, a more complex picture emerges here. As a soap opera, *The Archers* is clearly culturally marked as 'feminine'. Although *Inspector Morse* belongs to a genre traditionally considered 'masculine', the emphasis on the personal, the 'soap-like' structure of a long-running series and the 'new/old' masculinity represented by Morse, have the effect of feminising the text. In my empirical work I have interviewed a number of men who were willing to enter this feminine territory, suggesting that the cultural deval-orisation of the feminine is less prevalent than it once was. The *Morse* research telephone interviews (which are only partially analysed here) were conducted with six men and three women. Most of these men spoke at length about Morse's character and personal life, just as in the *Archers* focus groups Norman, Tim and Ben are on the whole happy to discuss character and relationships. Even in the *Archers* questionnaire one quarter of the sample were men. While I would be far from denying the importance of gender differences, I have found a less exact correspondence between gender and cultural taste than some previous research. This results in part from the intersectionality of determinants already discussed, but may also suggest the possibility of less rigid gender identities in at least some social contexts.

The interview with Mary and Ben was particularly interesting from this point of view. *Archers* fandom seemed to provide Ben not only with an ironic but implicated relationship to Englishness, but also with a way of constructing a form of masculinity likely to appeal to female professional colleagues, his feminist partner and her friends. Being a soap opera fan gave Ben access to a 'feminine' culture, while his academic background allowed him to participate in feminist analysis of the programme. However, perhaps the most striking aspect of his mode of talk about *The Archers* was the element of camp performance, which seemed to allow Ben to transgress at least some of the boundaries of conventional heterosexual masculinities. As Pamela Robertson has argued, camp 'enables not only gay men, but also heterosexual women and lesbian women, and perhaps heterosexual men, to express their discomfort and alienation from the normative gender and sex roles assigned to them by straight culture' (1999: 271). I would not evoke a fully Butlerian paradigm to describe this version of masculinity, or attribute to it quite the level of subversive potential which she has claimed for 'gender parody' in some of her writing (Butler, 1990). Nonetheless, it does seem to question conventional masculinities, and in that sense I would see it as a positive cultural development. As I have suggested earlier, this heterosexual male camp identity, constructed for a feminist audience, indicates that the questioning of gender identities is not the unique privilege of the social and cultural margins invoked both by Butler and by Schwichtenberg. Two further complications immediately spring to mind; the first of these is the role of ethnic and national identity, in that Ben's hybridity as a Jewish American living in Britain perhaps contributes as much to his ability to step outside cultural norms of masculinity as the 'vaguely academic and left-wing' milieu he inhabits. Evidence of such interrelationships seems to be a strength of empirical work, a useful corrective to the tendency of some theory to focus exclusively on gender and sexuality, as well as an area for further research.

The second point concerns the constraints and pressures imposed by the social context in which this 'new masculinity' emerged. Ben's feminised masculinity does not exist in a cultural vacuum, but in relation to his feminist audience. In a reversal of Bourdieu's paradigm, Ben's camp performance of soap opera fandom could be read as an object of exchange between the two women for whom he performs. Lovell asks: 'How may the existence of women as objects – as repositories of capital for someone else – be curtailing or enabling in terms of their simultaneous existence as capital-accumulating subjects?' (2000: 22). It does not seem excessively utopian to suggest that in the early twenty-first century in at least some social milieus both men and women can play object and subject, and that these roles might be interchangeable. However, Ben's success in appealing to a feminist audience needs to be read alongside Jim's failure. Jim is collectively rejected by the members of *Morse* group 2, understandably, on the grounds of his politics, but also because the version of masculinity he constructs (knowing the answer, knowing how things work) is deeply unappealing. On one level it seems a good thing that women no longer have to feign being impressed by men who don't impress them. On another, however, the analysis of this event leaves an uncomfortable feeling, like Seiter's troubling interview (Seiter, 1990). It is perhaps here, in the face of inequality, that feminism operates most clearly as a form of cultural capital.

Feminist cultural capital was also an issue in the interview with Louise, where the subtext seemed to be resistance to academic feminist textual analysis (though not to feminist politics). This resistance was expressed in part by reluctance to participate in the analysis of gender representation in the programmes, in part more directly, as a critique of left-wing intellectual appropriations of *The Archers*. Louise was aware of the importance of the 'quality' dimension of *The Archers* to such listeners and the disguised cultural élitism it implies. Similarly, the account Mary gave of her son Liam's views is telling: 'There really are poor people struggling in the countryside and you're spending your time playing academic games.' I am not suggesting that the kind of play around a media text which I have analysed here is morally or politically wrong; playing games with fictional narratives seems to me to be an innocent enough pleasure. These comments do, however, raise the broader question of contemporary feminisms' espousal of 'academic games'. If feminist play around a text is a well-established leisure activity, perhaps its dominance as a form of feminist intellectual intervention now needs to be questioned. This may involve carefully examining the methodologies of feminist academic work, and asking questions about its contribution to political, social and cultural change.

Reflection on my own methodology is the last, and clearly crucial, element of this conclusion. Many of my original centres of interest, it is now clear, were questioned by my empirical work, and, to a lesser extent, by the textual analysis. Questions of national and ethnic identity were at least as significant as gender in the talk about these texts. On one level this was to be expected: the most significant link between *Inspector Morse* and *The Archers* is the programmes' role in constructing national identity and in representing Englishness and, to some extent, Britishness, in both cases for national audiences and for *Morse* also in international contexts. Nonetheless, I was surprised by the enthusiasm generated by these representations, and by the lack of irony expressed in relation to Englishness both in *Morse* group 1 and Wood Norton group 2: 'I always did like them going, at the end of the programme, the episodes, went to the pub, I thought that was great, you know, just so human and real, British' (Matthew, *Morse* group 1). However, the research also explored more distanced, ambivalent and ironic responses to these representations. Further research, with a more ethnically diverse group of respondents, would be highly desirable, and would doubtless yield a still more complex picture.

In relation to both texts, as is evident from the discussion above, masculinities, and more specifically the relationship of masculinities to feminisms, became a more significant issue than I had imagined at the outset. The representation of the heterosexual couple, and of single people, which was my predominant concern at the beginning of the *Morse* research, faded into relative insignificance. The research revealed a match between my own ironic, and even slightly camp, mode of writing about these texts and the talk about them analysed in *Morse* group 2 and Chapter 6. However, the analysis of *Morse* group 1, the *Archers* fan club weekend, focus groups and questionnaire, and in a different way the interview with Louise, took me out of my own cultural milieu, into very different territory. A critical analysis of the feminist 'left-wing and vaguely academic' culture which I, like Ben, inhabit has emerged, an awareness of its constraints and limitations as well as its ability to question conventional gender identities. This awareness relies, in part, on the range of events analysed here: the contrast between the censorship of emotion in *Morse* group 2, and the expression of enthusiastic involvement in *Morse* group 1, the negotiation of the apparent contradiction between 'quality' text and addiction to a soap, the ability to enthuse about romance while describing one's own life-history in feminist terms. Without the empirical work, these complexities, and this range of readings, appropriations of media texts and cultural moments, would not have emerged. Whatever the shortcomings and difficulties of empirical audience research, at the end of this project I remain convinced of its value. I have been surprised by the data at many points, and some of my own prejudices and attitudes have been called into question: my account of the *Archers* fan club weekend is a case in point.

The multi-method approach adopted here has proved a useful way of collecting different kinds of responses to media texts, and, at times, of making comparisons. The questionnaire survey of *Archers* listeners gave access to a larger sample, and hence the possibility of 'grounding' the more detailed discussion of the focus groups and telephone interviews. However, in isolation, the questionnaire method would have had severe limitations. It seems important to note this, given the tendency to rely on written data in some feminist audience research. In both the telephone interviews and focus groups I have developed a method of analysis which combines numerical measures with careful reading and re-reading of transcripts and attention to linguistic features. The tapes were also listened to several times, and particular attention was paid to intonation, emphasis, unfinished phrases and sentences, interruptions, and so on. In all of these events, my own role as researcher was, in different ways, significant, and the analysis of this role, and of my own investments, has been central to this research. My final comment on all of this would be that at every level of this research, recruiting respondents, interviewing them or facilitating focus groups, and analysing the talk, the skills I have needed and have deployed have been those of femininity. Throughout, I felt conscious of a match between these skills, which I acquired in childhood and adolescence, and the requirements of my research. Perhaps the relatively high response rates in this research are in part a reflection of my desire to nurture my respondents and the positive reaction it inevitably produced. This was translated literally, in the *Morse* research, into providing food and wine for the focus groups; in the research on *The Archers* it was more a concern to avoid the uneven dynamics of

Morse group 2, to ensure that everyone felt their words were valued. Further reflection on the psychic and social resources one brings to this kind of project, on the gendered, classed and 'raced' persona of the researcher, as well as on her tasks, responsibilities and activities, would without doubt be beneficial. The parallels and differences between teaching and researching, in attention to group dynamics and to issues of equality for instance, are also a subject I would like to explore further.

The final phase of the research was perhaps the most testing in this respect. As the research progressed I became increasingly aware of the ethical dimension and concerned that my respondents should feel happy about their participation and about how they had been 'written up'. This was less a feature of the *Morse* research, than that on *The Archers*, partly because of the more longitudinal nature of the latter, and partly because of my growing awareness of research as a process. I therefore sent drafts of Chapters 5 and 6 to the people involved in each chapter. Of the eight 'Chapter 5' respondents, five replied with comments. Of these, four (Alice, Tim and Janet and Norman) commented positively on the chapter and on the way it had represented them as *Archers* fans. Tim and Janet commented: 'We do feel, Lyn, that you showed considerable perception in your assessment of our feelings concerning *The Archers*.' They went on to discuss recent storylines and concluded: 'perhaps we may meet up again at another *Archers* weekend'. Alice found herself 'quite amazed at the detailed analysis of what I thought was just a pleasant chat' and described other '*Archers* Addicts' events she had attended since.

It is clear from these responses that I am being addressed, in part at least, as a fellow fan. Viv was the only member of this group who seriously questioned my interpretations. Her main point concerned my suggestion that her choice of 'favourite characters' was connected with an identification with working-class or lower middle-class characters with Midlands accents – Sid and Hayley, and by extension, Sid's wife, Kathy. Viv disagreed: 'The fact that I have a special interest in Sid and Kathy is entirely due to the compelling (for me) storyline of Kathy's affair with Dave Barry and her subsequent break-up and reconciliation with Sid.' She goes on to attack the notion that there is a class- or region-based identification at stake: 'It was simply a good story and I'm sure I would have found it just as riveting had Sid been Welsh, a Yorkshireman, upper-class or even one of the Archer family.' Viv's comments (along with the others discussed below) indicate first of all the numerous possibilities of interpretation which research of this kind presents. It is a useful caution, reminding me, and other empirical researchers, of the partiality of our analyses, and of the need to declare this partiality, and their inevitable limitations. However, it also indicates both the sensitivity of the class issue in contemporary Britain, and the fact that people see themselves as individuals and are shocked to find themselves assigned to a category by a researcher, however tentatively. The fact that I had touched on a sensitive issue is revealed by other comments made by Viv. First, she commented that she lived in a village, not Wolverhampton, then that 'I do find it easier to express myself in writing so probably this is why I sounded "uneasy" on the tape. While I am conscious of my Midlands accent, I don't think it is a Brummie one.' All of this suggests that whatever Viv's motivations for her interest in characters such as Sid and Hayley, what I said in my discussion about the low status associated with Midlands accents was far from inaccurate, and indeed seems to be an issue for Viv. In reply I sent her a friendly letter, suggesting that my own Midlands background had perhaps influenced my interpretation of her responses. I have so far received no reply, which may mean that I have moved irrevocably into the researcher rather than fellow fan camp (until then Viv had been assiduous in replying to all communications).

Perhaps predictably, Mary, Ben, Jan and Louise all sent quite detailed comments. Ben described the experience of reading the chapter as 'weird and delicious', but it was Mary who eventually sent a long, typed letter. Most of Mary's comments were positive: 'I found it all fascinating and was intrigued by your account where it touched on the interactions between me and Ben and you too.' Like Viv, however, Mary found that in some ways my written text did not match up to her image of herself:

> I was rather horrified at how poorly my spoken text translates into written text on the page. The inarticulate utterances – no clear sentences, repeats, unfinished thoughts and so on – sat uneasily with your kind descriptions of me as some kind of thoughtful serious intelligent academic person!

Mary's point here raises a broader ethical question for empirical audience research – the representation of the respondents' spoken words in a written text. There is a conflict between the researcher's desire for accuracy and the need to avoid 'shaming' the respondents in the way Mary describes. I can think of at least one case in this research where I was tempted to correct someone's grammar, in order to pre-empt any negative judgements that might be made of the person. The rights and wrongs of this are a question for further debate, and are related to the 'nurturing femininity' mode of research mentioned above.

In one area, however, Mary was not happy with what I had written:

> What I do feel uncomfortable with, and I appreciate that this is integral to your thesis, is the description of me as 'Irish'. This isn't any kind of inaccuracy on your part, but rather a symptom of my own ambivalence about national identity.

She went on to discuss the issue in depth and eventually to provide the descriptors for herself, Ben and Jan which I use in the chapter, and which are much more nuanced in relation to ethnic and national identity than my original versions. Mary's letter confirms the importance of these questions here, and in the construction of identity in talk about media texts more generally. Like Viv she is reacting against the convenient labels used by researchers which ignore the complexity of lived experience: 'I feel too categorised'.

Jan had a generally positive and enthusiastic response, though she, like Mary, was concerned to nuance the image of her which I had presented: 'I came over as almost exclusively concerned with gender/sexuality, whereas I am very interested in class and in the marginalised in Ambridge.' She also made an interesting point in relation to Englishness, commenting that as her parents are Australian she is 'first generation English':

> I have struggled with this – particularly as I cannot identify as Australian in any meaningful way. ... I suspect I was drawn to *The Archers* as some kind of surrogate English family / community with which I could identify and – quite importantly – learn from.

Interestingly, Louise made a similar point:

> I grew up overseas, mainly in Hong Kong, and despite technically being 'fully' English I have never felt it ... perhaps one of the attractions for me is the creation of a family life and community life which is very alien to me but something I think it would be nice to have.

All of this supports the points made earlier about the importance of representations of Englishness in *The Archers*, and the reassurance they provide, even to listeners who would question their ideological basis.

Louise's response generally was the most challenging. She questioned my interpretation of her nervousness at the start of the interview (substantially re-written in the light of her comments). She also reacted to the fact that I had marked out the interview with her as different from those with the other respondents in the chapter:

> I'm not sure that I would consider myself less intellectual than other *Archers* listeners!! I just listen for entertainment. ... I've wondered about this and about how I am different from the other contributors. ... I think sometimes the analysis forgets this was a fairly short interview, we had never met before and I do not engage in discussions about *The Archers* in ways that some of your other contributors do.

Again there seems to be a reaction here against being 'categorised' by a researcher, even when the category consists of the respondent's own words: 'I'm not sure that I was constructing an identity as a TV soap person ... I think I was trying to situate myself for you in terms of my relationship with *The Archers*.' Like Viv, she also raised the issue of class, attributing the fact that she had mentioned her working-class origins to the stage she was at in her own academic work: 'If you had interviewed me a year earlier I may have said nothing about this at all.' Being the 'odd one out' in the chapter, despite my attempts to present the interview neutrally, and even my identification with her working-class roots and resistance to analysis, seems to have been a slightly uncomfortable, though interesting, experience for Louise: 'the process of being involved in your research has been very interesting and provided some useful points of consideration in teaching, particularly how it feels to have someone analyse what you say!'

Louise's comments touch on the crucial question of the desire to be open with, *and to please*, one's respondents, which the final stage of this research opens up. Again, femininity is in play. I was left wondering whether it was success or failure that most of my respondents were, in fact, happy with my portrayal of them. To what extent had I emphasised the positive in these interactions in order, in truly feminine mode, to keep the peace and protect vulnerable identities? Louise's comments do of course point out the limitations of research based on one or two interviews. As I have made clear throughout, the claims I make are in fact about these moments of communication, not about the individuals as 'whole people'. However, this is not how the process was experienced by the respondents, who were very concerned that I should represent their identities accurately, down to the last detail. If anything emerges in this research, it is the importance of identity to the participants. The comments on the draft chapters which I have analysed here, and the talk analysed in Chapters 4–6, seem to suggest that identity in lived experience is far more than the outmoded category envisaged by much postmodern and post-structuralist theory. Questions of class and of ethnic and national identity particularly have been seen to be highly sensitive issues in contemporary Britain, even in this relatively small sample. The gap between the contemporary theory and practice of identity which this research reveals, even among academics, seems worthy of further study. This, along with the complex dynamics and intersections of class, gender, sexuality, ethnicity and 'race' which are in play in talk about media texts, remains an empirical question.

The Archers Follow-up Questionnaire for Theatre Sample (Postal Survey)

Archers Research

Thank you very much indeed for agreeing to help me in my research on *The Archers*. I am enclosing the questionnaire and a stamped, addressed envelope for you to return it in.

Your replies will be treated with the utmost confidentiality, and no real names will be used in writing up the research.

I am interested in everything you write, so please feel free to answer as much, or as little, of the questionnaire as you want.

I look forward to reading your replies in the very near future.

Name

Please circle your age-group, and the word that best describes where you live:

below 25 / 26–35 / 36–45 / 46–55 / 56+

city / town / suburb / village / country

Male / Female

Occupation ....

If you are retired, please give your occupation prior to retirement.

How would you prefer to describe your ethnic origin:

1 How long have you been listening to *The Archers*?
2 What (if any) changes in the programmes have you noticed over the years? Have they been for better or worse?
3 What do you like about *The Archers*? (What makes you listen?)
4 Who is your favourite character (or characters)? What do you like about them?
5 Are there any characters you don't like? If so, why?
6 Which (if any) characters do you identify with? Why?
7 What do you think about the role of women in *The Archers*?
8 What do you think about the role of men in *The Archers*?
9 Is the portrayal of English traditions (village fêtes, cricket, etc.) an important part of the programmes for you? If so, why?
10 Is the rural setting something you enjoy? Why?
11 Are there any recent stories you have particularly liked? Why?
12 Are there any recent stories you have disliked or found boring? Why?
13 How often do you listen?
14 When and how do you listen (e.g. in the car, washing up, etc.) ?
15 Do you follow any other serials on TV or radio?
16 Are you a member of the '*Archers* Addicts'?
17 Please describe any activities organised by the '*Archers* Addicts' which you have participated in.
18 Do you read books about *The Archers* or collect memorabilia?
19 Do you have friends who are keen on *The Archers*? Are they mainly men or women?
20 Do you talk about *The Archers* with them? If so, what kind of things do you talk about?
21 Do you have any other comments on the programmes?

WITH **MANY THANKS** FOR YOUR HELP

NB: larger spaces were left for replies in the original.

Appendix Two

The Samples

Inspector Morse: The NFT Questionnaire

Analysis of the original thirty questionnaires suggests that the sample diverged considerably from *The Guardian*'s description of the *Morse* audience as 'ABC1 adults aged 35+' in terms of age, in that 75 per cent of respondents were under 35 (MacArthur, 1990: 25). This age-group is probably far more representative of cinema audiences in central London, than of the *Morse* audience or of television audiences generally. The sample was also predominantly female (60 per cent). The questionnaire did not ask respondents about their ethnicity, as I felt that this would be intrusive, and that the questionnaire may already be quite off-putting given the method of recruitment at an entertainment venue. While a more subtle analysis is therefore impossible, it was easy to observe that the audience was almost entirely white. It seems possible that the audience attracted by a screening of *Morse*, a well-known television programme rather than a film, may have been slightly more lower, as opposed to middle and upper middle class than would usually be expected at this venue. Some 20 per cent of the original sample were in professions such as doctor, lecturer or company director, 37 per cent in skilled or semi-professional work, e.g. nurse, secretary, electrician, 13 per cent unskilled clerical or shop work, 13 per cent students, and 3 per cent each for unskilled manual work or unemployed (around 10 per cent did not give their profession). This profile could be encompassed by the ABC1 description of the *Morse* audience, so that it may be mainly in terms of age that the respondents were atypical.

The 'NFT factor' may, however, be less evident in the focus groups, since the invitation was opened to friends of the respondents: in group 1, one person out of three, and in group 2, two out of five, were not present at the NFT screening. Nonetheless, the culture of both discussion groups was very clearly white and metropolitan, and a geographical location outside London or a greater ethnic diversity may well have produced very different results. It also seems likely that those who were sufficiently motivated to respond to two further invitations were in fact keen *Morse* fans, rather than just cinema-goers who happened to be at the NFT that evening, and the age distribution of the discussion groups (50 per cent under and 50 per cent over 35) seems to confirm that the composition of the group, as well, of course, as its size, has changed slightly since the original questionnaire (see Chapter 4 for details of the participants in the focus groups).

The '*Archers* Addicts' Weekend at Wood Norton Hall

There were twenty participants in the weekend – fifteen women and five men. Of the fifteen women at least seven were married (two were accompanied by their husbands). Two of the married women (whom I subsequently became friendly with – see Chapter 5) were old friends, for whom the weekend was an opportunity to meet up again and spend time together. Of the remaining eight women, seven were definitely single; the eight included one widow (who was with her daughter-in-law), two sisters and a mother and daughter. One third of the fifteen women had therefore come to the weekend alone, while two-thirds had come with a woman friend or relative, or their husband. The fact that there were three times as many women as men present, and that most of them had come with someone else, supports the general view of feminist researchers that soap opera attracts a predominantly female audience, and that relating to others through talk about it is more typical of 'female culture' than male (Brunsdon, 1981; Geraghty, 1991). All three of the single men had come alone. Two of these men were very keen *Archers* fans, while the third said he rarely listened, and seemed to be there mainly for the company.

As only the eight participants in the focus groups answered my questions about occupation and age, my profile of the participants in the weekend is based on what I could glean from observation and conversation, and therefore incomplete (because of the organiser's initial reluctance to give permission for the discussion groups, I decided that distributing a questionnaire to the whole group would be too intrusive). Three of the five men were retired (two from a class 11 occupation, and one from class 1; Standard Occupational Classification, HMSO, 1991). Of the two in work, one's occupation was unknown, the other was an electronics technician (class 11). Among the women, two were housewives (one a former secretary – class 11) and four were retired (one from a class 11 profession). 'Housewives' could, of course, count as unemployed, or more accurately unwaged. Four were in class 11 occupations, one in skilled manual work (111m), and one in a professional class 1 occupation. For three of the women I have no information. The inadequacy of these categories in relation to women who work in the home and retired people is manifest here (Abbott and Wallace, 1997: 56–8). Nonetheless, it seems possible to conclude that there was a middle-class majority, with the emphasis on 'middle': there were only two participants who would be placed in social class 1, and only one in class 111m.

Four of the men were in their forties or fifties, and the oldest man was in his seventies. Only four (less than one third) of the women were under forty. About the same number were in their forties, two in their fifties, one in her sixties and about four in their seventies. It is therefore possible to conclude that about half the group were in their forties or fifties. Slightly less than a quarter were under 40, and a quarter were in their seventies. This middle-class, middle-aged or older profile is consistent with the image of the Radio 4 audience, and of the *Archers* audience which is generally current in the press. It is also consistent with the BBC's own research (Prior, 1983). At least in the sense of conforming to this general view, and to the BBC's own statistics, the use of the term 'mainstream' to describe this group of *Archers* listeners seems justified.

All the participants were white, but lack of information prevents me from 'deconstructing whiteness' in detail (Hickman and Walter, 1995). It is likely, however, that the term does need such deconstruction; to my certain knowledge there was one American, one Irish and one Scottish woman, and it is quite possible that others in the group would not describe themselves as 'English'.

The Archers Questionnaire Survey

Tables

Theatre Royal Sample (Sample 1)

300 distributed, 158 returned (just over 50 per cent response). 120 women (76 per cent); 38 men (24 per cent).

Follow-up Questionnaire (Sample 2)

Sent out 158, 110 returned (response rate = 70 per cent). 86 women (78 per cent); 24 men (22 per cent).

Sample 1

Occupation	Men	(%)	Women	(%)
Professional (1)	5	13	10	8
Manage/tech (11)	18	47	63	52
Skilled non-manual 111N	8	21	14	12
Skilled manual 111M	1	3	1	0.8
Partly skilled 1V	1	3	–	–
Unskilled V	–	–	–	–
Retired	4	11	12	10
Unemployed	–	–	1	0.8
Housewife	–	–	8	7
Student	–	–	8	7
No answer	1	3	3	2.5

Age

under 25	1	3	4	3
26–35	3	8	26	22
36–45	13	34	27	22
46–55	12	31	39	33
55+	8	21	23	19
No answer	1	3	11	0.8

Questionnaire Follow-up (Sample 2)

Occupation	Men	(%)	Women	(%)
Professional (1)	2	8	5	6
Manage/tech (11)	15	62	42	49
Skilled non-manual 111N	4	16	13	15
Skilled manual 111M	1	4	1	1
Partly skilled 1V	–	–	–	–
Unskilled V	–	–	–	–
Retired	3	12	9	10
Unemployed	–	–	–	–
Housewife	–	–	9	10
Student	–	–	5	6
No answer	–	–	2	2

Age				
under 25	1	4	1	1
26–35	2	8	15	17
36–45	6	25	20	23
46–55	9	38	29	34
55+	6	25	21	24
No answer	–	–	–	–

Ethnicity				
White British	12	50	47	55
White English	7	29	19	24
Jewish	1	4	1	1
White European	2	8	9	10
Irish	1	4	1	1
Scottish	1	4	1	1
African Caribbean	–	–	1	1
White American	–	–	1	1
Latin American	–	–	1	1
No reply	–	–	5	6

Commentary

There are broad similarities between the original sample of 158 and the final questionnaire sample of 110, in terms of gender, age and social class. The data on the 158 can thus be read as a confirmation of the validity of the final sample, which I will concentrate on in this analysis. Caution should be exercised in portraying the sample as typical of the *Archers* audience, since the venue and the nature of the event, performed at a theatre in an Arts Festival, will both exert an important influence. It is likely that social classes 1 and 11 are particularly well represented in this sample, given the popularity of theatre-going in these classes. The radio audience is likely to have a somewhat broader constituency. The same comment could be made in terms of ethnicity and 'race': southern Britain, non-metropolitan venue may be a significant factor influencing the composition of the sample which is predominantly white British or English (respondents were asked to describe their ethnic origin in their own words). Only one respondent identified as black (African-Caribbean), two as Irish, two as Scottish, one as Latin American, one as American and two as Jewish: 8 per cent of the sample in total. Nine women and two men (10 per cent) identified as White European. The high percentage of 'White British' responses (54 per cent) may mask other identities: for example, Hickman (1995) has researched the tendency for Irish identity to become 'invisibilised' among the second generation.

In terms of class, then, this sample was dominated by social class 11 (62 per cent of men and 49 per cent of women). A further 8 and 6 per cent respectively belonged to social class 1, and 16 per cent of men and 15 per cent of women to class 111N (non-manual). Only one man (4 per cent) and one woman (1 per cent) were in skilled manual work (class 111M), and social classes 1V and V, and the unemployed were not represented. 12 per cent of men and 10 per cent of women were retired. 6 per cent of the women described themselves as housewives, and 2 per cent were students. This sample is thus different from the Wood Norton Hall group, which was dominated by people who were not in employment (60 per cent of men were retired and 40 per cent of women retired or housewives). Clearly, the much larger theatre sample is closer to the general population in this respect. The high number of retired people in the Wood Norton Hall group suggests that the availability of time and leisure is significant in determining the choice to participate in a residential weekend. Although the dominance of social class 11 is a feature in both cases, social class 111N (entirely absent at Wood Norton) was included in the theatre survey sample (15 per cent), again making the latter sample less atypical in relation to the general population.

The proportion of women in the sample was similar in both cases (75 per cent at Wood Norton, 78 per cent in the questionnaire survey), again reinforcing the notion that although men listen to *The Archers* and participate in fan cultures, they are in a minority, and these activities are predominantly feminine. It should be taken into account that given the dominant image of soap opera as a women's genre, men will have been less likely to return the questionnaire or take the initial enquiry form. However, the disparity in numbers is so great that even taking this variable into account, the gender bias remains. Clearly, the social construction of femininity, and soap opera's role in that context are crucial factors here (Geraghty, 1991).

The dominant age-group in this sample is 46–55 (38 per cent of men and 34 per cent of women, and about one quarter of the sample were over 55). Only 18 per cent of women and 12 per cent of men were under 35, suggesting that the older profile of the Radio 4 audience is also represented here. The high proportion of respondents in the 46–55 age range may be particularly significant in relation to *The Archers* since the programme itself is over fifty years old, and many of its listeners have been following it since childhood. As might be expected from the figures relating to retirement, this sample was slightly younger than the Wood Norton group, where 25 per cent were in their seventies, and only 25 per cent under 40 (as opposed to 41 per cent under 45 in this sample).

Appendix Three

Description of *Morse* Extracts Shown at Focus Groups

1 The Last Five Minutes of *The Dead of Jericho* (first broadcast on 6 January 1987)

Anne Staveley, whom Morse has met in a choir and befriended, hangs herself as a result of an unhappy love affair with Anthony Richards. Her voyeuristic neighbour, George Jackson, attempts to blackmail Richards, who subsequently murders him. In this scene Morse interviews the two Richards brothers, Alan and Anthony, and the wife of Anthony Richards, Adele. Although she is aware of the facts, Adele is colluding with the brothers' exchange of identity, which has provided Anthony with an alibi. In this scene, with the help of the timely arrival of Lewis, Morse realises that the Richards brothers have deceived him. He then identifies Anthony Richards as the person morally responsible for the death of his former mistress, Anne Staveley, and as the actual murderer of George Jackson. At the end of the extract Morse walks off alone, brooding on his romantic disappointment with Anne Staveley, who left a message for Richards, but not for him.

This extract was chosen because of its problematisation of heterosexual relations, and the binary opposition single/married which structures the narrative. Morse's moral integrity is seen in contrast to the extremely negative representation of the married couple, and particularly of the married man, Richards. The single woman, Anne Staveley is clearly a victim of all the male characters apart from Morse, and her financial independence and home which speaks of cultural interests and domestic comfort are to some extent negated by the impression of loneliness and vulnerability which she conveys.

2 Morse and Lewis Interviewing the Headmaster and his Family in *Last Seen Wearing* (first broadcast on 8 March 1988).

In this scene Morse and Lewis are investigating the disappearance of a schoolgirl, Valerie Craven, by conducting a series of interviews in the girls' public school which she attended. Here the idealised vision of the Headmaster's beautiful blonde wife and well-behaved children is compounded by the setting, an elegant wood-panelled room whose leaded windows look out onto the green expanse of the school grounds. All of this is undercut by the polite tension between husband

and wife, and our suspicions are definitely raised when the Headmaster declares that: 'We make it a policy to talk as a family.' It is no surprise then that he is implicated both in the death of his Deputy Headmistress, who for mainstream television is unusual in combining lesbianism with intelligence, charm and wit, and in Valerie's disappearance.

3 From the Same Programme

Morse interviewing the Deputy Headmistress, Miss Baines, in her house late at night, immediately prior to her death during a row with the Head, who pushes her downstairs. The scene is interesting because of its positive representation of a single woman, who we later learn is a lesbian, and the tone of the conversation which almost crosses the boundary into the private domain. On the plot level Baines confirms our negative impression of the Headmaster by describing his ruthless determination to win a fathers' race in the school sports day.

4 The Scene from *Dead on Time* (first broadcast on 26 April 1992), When Morse Entertains Susan, his Former Fiancée

Morse first met Susan when they were both students in Oxford, but she broke their engagement and married another man. Her terminally ill husband has recently died in suspicious circumstances and Morse is investigating the case. Prior to her arrival Lewis visits Morse, and on seeing Morse's agitation and romantic preparations, chooses not to give him some information which might implicate Susan. This is an emotionally intense moment, as it is made clear that Morse is still in love, after all those years.

Appendix Four

Codes for Topic Maps:
The Archers and *Morse*

1 Medium
2 Intertextual references and comparisons

3 Secondary literature
4 Quality
                         – c) character
                         – m) music
                         – ph) photography
                         – a) acting/actors
                         – e) Englishness
                         – s) script/dialogue
                         – pl) plot
                         – r) relevanve, realism
                         – d) directing

5 Agency/Production
                         – p) producer
                         – pc) production costs
                         – t) technical aspects of production
                         – a) acting/actors
                         – s) script/dialogue

6 Modality
                         – i) internal, i.e. codes and conventions make programme
realistic = +
unrealistic = -
                         – e) external, i.e. like real life
realistic = +
unrealistic = -

7 Narrative
                         – f) future storylines
                         – r) re-telling
                         – c) critique (boring or trivial storyline)

8 Character
                         – f) favourite
                         – d) disliked characters
                         – a) death of characters (Archers)
                         – d) disappearance or non-appearance of characters
                         – c) criticism of characters' behaviour

(n.b. Character is often linked to modality)

9 Audience (general references to)   – f) being a fan

                                        – a) Archers addicts/organised fan club activities

                                        – e) emotional involvement

                                        – h) histories of listening/viewing

                                        – l) learning from the programmes

10 Gender representation/The personal

Morse:	*The Archers*:
a) Morse single	a) single characters/romantic speculation
b) Morse/Lewis relationship	b) lack of romance
c) Morse's relationships with women	c) representation of women
d) Morse family	d) representation of men
	e) representation of lesbians and gay men

11 Modernity, keeping up with the   – e) enterprise
     times   – s) current social issues

12 Representation of tradition   – v) village life

                                        – e) Englishness

                                        – c) country life

Sample Topic Map: The Archers
Focus Group – Wood Norton Hall 2

Line Number	TOPIC	TOPIC CODE	INTRODUCED BY:
5 >	histories of listening	9h	ALICE
5>	emotional involvement	9e	ALICE
14>	character / romantic speculation	8 10a	ALICE
29>	modality	6e+ > –	JANET
40>	involvement / modality	9e 6e+	JANET
43>	country life	12 c	TIM
52>	character	8d	TIM
	quality – mystique	4	
65>	quality	4 s a d pl	ALICE
75	narrative – critique of pantomime story	7 c	ALICE
79	modality	6 e + > -	TIM
94>	gender modality	10 c 6 e +	TIM JANET ALICE
131	representation of women	10c	LYN
132>	representation of men > women	10 d > c	ALICE JANET
	modernity, modality, quality	11 6e 4	ALICE JANET
167	quality writing	4 s	TIM
170>	modernity	11 e s 4 9l	ALICE JANET
	quality, learning		
176	Ambridge women	10c	LYN
189	vintage Archers tapes	3	ALICE
203	character modality in Archers past	8 6e-	TIM
209	medium – radio more important in past	1	ALICE
213	audience size despite TV	9	TIM
216>	producer development of storylines / social issues, quality	5p 7 11s 4	ALICE
242	educational function	9l	ALICE

Line Number	TOPIC	TOPIC CODE	INTRODUCED BY:
250	narrative	7 r	JANET
254	modernity – too modern?	11	LYN
257>	modality	6e- > +	ALICE > JANET
273	retelling	7r	ALICE
292>	male characters	10d	LYN > TIM
300	female audience	9	TIM
319	character disliked	8d	ALICE
335>	business realistic	11e > 6i+	ALICE
345	narrative	7r	TIM
354	narrative > the weekend organiser 'Kathy'	7r > 9a	ALICE > TIM
362>	favourite character?	8f	LYN
377	career woman – children	10c	ALICE
387	modality character	6I+ 8	ALICE
393	romance narrative >	10 6e- 8	ALICE
398>	modality > character		
433	favourite character?	8f	LYN
469	character disliked	8d	JANET
482>	modality character	6e+ 8 > 6e-	ALICE
508	favourite scene or moment?		LYN
510>	narrative	7r	ALICE
522>	in tears recently? > Mark's death	9e > 8d	LYN > ALICE
530	*The Archers* too dramatic recently?	11	LYN
532	realistic	6e+	ALICE
541	possible educational function	9l	ALICE
545>	romance	10a	JANET
573>	weekend activity	9a 11s 6e+ 4	ALICE
	modernity, modality, quality		

Line Number	TOPIC	TOPIC CODE	INTRODUCED BY:
580>	business	11e	TIM > JANET > LYN ALICE
603	killing off Guy Pemberton too soon >romance >	7c 10a 8d	JANET
619	modality		ALICE
622>	Archers addicts?	9a	LYN
650	actors / characters	5a	ALICE
676 >	characters as they imagine them?	1 9	TIM
701	country village?	12v	LYN
725	modality	12v 6e-	ALICE
736>	Englishness	12e v	LYN

Notes

Introduction

1 This idea of a shared repertoire or resource seems to bear some resemblance to the concept of the 'interpretive community' developed by Stanley Fish, and applied in Janice Radway's study of readers of romantic fiction, and Henry Jenkins's work on fandom (Fish, 1980; Radway, 1984; Jenkins, 1992). It does not, however, necessarily imply the complete evacuation of the text which Fish's argument seems to rely on. Barker and Brooks comment: 'The idea of "interpretive community" has much mileage in it, but mainly in so far as it sheds certain inbuilt tendencies to tell us in advance what a "community" is, and what it means to belong to one, or of course, more than one' (1998: 104).

2 Characters such as Hayley Jordan, Sid Perks, Usha Gupta and Jason.

3 *Crossroads* (ATV / Central Independent Television, 1964–88); *Coronation Street* (Granada, 1960–); *EastEnders* (BBC, 1985–); *Brookside* (Mersey / Channel 4, 1982–).

4 The inverted commas here and in the title of the book indicate that I am using the word 'quality' to present a discursive construction rather than a positive evaluation of the texts under discussion.

5 Both *Inspector Morse* and *The Archers* can be described as 'mainstream' in that they are produced by institutions which are at the centre of the British media industry (Central Independent Television and the BBC), and in that relative to other programmes in the same medium they both attract large audiences.

6 See Moores (1988) and Tacchi (2000) for historical and contemporary studies (respectively) of the role of radio in everyday life.

7 See Chapter 1 for a discussion of feminist post-structuralist deconstructions of the term 'identity' and its precise meaning and implications here.

8 For example, lines 272–6 of *Morse* focus group 2:

> *Sue*: He's a complete shit, he's having an affair with somebody else, she doesn't want to admit it, but when it comes to a public face they're colluding and pretending they're having a wonderful time.
>
> *Sarah*: Calling each other darling all the time and just, oh
>
> *Jim*: Well, there are people
>
> *Sue*: Maybe that's the kind of marriage the *Archers* have.

[*Female laughter*]

Sarah: and quite often the plot does depend on Mrs Lewis doing something new like deciding to learn Greek.

[*Laughter*]

Sarah: So, it's like the person you never see but on whom the whole thing pivots.

Lyn: Bit like Prue in *The Archers*.

[*Laughter*]

Sarah: Yes, yes.

(683–8)

Lisa: To kind of go round and in a way, sort of, I don't know, I think it would actually spoil the programmes to have been round everywhere. For me I think that would destroy

Sarah: Like going to Ambridge or something.

[*Laughter*]

Sarah: That's weird, isn't it? It's near Birmingham, Sussex, Scotland.

(864–9)

Chapter 1 Bourdieu, Butler and Beyond

1   Ann Curthoys, for instance, has argued that reading Beauvoir's autobiographies as a student in Sydney in the 1970s provided her with the role-model of an intellectual woman which was entirely absent from Australian society (Curthoys, 2000; see also Moi, 1994).

2   Even Frow, who is generally highly critical of Bourdieu's text, finds the correlation between educational and cultural capitals uncontroversial, though, as he says, the relationship with economic capital is more complex (1987: 67).

3   For Butler's critical comments on Bourdieu see Butler (1997) *Excitable Speech: A Politics of the Performative*, New York and London: Routledge.

4   Alldred uses 're-presentation' to emphasise the active process of production of the research account by the researcher and the fact that it embodies her perspective. 'Re/presentation' is used to emphasise 'its significance for cultural politics' (1998: 149).

Chapter 2 'Quality' Media: Critical Debates, Texts and Contexts

1   The nature of the engagement of international audiences with *Morse* is beyond the scope of this study; it would, however, be an interesting topic for future research.

2   The voice of Bob Arnold (Tom Forrest) was a further, important example, until the actor's death in 1998. For thirty years, Bob Arnold, as Tom Forrest, set the scene for the Omnibus edition, with 'a nugget of topical country folklore' (Willmott and Niklaus, 2000: 53). He was already well known on radio as a 'Cotswolds character' when he began to play Tom Forrest. The fact that his voice could still be heard until 1998 clearly added to the heritage dimension of *The Archers*.

3   On 21 May 2000, the extent of Ruth's anxiety about finding a lump in her breast was emphasised by her lack of interest in David's description of the beautiful countryside around them; David's reference to the scent of the honeysuckle added another dimension to the visual image. In this case the description created a contrast between the beautiful image and the worrying plot development, reminiscent of the crimes in beautiful settings aspect of *Inspector Morse*.

4   This kind of imagery was returned to at Christmas 2001/2 when Siobhàn began an affair with Brian Aldridge, and thus took up the *femme fatale* of Ambridge role. At one Christmas party she wore a low-cut green top – which caused Jennifer Aldridge to remark that the colour made 'us blondes' look sea-sick but really suited Siobhàn. Jennifer's phrase seems to exclude Siobhàn from the normally all-inclusive Englishness of Ambridge, while the colour green has obvious Irish connotations. Later, at the Lower Loxley masked ball, Siobhàn's glamorous appearance – she was instantly recognisable because of her hair – was again commented on, constructing her as an exotic Other. One could argue that this represents a shift from the invisibilisation discussed here, though it is perfectly possible for the two tendencies to run in tandem as contradictory discourses within the dominant ideology of Englishness.

5   The problem clearly extends far beyond *The Archers*. In 1999, writing in *The Guardian* about Radio 4, Anne Karpf questioned how in the 1990s a national radio station can still sound so white (Karpf, 1999). Discussing the whiteness of the British public sphere, Morley commented: 'When the culture of the public sphere is in effect "racialised" by the naturalisation of one (largely unmarked and undeclared) form of ethnicity, then only some citizens of the nation find it a homely and welcoming place' (2000: 118).

6   I refer here to Sid's affair with Jolene Rogers, which was greeted in the press by headlines such as 'Perky Sid's soapy slip-up' (N. Fountain, *The Guardian* 2000: 6), or 'Now *The Archers*: Rumpy pumpy tum-ti-tum' (D. Lister, *The Independent* 2000: 1).

7   In March 1999 this scene won Radio 4's *Pick of the Week* Red Nose Day competition where extracts from *The Archers* were played to listeners who phoned in.

Nelson announced 'I have been wearing the shoes and I have been measured for a gown' to a horrified Julia. 4282 listeners voted for the red shoes extract.

8 The difficulties in representing the overwhelming attractions of Jolene Rogers on radio are a case in point. References to fur mini-skirts with matching hats, or 'The Bull' being crowded with lascivious men when she worked there as a barmaid, may have less objectifying power than the camera.

Chapter 3 Introducing the Audience Study

1 Demographic details of all samples can be found in Appendix 2 and the *Archers* postal questionnaire can be found in Appendix 1.

2 The performance was almost identical to that given at the Wood Norton weekend, but with different actors (Carole Boyd alias Lynda Snell and Jack May alias Nelson Gabriel). There was also a different scriptwriter – Caroline Harrington.

3 The *Annual Review of BBC Broadcasting Research Findings* published in 1983 comments: 'the audience profile for listeners of *The Archers* tends to be predominantly female and aged 50+' (Prior, 1983: 75). This is based on a sample of 1287 – i.e. the 46 per cent of the BBC's Listening Panel of 3000 (recruited according to quotas of age, sex and region) who replied that they were *Archers* listeners.

4 It may well be a dangerous assumption to link the ethnic profile of a media text to that of its characters in any simplistic way. Buckingham sounds a note of caution about these kinds of assumptions in his *EastEnders* research:

> the girls are extremely critical of what they regard as Michelle's selfishness, which is surprising given that they are very close to her in terms of age, gender and class background. This would suggest that the notion that viewers will automatically 'identify' with characters who are like them-selves is perhaps an oversimplification.
>
> (1987: 173)

Nonetheless the 'whiteness' of *The Archers* is an issue in this research.

5 After some deliberation I decided to refer to the encounter with Mary and Ben as an interview rather than a focus group, even though it involved only one less respondent than two of the focus groups. I have done this since it was not set up in the same way: unlike the respondents in the focus groups Mary and Ben were not invited to participate in a group in a public space. The fact that the interview took place in their home and that Mary and Ben clearly knew each other much better than the majority of participants in the focus groups was thus a differentiating feature of this event.

Chapter 4 In Love with Inspector Morse

1 Barrington Pheloung was interviewed by Sabine Durrant: Durrant (1991) 'Medium with a message', *The Independent* 10 May. In this piece we learn that

Morse's tastes 'could be said to have subtly developed from Mahler to Mozart' and that Pheloung, like Morse, 'has a penchant for good reading, fine wine and the classics'. Thus, both character and composer are distinguished by 'quality' interests.

Chapter 5 '*Archers* Addicts'

1 Barker and Brooks note that there has been very little work on the distinction between high and low investment in a media text, and on the relationship of this to willingness to participate in research (1998: 237).

2 I have already described the negative representation of fandom in the two articles on the weekend. It is, however, possible to distinguish between the two articles: while Ameghino, who was only present during the Saturday morning coach trip, maintains an ironic distance, Graham identifies with the fans, and repeatedly uses the pronoun 'we' to refer to the weekend's participants. She concludes triumphantly: 'We will have something in common for ever, something more unifying than geography or profession: for we are the *Archers* Addicts.' This approach may have contributed to my sense that Graham was accepted into the group slightly more readily, or at least sooner, than I was.

3 Although the venue was neutral in terms of my role (I was as much a stranger at Wood Norton as my respondents), clearly as a BBC centre hosting a BBC-organised weekend it was far from neutral in other respects.

4 Examples from the 1960s would be Beryl Reid's 'Marlene', Janice on *Juke Box Jury* whose 'I'll give it foive' made headline news. More recently Harry Enfield's series of 'we're much richer than yow' sketches. Jasper Carrott, like his daughter, seems to be contributing to the recent nuancing of these stereotypes, since he presents an ironic and middle-class version of Birmingham culture.

5 In subsequent correspondence Viv commented, however: 'Finally, I can't believe I'm saying this, but I have warmed to Julia Pargetter over the last few weeks. Her antics with the builders and her success with the art sale plus the amusing episodes with her novel tapes have made her seem more appealing' (letter, April 1999). This change of view is a useful reminder of the fluctuating nature of the identifications and opinions expressed in events such as these, and their specificity to these particular social contexts.

6 The 'flexibility' of the discourse of modality is also demonstrated by *Morse* focus group 2, where critique of the representation of women in the programmes was couched in similar terms. External modality is a term used in audience studies to describe comparisons of the text with 'real life', while 'internal modality' describes discussions of realism within the terms of the diegesis. Discussion of whether a character's behaviour is consistent would fall into this category, for instance (see Buckingham, 1993d: 47).

7 For instance on page two of the transcript I asked: 'Has anybody else got something they don't like?' and after one response I reiterated the question: 'Has anyone else got anything else that they don't like, or they haven't liked?'

8 The first part of the telephone interview with Elspeth was spent discussing how she would record the programmes and listen to them in the early hours of the morning to avoid being interrupted by telephone calls from patients, thus confirming the impression of a hectic life.

9 Barker and Brooks describe the opposite of 'sad' as 'trash culture' which is 'knowing about the world, but always with an ironic tone' (1998: 175). Their definition does not seem to match Viv's position here, but she is demonstrating an awareness of a wider popular culture, perhaps in response to the 'stick' she described herself receiving from her sons (telephone interview, March 1999).

10 The competition for space in a larger group is illustrated by the fact that the most dominant group members in focus group 1 (Viv and Joan) spoke considerably less (157 and 199 lines respectively) than the dominant participant here (Alice – 337 lines).

11 Although there have been no lesbian characters in *The Archers* in recent years, Nye *et al.* comment that in 1952 Christine Archer had an affair with an older woman. It is possible that Joan remembers this (2000: 74).

12 Tacchi comments: 'I have found that men are more likely to rationalise their listening, while women more frequently talk about their radio listening in relation to their emotional life, how they feel or have felt, in romantic terms' (2000: 161).

Chapter 6 Feminisms, Fans and Country Folk

1 The question here was asked in an open way ('What changes have you noticed over the years? Have they been for better or worse?') in order to avoid suggesting or dictating responses. As a result, the answers to this question are less focused than they might have been if I had asked directly about approval or disapproval of the modernisation of the programmes. However, my concern was not to ascertain reactions to recent production policies, but to allow space for culturally significant discourses to emerge. Interestingly, many respondents identified modernity and modernisation as an issue and a significant change, without necessarily 'voting for or against'. In some ways, these less directed responses may be more significant than the positive replies to very direct, closed questions such as questions nine and ten, and the percentages should be read in this light (see Appendix 1 for the full questionnaire text).

2 Narrative occurs second on the topic map (twenty references), and character fourth with ten.

3 The terms 'English' and 'Englishness' are probably more accurate than British and Britishness in relation to *The Archers* in that the latter might encompass a whole range of ethnic and national identities. Ben is referring to cultural stereotypes which are only associated with the English inhabitants of Britain (that is a clipped, emotionally repressed style of speech which perhaps reached its apogee in earlier decades of this century, as exemplified in films such as *Brief Encounter*).

4 See Chapter 2 for a discussion of Nelson's almost transgressively camp persona.

5 The 'people on this list' are Mary's friends and colleagues who she thought might be willing to talk about *The Archers*. The interviews with two of them, Jan and Louise, are the topic of the rest of this chapter.

6 The discussion or speculation about Debbie becoming a lesbian character later moves back into the diegesis. The level of collusion between Jan and myself is quite striking:

> *Jan*: ... I've never felt we've really travelled with Debbie, like we have with, say, Shula. And other characters.
>
> *Lyn*: Yes. Yes, it's quite unrealistic in a way, isn't it, because, you know, for a young woman of her age, the notion that she just does this farm work –
>
> *Jan*: I know, and she's not dating, is she?
>
> *Lyn*: No.

7 Mary wrote about watching *EastEnders* with her son before he left home in her questionnaire. She and Ben did make intertextual comparisons with other soaps, but did not seem to be following them in the same way.

8 One is of course on difficult ground in making assumptions about people's sexuality; equally it would have been extremely difficult and detrimental to the research in the context of the Wood Norton weekend to ask a direct question on this. However, in group 2 the married couple – Tim and Janet – constituted the 'majority', and in group 1 there were two married women and one widow. In relation to the others in the group nothing is known – but if there were lesbian or gay participants they were not open about this in the way that Jan was, and this is a significant difference in cultural terms.

9 The extract from the transcript demonstrates these collusive pleasures, and also the association of this kind of writing with quality – see particularly the bold sections:

> *Ben*: – there are a couple of – you know, there's this book *Unheard in Ambridge* which is a whole – because you bought me that, didn't you – someone did. I'll show it to you. It's basically a cartoon book, constructing an entire storyline solely using people who never speak in *The Archers*. [*laughter*] So there's Prue Forest, there's, um, Jean Paul – who now speaks but for a long time didn't –
>
> *Mary*: Not very often, no.
>
> *Ben*: Mainly when he's throwing knives in the kitchen, and lots of other people who get referred to, but the classic thing was this week when, you know there was this thing about these embroidered cushions, that

William nicked from a craft fair somewhere and then Joe and Eddie flogged them as if they were Clarrie's own work, and, anyway. There was this wonderful – **I'm sure they loved playing these games**, which is Clarrie saying, 'What have you got to say for yourself?' Now a word is never spoken, it's William who has the speaking part who's recently acquired a very de..e..p voice, but Edward has never spoken, I think, for 12 – however, old Edward is, he's never spoken. 'Edward, what have you got to say for yourself?' And there's a kind of [*laughter*] 'I should think not – I'm not surprised you've got nothing to say for yourself – William.' [*lots of laughter*] I just bust a gut. Cos –

Lyn: **That was the one piece of witty writing this week**.

Chapter 7 Conclusion

1   One of my respondents, Mary, clearly shares my view; she commented in her final letter to me: 'What about Eddie Grundy then? And the discussions about "being a man" that Clarrie has with William? Definitions of masculinity? Next we know they'll be saying *The Archers* has been taken over by Queer Theorists' ...

2   Note, for instance, how Mary and Ben commented on the negative attitude of other left-wing intellectuals to soap opera.

Bibliography

Abbott, P. and Wallace, C. (1997) *An Introduction to Sociology: Feminist Perspectives*, London and New York: Routledge.

Alldred, P. (1998) 'Ethnography and discourse analysis: dilemmas in representing children', in J. Ribbens and R. Edwards (eds) *Feminist Dilemmas in Qualitative Research*, London, Thousand Oaks and New Delhi: Sage.

Allen, L. (1997) *The Lesbian Idol: Martina, kd and the Consumption of Lesbian Masculinity*, London and Herndon, VA: Cassell.

Ameghino, J. (1997) '*Archers* fans all a-quiver', *The Birmingham Post*, 25 January: 37–8.

Ang, I. (1985) *Watching 'Dallas': Soap Opera and the Melodramatic Imagination*, London: Methuen.

—— (1989) 'Wanted: audiences. On the politics of empirical audience studies', in E. Seiter, H. Borchers, G. Kreutzner and E.-M. Warth (eds) *Remote Control: Television, Audiences and Cultural Power*, London and New York: Routledge.

Ang, I. and Hermes, J. (1991) 'Gender and/in media consumption', in J. Curran and M. Gurevitch (eds) *Mass Media and Society*, London: Edward Arnold.

Baehr, H. and Dyer, G. (eds) (1987) *Boxed-in: Women and Television*, London: Pandora.

Barker, M. (1993) 'The Bill Clinton fan syndrome', *Media, Culture and Society* 15, 4: 669–74.

Barker, M. and Beezer, A. (1992) *Reading into Cultural Studies*, London and New York: Routledge.

Barker, M. and Brooks, K. (1998) *Knowing Audiences: Judge Dredd, its Friends, Fans and Foes*, Luton: University of Luton Press.

BBC Radio 4 Marketing (1999) *Listener Report*, London: BBC.

Beauvoir, Simone de (1949) *Le Deuxième Sexe*, Paris: Editions Gallimard.

Birt, J. (1998) *The Director General's Annual Report*, www.bbc.co.uk.

Bobo, J. (1988) '*The Color Purple*: black women as cultural readers', in E.D. Pribram (ed.) *Female Spectators: Looking at Film and Television*, London and New York: Verso.

—— (1995) *Black Women as Cultural Readers*, New York: Columbia University Press.

Bobo, J. and Seiter, E. (1997) 'Black feminism and media criticism: *The Women of Brewster Place*', in C. Brunsdon, J. D'Acci and L. Spigel (eds) *Feminist Television Criticism: A Reader*, Oxford and New York: Oxford University Press.

Bourdieu, P. ([1979] 1984) *Distinction: A Social Critique of the Judgement of Taste*, Paris: Les Editions de Minuit, trans. R. Nice (1984) London: Routledge and Kegan Paul.

—— (1986) 'The forms of capital', in J. Richardson (ed.) *Handbook of Theory and Research for the Sociology of Education*, New York: Greenwood Press.

—— (1998) *Masculine Domination*, Paris: Editions du Seuil, trans. R. Nice (2001) Oxford and Cambridge: Polity Press.

Bourdieu, P. and Passeron, J.-C. (1977) *Reproduction in Education, Society and Culture*, trans. R. Nice, London: Sage.

Brandt, G. (ed.) (1993) *British Television Drama in the 1980s*, Cambridge: Cambridge University Press.

Brockes, E. (2001) 'A long way from Ambridge', *The Guardian* 10 October, G2: 2–3.

Brower, S. (1992) 'Fans as tastemakers: Viewers for Quality Television', in L. Lewis (ed.) *The Adoring Audience: Fan Culture and Popular Media*, London and New York: Routledge.

Brunsdon, C. (1981) '*Crossroads*: notes on a soap opera', *Screen* 22, 4: 32–7.

—— (1987) 'Men's genres for women', in H. Baehr and G. Dyer (eds) *Boxed-in: Women and Television*, London: Pandora.

—— (1990) 'Problems with quality', *Screen* 31, 1: 67–90.

—— (1991) 'Pedagogies of the feminine: feminist teaching and women's genres', *Screen* 32, 4: 364–81.

—— (1993) 'Identity in feminist television criticism', *Media, Culture and Society* 15: 309–20.

—— (1998) 'Structure of anxiety: recent British television crime fiction', *Screen* 39, 3: 223–43.

—— (2000) *The Feminist, the Housewife and the Soap Opera*, Oxford and New York: Oxford University Press.

Brunsdon, C., D'Acci, J. and Spigel, L. (eds) (1997) *Feminist Television Criticism: A Reader*, Oxford and New York: Oxford University Press.

Brunsdon, C. and Morley, D. (1978) *Everyday Television: 'Nationwide'*, London: BFI.

Buckingham, D. (1987) *Public Secrets: 'EastEnders' and its Audience*, London: BFI.

—— (ed.) (1993a) *Reading Audiences: Young People and the Media*, Manchester: Manchester University Press.

—— (1993b) 'Boys talk: television and the policing of masculinity', in D. Buckingham (ed.) *Reading Audiences: Young People and the Media*, Manchester: Manchester University Press.

—— (1993c) 'Conclusion: re-reading audiences', in D. Buckingham (ed.) *Reading Audiences: Young People and the Media*, Manchester: Manchester University Press.

—— (1993d) *Children Talking Television: The Making of Television Literacy*, London: The Falmer Press.

Burman, E. (1992) 'Feminism and discourse in developmental psychology: power, subjectivity and interpretation', *Feminism and Psychology* 2, 1: 45–60.

Butler, J. (1990) *Gender Trouble: Feminism and the Subversion of Identity*, London and New York: Routledge.

—— (1992) 'The body you want: interview with Liz Kotz', *Artforum*, November: 82–9.

—— (1993) *Bodies that Matter*, London and New York: Routledge.

—— (1997) *Excitable Speech: A Politics of the Performative*, London and New York: Routledge.

Cameron, D. (1985) *Feminism and Linguistic Theory*, London and Basingstoke: Macmillan.

Cameron, D., Frazer, E., Harvey, P., Rampton, M.B.H. and Richardson, K. (1992) *Researching Language: Issues of Power and Method*, London and New York: Routledge.

Chandler, D. (1996) 'Postcards from the edge', in M. Power *The Shipping Forecast*, London: Zelda Cheatle Press.

Cleto, F. (ed.) (1999) *Camp, Queer Aesthetics and the Performing Subject: A Reader*, Edinburgh: Edinburgh University Press.

Code, L. (1993) 'Taking subjectivity into account', in L. Alcoff and E. Potter (eds) *Feminist Epistemologies*, London and New York: Routledge.

Corner, J. and Harvey, S. (eds) (1991a) *Enterprise and Heritage: Crosscurrents of National Culture*, London and New York: Routledge.

—— (1991b) 'Mediating tradition and modernity: the heritage / enterprise couplet', in J. Corner and G. Harvey (eds) *Enterprise and Heritage: Crosscurrents of National Culture*, London and New York: Routledge.

Corner, J., Harvey, S. and Lury, K. (1994) 'Culture, quality and choice: the re-regulation of TV 1989–91', in S. Hood (ed.) *Behind the Screens: The Structure of British Broadcasting in the 1990s*, London: Lawrence and Wishart.

Craig, C. (1991) 'Rooms without a view', *Sight and Sound* 1, 2: 10–13.

Crisell, A. ([1986] 1994) *Understanding Radio*, London and New York: Routledge.

Cruz, J. and Lewis, J. (eds) (1994) *Viewing, Reading, Listening: Audiences and Cultural Reception*, Boulder, CO: Westview Press.

Curthoys, A. (2000) 'Adventures of feminism: Simone de Beauvoir's autobiographies, women's liberation and self-fashioning', *Feminist Review* 64: 3–18.

D'Acci, J. (1987) 'The case of *Cagney and Lacey*', in H. Baehr and G. Dyer (eds) *Boxed-in: Women and Television*, London: Pandora.

—— (1994) *Defining Women: Television and the Case of Cagney and Lacey*, Chapel Hill, NC: University of North Carolina Press.

Davies, B. (1993) *Shards of Glass*, St Leonards, NSW: Allen and Unwin.

Dawson, G. (1994) *Soldier Heroes: British Adventure, Empire and the Imagining of Masculinities*, London and New York: Routledge.

Denzin, N. and Lincoln, Y. (eds) (1998) *The Landscape of Qualitative Research*, London, Thousand Oaks and New Delhi: Sage.

DiMaggio, P. (1979) 'Review essay: on Pierre Bourdieu', *American Journal of Sociology* 84, 6: 1460–74.

Douglas, S. J. (1999) *Listening In: Radio and the American Imagination, from Amos 'n' Andy and Edward R. Murrow to Wolfman Jack and Howard Stern*, New York and Toronto: Random House.

Dyer, R. (ed.) (1981) *Coronation Street*, London: British Film Institute

—— (1992) 'Quality pleasures', in R. Dyer *Only Entertainment*, London and New York: Routledge.

—— (1996) '"There's nothing I can do": femininity, seriality and whiteness in *The Jewel in the Crown*', *Screen* 37, 3: 225–39.

Ernaux, A. (1997) *La Honte*, Paris: Gallimard.

Esposito, M. (2001) 'Jean de Florette', in L. Mazdon (ed.) *France on Film: Reflections on Contemporary French Cinema*, London: Wallflower Press.

Fairclough, N. (1989) *Language and Power*, London: Longman.

Felski, R. (1989) *Beyond Feminist Aesthetics: Feminist Literature and Social Change*, London: Hutchinson Radius.

Feuer, J. (1986) '*Dynasty*', paper presented at the International Television Studies Conference, London.

Fish, S. (1980) *Is There a Text in this Class? The Authority of Interpretive Communities*, Cambridge, MA and London: Harvard University Press.

Fountain, N. (2000) 'Perky Sid's soapy slip-up', *The Guardian* 28 January: 6.

Frow, J. (1987) 'Accounting for tastes: some problems in Bourdieu's sociology of culture', *Cultural Studies* 1, 1: 59–73.

—— (1995) *Cultural Studies and Cultural Value*, Oxford and New York: Oxford University Press.

Gamman, L. (1988) 'Watching the detectives: the enigma of the female gaze', in L. Gamman and M. Marshment (eds) *The Female Gaze*, London: The Women's Press.

Gamman, L. and Marshment, M. (eds) (1988) *The Female Gaze*, London: The Women's Press.

Garnham, N. and Williams, R. (1980) 'Pierre Bourdieu and the sociology of culture: an introduction', *Media, Culture and Society* 2: 209–23.

Gedalof, I. (2000) 'Power, politics, performativity: some comments on Elisa Glick's "Sex-Positive"', *Feminist Review* 64: 49–52.

Geraghty, C. (1991) *Women and Soap Opera: A Study of Prime-time Soaps*, Cambridge: Polity Press.

—— (1997) 'Audiences and "ethnography": questions of practice', in C. Geraghty and D. Lusted (eds) *The Television Studies Book*, London: Edward Arnold.

Gledhill, C. (ed.) (1991) *Stardom Industry of Desire*, London and New York: Routledge.

Glick, E. (2000) 'Sex positive: feminism, queer theory and the politics of transgression', *Feminist Review* 64: 19–45.

Graham, A. (1997) 'Addicted to Ambridge', *Radio Times* 14–20 June: 26–7.

Gray, A. (1987) 'Behind closed doors: video recorders in the home', in H. Baehr and G. Dyer, (eds) *Boxed-in: Women and Television*, London: Pandora.

—— (1988) 'Reading the readings: a working paper', unpublished paper presented at the 1988 International Television Studies Conference.

Greene, P., Collingwood, C. and Niklaus, H. (1994) *The Book of the Archers*, London: Michael Joseph.

Gruner, P. (1996) 'Diana's lawyer says: I will go to court to help the Grundys', *The Evening Standard* 13 December: 6.

Hall, C. (1992) *White Male and Middle Class*, Cambridge: Polity Press.

Hall, S. ([1973] 1996) 'Encoding/decoding', in P. Marris and S. Thornham (eds) *Media Studies: A Reader*, Edinburgh: Edinburgh University Press.

Hamilton, G. (1995) *Geoff Hamilton's Cottage Gardens*, London: BBC Books.

Härnsten, G. (1994) *The Research Circle: Building Knowledge on Equal Terms*, Stockholm: The Swedish Trade Union Conference.

Hartley, J. (1987) 'Invisible fictions: television audiences, paedocracy, pleasure', *Textual Practice* 1, 2: 121–38.

Haug, F (ed.) (1983) *Female Sexualisation: A Collective Work of Memory*, trans. E. Carter (1987) London: Verso.

Heide, M. (1995) *Television Culture and Women's Lives: 'Thirtysomething' and the Contradictions of Gender*, Philadelphia: University of Pennsylvania Press.

Hendy, D. (2000) *Radio in the Global Age*, Cambridge: Polity Press.

Hennessy, R. (1993) *Materialist Feminism and the Politics of Discourse*, London and New York: Routledge.

—— (1996) 'Queer theory, left politics', in S. Makdisi, C. Casarino and R.E. Karl (eds) *Marxism beyond Marxism*, New York: Routledge.

Hewison, R. (1987) *The Heritage Industry*, London: Methuen.

—— (1991) 'Commerce and culture', in J. Corner and S. Harvey (eds) *Enterprise and Heritage: Crosscurrents of National Culture*, London and New York: Routledge.

Hickman, M. (1995) *Religion, Class and Identity: The State, the Catholic Church and the Education of the Irish in Britain*, Aldershot: Avebury.

Hickman, M. and Walter, B. (1995) 'Deconstructing whiteness: Irish women in Britain', *Feminist Review* 50: 5–19.

Higson, A. (1993) 'Re-presenting the national past: nostalgia and pastiche in the heritage film', in L. Friedman (ed.) *British Cinema and Thatcherism: Fires Were Started*, London: UCL Press.

Hobson, D. (1982) *'Crossroads': The Drama of a Soap Opera*, London: Methuen.

—— (1989) 'Soap operas at work', in E. Seiter, H. Borchers, G. Kreutzner and E.-M. Warth (eds) *Remote Control: Television, Audiences and Cultural Power*, London and New York: Routledge.

Hollway, W. (1992) 'Gender difference and the production of subjectivity', in H. Crowley and S. Himmelweit (eds) *Knowing Women: Feminism and Knowledge*, London: Polity Press and The Open University.

Jenkins, H. (1992) 'Strangers no more, we sing: filking and the social construction of the science fiction fan community', in L. Lewis (ed.) *The Adoring Audience: Fan Culture and Popular Media*, London and New York: Routledge.

Jenson, J. (1992) 'Fandom as pathology: the consequences of characterization', in L. Lewis (ed.) *The Adoring Audience: Fan Culture and Popular Media*, London and New York: Routledge.

Jones, A. R. (1986) 'Mills and Boon meets feminism', in J. Radford (ed.) *The Politics of Popular Fiction*, London: Routledge and Kegan Paul.

Joseph, J. (1994) 'Archers go to the top to save Susan', *The Times* 10 January: 1.

Kaplan, C. (1986) *'The Thorn Birds*: fiction, fantasy, femininity', in C. Kaplan *Sea Changes: Essays on Culture and Feminism*, London: Verso.

Kaplan, C. and Glover, D. (1996) 'Editorial', *New Formations: Conservative Modernity* 28: 1–2.

Karpf, A. (1999) 'Stop this water torture', *The Guardian* 4 September.

Kockenlocker (1986) 'High tecs', *Sight and Sound* 55, 4: 240.

Kuhn, A. (1984) 'Women's genres: melodrama, soap opera, and theory', *Screen* 25, 1: 18–28.

Lawson, M. (2001) 'The plot thickens', *The Guardian* 16 February, G2: 3.

Lewis, L. (ed.) (1992) *The Adoring Audience: Fan Culture and Popular Media*, London and New York: Routledge.

Lewis, P. and Booth, J. (1989) *The Invisible Medium: Public, Commercial and Community Radio*, Basingstoke and London: Macmillan.

Liebes, T. and Katz, E. (1990) *The Export of Meaning: Cross-Cultural Readings of 'Dallas'*, Oxford: Oxford University Press.

Light, A. (1984) '"Returning to Manderley": romance fiction, female sexuality and class', *Feminist Review* 16: 7–25.

—— (1991a) *Forever England: Femininity, Literature and Conservatism between the Wars*, London and New York: Routledge.

—— (1991b) 'Englishness', *Sight and Sound* 1, 3: 63.

Lister, D. (2000) 'Now *The Archers*: Rumpy pumpy tum-ti-tum', *The Independent* 28 January: 1.

Lofgren, O. (1995) 'The nation as home or motel? Metaphors of media and belonging', unpublished paper, Department of European Ethnology, University of Lund, Sweden.

Lovell, T. (2000) 'Thinking feminism with and against Bourdieu', *Feminist Theory* 1, 1: 11–32.

Lury, C. (1995) 'The rights and wrongs of culture: issues of theory and methodology', in B. Skeggs (ed.) *Feminist Cultural Theory: Process and Production*, Manchester: Manchester University Press.

—— (1996) *Consumer Culture*, Oxford and Cambridge: Polity Press.

MacArthur, B. (1990) 'Watching the detectives', *The Guardian* 10 December: 25.

Mander, M. (1987) 'Bourdieu, the sociology of culture and cultural studies: a critique', *European Journal of Communications* 2: 427–53.

Mauthner, N. and Doucet, A. (1998) 'Reflections on a voice-centred relational method: analysing maternal and domestic voices', in J. Ribbens and R. Edwards (eds) *Feminist Dilemmas in Qualitative Research*, London, Thousand Oaks and New Delhi: Sage.

McRobbie, A. (1991) *Feminism and Youth Culture*, London: Macmillan.

Mellor, A. (1991) 'Enterprise and heritage in the dock', in J. Corner and S. Harvey (eds) *Enterprise and Heritage: Crosscurrents of National Culture*, London and New York: Routledge.

Mepham, J. (1990) 'The ethics of quality in TV', in G. Mulgan (ed.) *The Question of Quality*, London: BFI.

Mitchell, C. (2000) *Women and Radio: Airing Differences*, London and New York: Routledge.

Modleski, T. (1986) 'Introduction', in T. Modleski (ed.) *Studies in Entertainment: Critical Approaches to Mass Culture*, Bloomington: Indiana University Press.

Moi, T. (1994) *Simone de Beauvoir: The Making of an Intellectual Woman*, Oxford and Cambridge, MA: Blackwell.

Monk, C. (1995) 'Sexuality and the heritage', *Sight and Sound* 5, 10: 32–4.

—— (1999) 'Heritage films and the British cinema audience in the 1990s', *Journal of Popular British Cinema* 2: 22–38.

Moores, S. (1988) '"The box on the dresser": memories of early radio and everyday life', *Media, Culture and Society* 10, 1: 23–40.

—— (1993) *Interpreting Audiences: The Ethnography of Media Consumption*, London, Thousand Oaks and New Delhi: Sage.

Morley, D. (1980) *The 'Nationwide' Audience*, London: The British Film Institute.

—— (1986) *Family Television: Cultural Power and Domestic Leisure*, London: Comedia.

—— (1989) 'Changing paradigms in audience studies', in E. Seiter, H. Borchers, G. Kreutzner and E.-M. Warth (eds) *Remote Control: Television, Audiences and Cultural Power*, London and New York: Routledge.

—— (1992) *Television, Audiences and Cultural Studies*, London and New York: Routledge.

—— (2000) *Home Territories: Media, Mobility and Identity*, London and New York: Routledge.

Mulgan, G. (ed.) (1990) *The Question of Quality*, London: BFI.

Mulvey, L. (1975) 'Visual pleasure and narrative cinema', *Screen* 16, 3: 6–18, republished in L. Mulvey (1989) *Visual and Other Pleasures*, Basingstoke and London: Macmillan.

Murdock, G. (1997) 'Thin descriptions: questions of method in cultural studies', in J. McGuigan (ed.) *Cultural Methodologies*, London, Thousand Oaks and New Delhi: Sage.

Naughton, J. (1987) 'Ahead of the pack', *The Listener* 117, 2995: 36.

Neale, S. (1980) *Genre*, London: British Film Institute.

Newnham, D. (1992) 'Goofy over Mickey Morse', *The Guardian* 27 February: 29.

Nye, S., Godwin, N. and Hollows, B. (2000) 'Twisting the dials: lesbians on British radio', in C. Mitchell (ed.) *Women and Radio: Airing Differences*, London and New York: Routledge.

Oakley, A. (1981) 'Interviewing women: a contradiction in terms', in H. Roberts (ed.) *Doing Feminist Research*, London: Routledge and Kegan Paul.

Osborne, P. (1996) 'Times (modern), modernity (conservative)? Notes on the persistence of a temporal motif', *New Formations* 28: 132–41.

Pearson, A. (1994) 'That *Archers* Woman', *Radio Times* 26 February–4 March: 36–7.

Potter, J. and Wetherell, M. (1987) *Discourse and Social Psychology: Beyond Attitudes and Behaviour*, London: Sage Publications.

Press, A. and Cole, E. (1999) *Speaking of Abortion: Television and Authority in the Lives of Women*, Chicago and London: University of Chicago Press.

Prior, L. (1983) '*The Archers* in the 1980s', BBC Broadcasting Research Findings 8: 68–74.

Purdie, S. (1992) 'Janice Radway, *Reading the Romance*', in M. Barker and A. Beezer (eds) *Reading into Cultural Studies*, London and New York: Routledge.

Radway, J. (1984) *Reading the Romance: Women, Patriarchy and Popular Literature*, London and New York: Verso.

—— (1994) 'Romance and the work of fantasy: struggles over feminine sexuality and subjectivity at century's end', in J. Cruz and J. Lewis (eds) *Viewing, Reading, Listening: Audiences and Cultural Reception*, Boulder, CO: Westview Press.

Ribbens, J. and Edwards, R. (eds) (1998) *Feminist Dilemmas in Qualitative Research*, London, Thousand Oaks and New Delhi: Sage.

Richards, C. (1993) 'Taking sides? What young girls do with television', in D. Buckingham (ed.) *Reading Audiences: Young People and the Media*, Manchester: Manchester University Press.

Roberts, H. (ed.) (1981) *Doing Feminist Research*, London: Routledge and Kegan Paul.

Robertson, P. (1999) 'What makes the feminist camp?', in F. Cleto (ed.) *Camp, Queer Aesthetics and the Performing Subject: A Reader*, Edinburgh: Edinburgh University Press.

Roseneil, S. and Seymour, J. (eds) (1999) *Practising Identities: Power and Resistance*, Basingstoke and London: Macmillan.

Ross, A. (1989) *No Respect: Intellectuals and Popular Culture*, London and New York: Routledge, Chapman and Hall.

Samuel, R. (1994) *Theatres of Memory*, vol. 1 *Past and Present in Contemporary Culture*, London and New York: Verso.

Sanderson, M. (1991) *The Making of 'Inspector Morse'*, London and Basingstoke: Macmillan.

Scannell, P. (1988) 'Radio times', in P. Drummond and R. Paterson (eds) *Television and its Audience*, London: British Film Institute.

—— (1996) *Radio, Television and Modern Life*, Oxford: Blackwell.

Scannell, P. and Cardiff, D. (1991) *A Social History of British Broadcasting: Serving the Nation, 1923–39*, Oxford: Basil Blackwell

Schwichtenberg, C. (1994) 'Reconceptualizing gender: new sites for feminist audience research', in J. Cruz and J. Lewis (eds) *Viewing, Reading, Listening: Audiences and Cultural Reception*, Boulder, CO: Westview Press.

Seiter, E. (1989) '"Don't treat us like we're so stupid and naïve": towards an ethnography of soap opera viewers', in E. Seiter, H. Borchers, G. Kreutzner and E.-M. Warth (eds) *Remote Control: Television, Audiences and Cultural Power*, London and New York: Routledge.

—— (1990) 'Making distinctions in audience research: case study of a troubling interview', *Cultural Studies* 4, 1: 61–84.

—— (1999) *Television and New Media Audiences*, Oxford and New York: Oxford University Press.

Seiter, E., Borchers, H., Kreutzner, G. and Warth, E.-M. (eds) (1989) *Remote Control: Television, Audiences and Cultural Power*, London and New York: Routledge.

Silverman, D. (1993) *Interpreting Qualitative Data: Methods for Analysing Talk, Text and Interaction*, London, Thousand Oaks and New Delhi: Sage.

Skeggs, B. (ed.) (1995) *Feminist Cultural Theory: Process and Production*, Manchester: Manchester University Press.

—— (1997) *Formations of Class and Gender: Becoming Respectable*, London, Thousand Oaks and New Delhi: Sage.

Skirrow, G. (1987) 'Women / acting / power', in H. Baehr and G. Dyer (eds) *Boxed-in: Women and Television*, London: Pandora.

Smethurst, W. (1996) *'The Archers': The True Story*, London: Michael O'Mara Books.

Sontag, S. ([1964] 1999) 'Notes on "camp"', in F. Cleto (ed.) *Camp, Queer Aesthetics and the Performing Subject: A Reader*, Edinburgh: Edinburgh University Press.

Sparks, R. (1993) '*Inspector Morse*: "The Last Enemy" (Peter Buckman)', in G. Brandt (ed.) *British Television Drama in the 1980s*, Cambridge: Cambridge University Press.

Stacey, J. (1993) 'Textual obsessions: methodology, history and researching female spectatorship', *Screen* 34, 3: 260–74.

—— (1994) *Stargazing: Hollywood Cinema and Female Spectatorship*, London and New York: Routledge.

Stanley, L. and Wise, S. (1993) *Breaking Out Again*, London and New York: Routledge.

Steedman, C. (1986) *Landscape for a Good Woman: A Story of Two Lives*, London: Virago.

Tacchi, J. (2000) 'Gender, fantasy and radio consumption: an ethnographic case-study', in C. Mitchell (ed.) *Women and Radio: Airing Differences*, London and New York: Routledge.

Tasker, Y. (1993) *Spectacular Bodies: Gender, Genre and the Action Cinema*, London and New York: Routledge.

Taylor, H. (1989) *Scarlett's Women: 'Gone with the Wind' and its Female Fans*, London: Virago.

Thomas, L. (1995) 'In love with *Inspector Morse*: feminist subculture and quality television', *Feminist Review* 51: 1–25; republished in C. Brunsdon, J. D'Acci and L. Spigel, (eds) (1997) *Feminist Television Criticism: A Reader*, Oxford and New York: Oxford University Press.

Thornton, S. (1995) *Club Cultures: Music, Media and Subcultural Capital*, Oxford and Cambridge, MA: Blackwell.

—— (1997) 'The social logic of subcultural capital', in K. Gelder and S. Thornton (eds) *The Subcultures Reader*, London and New York: Routledge.

Treacher, A. (1988) 'What is life without my love?: desire and romantic fiction', in S. Radstone (ed.) *Sweet Dreams: Sexuality, Gender and Popular Fiction*, London: Lawrence and Wishart.

Tulloch, J. (1989) 'Approaching the audience: the elderly', in E. Seiter, H. Borchers, G. Kreutzner and E.-M. Warth (eds) *Remote Control: Television, Audiences and Cultural Power*, London and New York: Routledge.

Van Zoonen, L. (1994) *Feminist Media Studies*, London, Thousand Oaks and New Delhi: Sage Publications.

Vincendeau, G. (1995) 'Unsettling memories', *Sight and Sound* 5, 7: 30–2.

Walkerdine, V. (1986) 'Video replay: families, films and fantasy', in V. Burgin, J. Donald and C. Kaplan (eds) *Formations of Fantasy*, London: Routledge and Kegan Paul.

Weedon, C. ([1987] 1997) *Feminist Practice and Poststructuralist Theory*, Oxford and Cambridge, MA: Blackwell.

Wheeler, W. (1994) 'Nostalgia isn't nasty', in M. Perryman (ed.) *Altered States*, London: Lawrence and Wishart.

—— (1999) *A New Modernity: Changes in Literature, Science and Politics*, London: Lawrence and Wishart.

Whitburn, V. (1996) *'The Archers': The Changing Face of Radio's Longest Running Drama*, London: Virgin Books.

Williamson, J. (1991) '"Up where you belong": Hollywood images of big business in the 1980s', in J. Corner and S. Harvey (eds) *Enterprise and Heritage: Crosscurrents of National Culture*, London and New York: Routledge.

Willmott, K. and Niklaus, H. (2000) *The Archers Annual 2000*, London: BBC Publications.

Wilson, E. (1988) 'The counterfeit detective', in E. Wilson *Hallucinations: Life in the Post-Modern City*, London: Radius.

Wollen, T. (1991) 'Over our shoulders: nostalgic screen fictions for the 1980s', in J. Corner and S. Harvey (eds) *Enterprise and Heritage: Crosscurrents of National Culture*, London and New York: Routledge.

Wright, P. (1985) *On Living in an Old Country: The National Past in Contemporary Britain*, London: Verso.

Index